MW01007088

The Enduring Promise of America's Great City Schools

MICHAEL CASSERLY

HARVARD EDUCATION PRESS
CAMBRIDGE, MASSACHUSETTS

Copyright © 2025 by the President and Fellows of Harvard College

All rights reserved. No part of this publication may be reproduced or transmitted in any form or by any means, electronic or mechanical, including photocopy, recording, or any information storage and retrieval systems, without permission in writing from the publisher.

Paperback ISBN 9781682539316

Library of Congress Cataloging-in-Publication Data

Names: Casserly, Michael D., author.
Title: The enduring promise of America's great city schools / Michael Casserly.
Description: Cambridge, Massachusetts : Harvard Education Press, [2024] |
    Includes bibliographical references and index.
Identifiers: LCCN 2024017065 | ISBN 9781682539316 (paperback)
Subjects: LCSH: Education, Urban—United States. | Educational equalization—
    United States. | Urban schools—United States. | Public schools—United States. |
    Social distancing (Public health) and education—United States.
Classification: LCC LC5131 .C378 2024 | DDC 370.973/091732—dc23/eng/20240619
LC record available at https://lccn.loc.gov/2024017065

Published by Harvard Education Press,
an imprint of the Harvard Education Publishing Group

Harvard Education Press
8 Story Street
Cambridge, MA 02138

Cover Design: Jackie Shepherd Design
Cover Images: FatCamera via iStock, releon8211 via Shutterstock

The typefaces in this book are Minion Pro and ITC Stone Sans.

This book is dedicated to the nation's urban
public school educators and the millions
of students they serve.

Contents

Contents

Foreword

Running a large, urban school district is among the more challenging jobs in America. It is challenging enough for school superintendents to support learning and drive positive outcomes for increasingly diverse student populations. School leaders must also ensure that kids are safe, healthy, and well fed, that their parents feel welcomed and included, that their teachers feel valued and motivated, and that school board members and elected officials who provide the funding feel the funding is justified and the results are positive. These challenges are exponentially greater when the student population approaches that of a midsize American city.

Thankfully, for the last thirty-plus years, urban school leaders have had Mike Casserly watching our backs in Washington, D.C., and giving voice to our collective needs and concerns. As the head of the Council of Great City Schools, Mike Casserly also brought us together to share best practices and learn from each other.

In this important book, Mike shines a light on school reforms of the last twenty years, separating the facts from fiction to draw insights and lessons that can inform the next generation of school superintendents. Examining both hard data and qualitative case studies, Mike highlights success stories that turned some urban districts into the fastest-improving schools in the country, while also being open and honest about some of the less successful efforts.

He also digs deep into what was one of the most disruptive events in the history of public education—the 2020 pandemic that forced schools across the United States to close and forced teachers and students to shift to online learning. Mike tells how the pandemic distracted the education sector from implementing proven education reforms that generated measurable and meaningful academic progress.

As we all know, many kids suffered under online learning conditions. But it is worth noting that many school districts, including the one that I ran in Chicago, are well on their way to erasing COVID-related learning loss. Mike played a key role in helping big-city districts manage the pandemic, convening weekly calls with urban superintendents to share information and stay abreast of the latest research.

Today American public schools confront new issues from culture war debates around race and gender to pedagogical debates about how to teach reading and history. There is a chronic shortage of teachers in areas like bilingual and special education and, despite all our best efforts, there are continuing inequities in student outcomes.

As today's school leaders wrestle with these and other topics, I encourage them to regularly consult Mike Casserly's thoughtful insights. What they will find is what I found when I first started running a big-city school system: a savvy, clear-headed thinker with an optimistic slant driven by the singular mission of providing America's children with the very best education possible.

—Arne Duncan, Chicago Public Schools CEO (2001–2008)
US Secretary of Education (2009–2015)

1

Why Urban Education Matters

The three years between 2020 and 2023 brought unprecedented challenges to America's system of public education, particularly in the nation's big cities. A global pandemic swept the nation, killing over a million citizens. Students lost ground academically. The number of shootings and the amount of violence escalated. Staff shortages left classrooms unsupervised. School board meetings descended into shouting matches. Enrollment in traditional public schools plummeted. Critical race theory tore apart the citizenry. Parents were at each other's throats about whether to open school buildings or leave them shuttered. School staff were exhausted.

The teacher unions demanded safety above all else. Watchdogs pulled library books off the shelves. A national school boards organization splintered. Achievement gaps persisted. Scholars declared the national standards movement dead. Partisan interests seized on the challenges to further their own agendas. Charter schools and homeschooling expanded. And the school choice movement and conservative parent rights groups licked their chops.

All of this was on top of the usual array of issues that dominate urban school agendas: budget fights, proposals to take over districts or break them up, natural disasters, court orders, the threat of strikes, and assorted scandals. Was it any wonder that a *Washington Post* analysis of the Bureau of

Labor Statistics' American Time Use Survey data found that educators reported being under more stress than most other professions?[1]

"PUBLIC SCHOOLS FACING A CRISIS OF EPIC PROPORTIONS," screamed a front-page article in late January 2022 in the *Washington Post*. Smelling blood, advocates called for the breakup of school systems, the dismantlement of public education, the election of school boards on partisan slates, and the rise of parental choice as the organizing principle behind elementary and secondary schools nationally. Critics argued that public education had squandered the confidence of the citizenry and school systems were wasting the billions of dollars that Congress had allocated to get them through the pandemic. It was not an uplifting period.

If the next *Washington Post* headline read, "PUBLIC EDUCATION IN THE 50 STATES DISMANTLED," would you notice? If public schools as we know them went away, replaced by a patchwork of private or locally chartered and independent institutions that set their own entrance requirements, eligibility criteria, curriculum, and standards for student learning, would it matter to you? It might not. Most of the population does not have a child in a public school. Unless you worked in one of these schools, you would get up at the same time tomorrow morning and go to work. You would shop at the same grocery store on Saturday morning. You would still have to pay the rent and try to put away a few dollars at the end of the month.

Suppose the headline was slightly different and it read, "PUBLIC SCHOOL DISTRICTS IN THE MAJOR CITIES DISMANTLED." Would you care then? Unless you lived in one of the nation's largest urban areas and sent your child to a traditional public school, you might not pay attention. You also might not care. These schools may serve parents and children who do not look like you, go to the same church, or even speak the same language. Roughly 44 percent of the students in these urban public schools are Hispanic, 26 percent are African American, over 72 percent are from families with low incomes, and 17 percent do not speak English as a first language.[2] Cities and their public schools tend to be larger, more complicated, messier, and more diverse than one sees elsewhere. Academic performance on most standardized measures is not as high as the national average in many cities. And voters there tend to be more progressive politically.

THE ROLE OF PUBLIC SCHOOLS IN A TIME OF CRISIS

These questions about the continued existence and viability of public schools, particularly in urban areas, are not entirely academic, as we saw in March 2020. As governors and mayors closed schools at the beginning of the pandemic, the nation's largest city school superintendents, chief executive officers, and chancellors debated a range of existential questions, shared ideas, and developed next steps on weekly Zoom calls convened by the Council of the Great City Schools, the nation's primary coalition of large city public school districts.[3]

How essential are we as large city public school systems? What responsibility do we have to our students, staff, parents, and communities in a situation like this? Is access to free, public education a right of citizenship in this country, even if it is not in this nation's constitution? What are the effects on our students if instruction is put on hold? How do we balance the need for public safety and our students' needs to be prepared for the future? What are the implications for the nation if students lack the education to meet the demands of a rapidly changing world? Should we close our school systems as part of a broader national public health emergency?

If we close our schools or we are told by a higher authority to close them, should we teach our students at a distance, knowing that online learning is a poor substitute for in-person instruction? How should we deal with the internet deserts that exist in large swaths of our cities, which will make access to online learning inequitable? How can we possibly ensure adequate instructional quality with remote instruction? How will we prepare parents to work with their children on their lessons? Would we be better off closing our doors for the duration of the pandemic rather than subjecting ourselves to the inevitable public criticism we will face? When should we reopen and under what conditions? Who will make the decision? What will it take to get these issues even partially right?

The leaders of these school systems knew that how we answered these and other questions and how we handled a crisis for which there was no playbook were central to the future of large urban school districts. Moreover, underlying these questions about the role of public schools was yet another fundamental issue about our role as educational leaders. As we discuss later, progress over the past several decades has revealed a central paradox facing school district leaders—particularly those in the nation's largest cities.

These leaders are constantly in the crosshairs of whatever economic, political, and social battles are raging throughout the country. They face a constant stream of crises—school shootings and community violence, labor disputes, crumbling school facilities, and a host of other fires that must be extinguished daily. Urban educators usually have procedures for handling many of these predictable crises or experiences dealing with them. There was no manual to consult, however, for how to manage a global pandemic.

At the same time, the data are clear that school district leaders need to think strategically about instructional improvement to effectively advance long-term academic and social outcomes. Simply put, they need to *focus* on student achievement to *impact* student achievement. If they let the routine crisis management aspect of their roles take center stage, they would be unable to fulfill their larger mission of improving academic achievement.

At the outset of the COVID-19 crisis, district leaders had to decide whether and how to do just that. To meet the immediate needs of their students and communities, they would need to step fully into the role of crisis managers, putting on hold their long-term academic vision for improvement in order to provide fundamental support and services in addition to instructional continuity. Should they take on this kind of mission?

Warning signs for school leaders were flashing amber. Most states had not designated schools and their staff as essential workers alongside hospital staff, health care workers, police, and fire/rescue workers. Some states encouraged local school systems to provide meals and childcare services to essential workers, but they did not tag schools or school personnel themselves as essential. There is no federal obligation to provide public education. It was not even clear what compulsory attendance in schools meant in these circumstances. So, the question remained: What should we do?

What urban education leaders knew—firsthand—which advocates, commentators, critics, and others did not pay much attention to—was that families, particularly in the nation's major cities, relied on their schools for much more than just academic instruction. Schools were often the central pillars of their communities, providing information and access to resources, food, devices, special education, mental health services and counseling, language translation services, immigration aid, clothing and laundry services, social services, housing assistance, and health services at the neighborhood level that few other institutions could at the same scale.

Along with that understanding, however, was the realization that schools, their personnel, and their resources could not single-handedly mitigate the impact of the pandemic. Learning would be lost. People would get sick. Parents and guardians would be frustrated and exhausted. Unions would make unreasonable and ever-changing demands. Food deliveries might be uneven. School board meetings might be impossible to manage. The press would pounce on any inconsistency. Websites would break down. Call-in services would get clogged. Devices would be stolen and pawned. Federal and state governments would send contradictory messages. Some parents would want to send their children back into school buildings sooner than others. Congress and state legislatures might not fund any of the efforts school leaders would have to undertake. There were trap doors everywhere. Critics would have ample ammunition for their condemnations. And the press would see disaster, controversy, and chaos everywhere. The risks of failure were high.

Nonetheless, leaders of the nation's urban public school systems agreed on these weekly calls that there was no choice but to do everything we could for the students and families we served. Michael Hinojosa, the superintendent of the Dallas Independent School District, saw this as a defining moment for public education. The stakes would be particularly high for school systems in the big cities, where public scrutiny was always intense. It would not matter that schools were not officially deemed essential. The public knew better and so did school leaders. Schools were critical to the health and well-being of the community. If schools, particularly in the big cities, did not stand up and meet the moment, children and families would be harmed, and the nation itself would be jeopardized.

School superintendents, school boards, and staff decided at these weekly sessions that they would do everything they could to address the crisis, putting their reputations and the reputations of their school systems on the line, as best they could, to meet the needs of their families and children. The decision would prove fateful.

THE QUESTION OF REMOTE INSTRUCTION AND LOST TIME

In March 2020 at least one question was definitively answered for education leaders throughout the nation. Schools were shuttered, and district leaders were faced with a previously unimaginable scenario: the only way for instruction to continue would be to shift to distance learning.

Haunting all big-city school leaders at this point was the research that they were all familiar with, showing that remote instruction was a poor substitute for in-person classes, where teachers had the flexibility to address individual student needs as they emerged. And there was the rub. Remote instruction was a short-term answer to a crisis, not an effective or sustainable approach to supporting, advancing, or improving student achievement, particularly in school systems with large numbers of students from low-income families, English language learners, and students with disabilities.

Even in the best circumstances studies demonstrated that, on its own, online teaching produced inferior results compared to face-to-face teaching. A review of studies done by Rick Hess, a scholar at the American Enterprise Institute, concluded that online instruction of students showed equal or better outcomes for some high-achieving students who worked well independently but that it resulted in inferior academic performance for other students.[4] He cited a 2017 study published in the *Journal of Research on Educational Effectiveness*.[5] It assessed remedial algebra classes in seventeen Chicago high schools and showed that students randomly assigned to online instruction learned less than their peers.

Superintendents in the nation's major city school systems knew about these and other studies. And they knew from their own experiments and experience that online instruction and lost learning time were likely to result in lower student performance. In addition, not everyone had a computer at home or knew how to use one. Many families did not have access to the internet. This would need to be addressed. Devices would need to be purchased and distributed, and lost time would need to be recaptured. Professional development would need to be deployed to prepare teachers for new modes of instruction. Parents, some of whom quit their jobs to support their children with remote schoolwork, would need training on how to best help. Teacher contracts would have to be amended to accommodate new instructional expectations and workloads. And procedures would have to be set up to manage broken or lost equipment.

Should school leaders even try this approach—knowing that the results were likely to be subpar? Would it be better to shut the institution down along with all the other services and companies that were being closed? It would not be until later that districts would face the question of whether to offer remote instruction or reopen schools. At this point, however, they were facing a more basic question: Would it be better to do nothing?

Perspectives on this question differed among school leaders when the pandemic started. Eric Gordon, the chief executive officer of the Cleveland municipal school district in Ohio, wondered if school systems and the children they served would be better off if the school systems were declared part of the public health emergency and were shut down entirely like corporations and businesses. At that time, Gordon was one of the longest-serving big-city school superintendents in the nation and was widely respected by his colleagues for his intelligence, strategic thinking, and wicked self-deprecating sense of humor. He led a public school system that was among the poorest in the nation and had little capacity to provide electronic devices to students to teach them remotely. He feared that public education was in a no-win situation.

This hesitation was not a matter of defeatism or a lack of commitment to the community. It was an uncertainty over the fate of our schools. But within days of Ohio's governor shutting the state's schools down for an extended three-week "spring break," the Cleveland public schools had set up sanitation procedures; outlined handwashing practices; suspended professional travel; curtailed after-school events; set up twenty-two food service sites with citywide transportation that provided two meals a day to anyone who showed up, including students from charter and private schools; distributed three days of teacher-prepared learning packets; and launched a system-wide information campaign to keep the public informed about steps the district was taking.

What Gordon was leery of, however, was promising the public that the school system could pivot quickly to remote learning with such a wide digital divide among residents of his city. Many leaders like those in Baltimore and Detroit, whose school systems were not fully prepared to jump into remote instruction, shared Gordon's reservations. Besides, it was not clear in the early days of the pandemic how long the lockdowns would last. Some states, like Ohio, were treating the situation as a hiccup in the regular school schedule and expected that students would be back in classes by late spring. Other states were signaling that schools would close for the remainder of the school year.

School leaders who ran systems with greater technological capacity were already moving in the early days of the pandemic to set up remote instruction. They typically had more wherewithal. The Miami-Dade County public schools, which had already been integrating computer use into their instructional programs, were an example of this. By mid-March 2020, the Miami school system had moved to universal remote instruction, given out fifty-two thousand devices, and seen one million logins from students and staff within the first week, according to district superintendent Alberto Carvalho. An impeccably dressed, oratorically gifted, self-assured leader with an impressive track record of results, Carvalho, along with his team, began planning a month before the pandemic hit full force. When it arrived, the district had already provided online professional development for teachers and staff, served one hundred thousand meals with no questions asked, and set up childcare centers for health workers across the city.

PLAYING THE HAND WE WERE DEALT

What these and so many other school systems did to support their local students and families over the subsequent two years following the first shutdowns in March 2020 was remarkable indeed. On a "60 Minutes" program at the beginning of the pandemic, we heard how corporate giants like Ford Motor Company and Amazon had mounted crash production and distribution efforts, and viewers marveled at their capacity and expertise. I am not sure that any of them held a candle to what big-city public schools were doing at the time.

The schools' efforts began in March 2020 with districts putting their instructional materials online, setting up remote instructional systems, packaging teaching lessons, providing professional development on virtual instructional techniques, informing parents, and redeploying personnel. Most systems had their remote instruction up and running, at least in rudimentary form by the first week in April, just two weeks after the districts had been shut down.[6] Even in places where technology was sparse, the districts packaged paper lessons or instructional packets to facilitate learning as best as possible.

San Antonio bundled their lessons a week at a time; Philadelphia created learning guides and translated them into multiple languages; Baltimore created daily videos that parents and students could use on any electronic platform or on television; the District of Columbia made sure that all their teachers had laptops and that students from low-income families and English language learners (ELLs) were served first; Kansas City began setting up cross-school online professional learning communities; and Long Beach set up crowd-sourcing strategies so that teachers could help each other in lesson planning.

Nearly everyone, including New York City, had surveyed their parents to determine their technology capacity and other needs. Principals were coordinated in every district to monitor instruction and family needs. And leaders began almost immediately to think about their summer schools, graduation ceremonies, the extent of unfinished learning, new grading and attendance procedures, student testing, staff evaluations, instructional monitoring, and the thousand and one details that were required to provide instruction at the highest quality possible.

While the instructional pieces were being put into place, operational teams were marshalled to develop safety, health, and cleaning protocols, purchase masks and gloves, retain bus drivers, and set up new security systems. And the districts immediately implemented procedures for providing meals to students and families that were likely to go without.

By the time all was said and done, the Los Angeles Unified School District, for instance, had provided 72,970,000 meals to students and another 21,891,000 meals to adults in the community in the two years after the pandemic started. In St. Petersburg, Florida, the Pinellas County public schools served 1,137,000 meals to students over the same period. The Denver public school district served 6,111,000 breakfasts and lunches to students. The Albuquerque public schools in New Mexico provided over 13,324,000 breakfasts, lunches, and snacks. The Charleston, South Carolina, public schools served about 7,321,000 meals. The Richmond, Virginia, public schools provided 4,881,000 meals. And the San Diego public schools distributed approximately 21,303,000 meals.

Every major urban school system in the nation had elaborate systems in place to feed students, families, and community members throughout the pandemic, regardless of whether schools were open or closed. They used their buses and other vehicles, retrofitted many of them with refrigerators and ovens, set up regular feeding stations throughout their communities, dropped off food at bus stops, packaged multiple meals per box to make sure that all family members would eat for several days, and provided staff and volunteers despite the risks of getting sick.

In addition, these school systems stepped up almost single-handedly to narrow the digital divide in their communities—not knowing whether they would ever get reimbursed by their states or the federal government. The Columbus Public Schools in Ohio purchased and delivered nearly 45,000 Chromebooks and distributed about 2,000 hotspots to ensure that every student had access to the internet and the lessons that the district provided. The Oklahoma City public schools procured 12,000 iPads and Chromebooks and 7,000 hotspots to make sure that every student in the district had access to learning. On the other side of the country, the San Francisco public schools bought and distributed 36,300 devices and 15,300 hotspots. In Fresno, California, the public schools provided 60,000 laptops, 12,000 tablets, and 8,500 hotspots. Almost everyone retrofitted their buses with internet capacity and parked them near public housing to provide residents with connections they would not have otherwise had.

There was not a major city school system in the nation that did not do something similar to make sure that their students had food and access to materials and teachers. They stepped up with devices, hotspots, and at least rudimentary training on their use.

At the same time, the nation's urban schools were devising new strategies to address the mental health needs of their students and families. The Cleveland school district established Rapid Response Teams to handle suicide issues, grief counseling, community violence, and social-emotional wellness strategies. Every school in the district was paired with community agencies to support family wellness.

In Broward County, Florida, the school district immediately set up mental health and social emotional counseling call-in services via telephone and online, and it expanded its Family Counseling Program. Within weeks of the pandemic's start, the district had provided mental health services to approximately nine thousand individuals.

In Los Angeles, the public school system, led by Austin Beutner at the time, set up extended-hour hotlines in multiple languages to address student and family mental health needs and provide information on obtaining food, clothing, housing, and other social services. And in Tulsa, Oklahoma, where Deborah Gist ran the schools, the public school district set up a Wellness Care Line that provided mental health support to thousands of children and families as they were grappling with the pandemic. In addition, every school in Tulsa had a wellness team that called on students daily to ensure they were doing all right.

Big-city school districts all over the country were putting into place similar strategies, and communities everywhere were looking to them for examples. And they were sharing their ideas with each other on their weekly calls.

These and other big-city school districts were also among the most aggressive in the nation regarding requiring face masks for students and staff. A study across nine states conducted by researchers at Duke University and published in the journal *Pediatrics* found that schools that required universal masking for adults and students saw 72 percent fewer secondary infections than did schools that had no mask requirements or only partial masking.[7] The study concluded that once school size, vaccination rates, and other characteristics were considered, schools with universal masking had nearly 90 percent lower infection rates.

A separate study in Arkansas by the Centers for Disease Control and Prevention yielded comparable results. In other words, aggressive but often unpopular urban school policies on masking prevented disease transmission and saved lives across the country. As it turned out, schools were not the super-spreaders of COVID-19 that many other settings were, partly because youth were not as susceptible as the elderly and partly because schools were being extra cautious—some would say too cautious.

As the first COVID-19 vaccines became available in December 2020, big-city public school systems marshalled their expertise and capacity to help vaccinate not only students but also the general population. The Anchorage, Alaska, school district was one of the first school districts in the nation to begin providing vaccines to city residents, along with snacks and transportation. The Albuquerque public school system was also an early provider, including services for nearby Native American reservations.

The Detroit community school district set up its Teens for Vaccines program that became a model for school districts across the country. The Guilford County schools in Greensboro, North Carolina, used their school buses to transport students (with parent permission) from high schools to the Greensboro mass vaccination site and also hosted weekday and weekend mobile clinics at local schools, particularly in underserved neighborhoods and communities where vaccination rates had been low. In Texas's El Paso Independent School District, leaders held "Vaccinate Before You Graduate" clinics at its high schools for students ages twelve and up.

While all this was happening, big-city school systems in the United States stepped up to take in refugee children from Afghanistan following the Biden administration's evacuation of that country. Today, many are starting to see new arrivals from Ukraine as well. The school districts were providing newcomer aid, instruction, and social services to the new arrivals. In Kansas City, Missouri, the public school system hosted weekly joint educational orientations with local refugee resettlement agencies for families and children, along with enrolling and screening students. The Indianapolis public schools conducted one-on-one interviews with all incoming families and children; administered subject-matter assessments; and awarded credit for education already received. The Nashville public schools coordinated with local resettlement agencies to provide orientations, counseling, social work services, and housing to newly arrived Afghan families. The Oakland public schools also provided these services along with housing support, immunizations, legal and social-emotional supports, and translation and language instruction services.

In many ways, none of this was unusual. Big-city school systems across America have provided services to newly arrived immigrant and refugee children and families since the earliest days of the twentieth century. Even more recently, the nation's urban public schools have opened their doors to families from Cuba, Haiti, Afghanistan, Ukraine, Guatemala, Vietnam, Sudan, and many other countries, including some fifty-eight thousand unaccompanied minors, as they were seeking refuge, freedom, and a better tomorrow. These big-city school systems are now not simply meeting their legal obligations to serve these children but are working to make them feel welcomed and give them a promising future. And they were even doing this during a global pandemic.

At the same time that the pandemic was beginning, the United States was conducting its regular census count and our nation's big-city schools distributed materials in multiple languages, set up information booths in local grocery stores and barber shops, and did everything they could to ensure that everyone was counted.

Deputy US Secretary of Education Cindy Marten, who was the former superintendent of the San Diego Unified School District in California, described it well when she asserted at a conference of big-city school leaders in March 2022 that, during the pandemic, our "urban schools were the largest relief efforts in our communities."[8]

As the months ticked by during the pandemic, the nation was convulsed by the killing of George Floyd along with the ensuing protests, two unprecedented impeachments occurred, the US Capitol was sacked, and the nation's urban school leaders spoke out on behalf of their urban communities on the issues that were rocking the nation. Their perspectives may not have been shared by those outside the big cities—and not everyone inside of them either—but district leaders made it clear that their public schools shared many of the same concerns that their parents did about the state of our democracy and the imperative for equity.

URBAN SCHOOLS MAKE THEIR MARK

The truth is that urban public schools have contributed to and helped the country in large ways and small both during the pandemic and over the years:

- When hurricanes devastated New Orleans and Puerto Rico, urban school districts sent in teams of facilities specialists and engineers at no cost to their districts to assess the damage and develop long-range recovery strategies.
- When Houston was flooded after Hurricane Harvey, the big-city schools all over the country set up donation boxes in their hallways and shipped clothing and goods to grateful Houston students and families.
- When terrorists attacked New York City on 9/11, the big-city schools sent mental health workers to the city to assist traumatized students and staff.
- When the nation was debating whether the nation's big-city mayors should run its public schools, the Council of the Great City Schools and US Conference of Mayors held the country's first and only summit of urban school superintendents and mayors to work out differences and unify around a single vision for our public schools.
- When the nation's urban schools increased their graduation rates from around 65 percent in 1990 to some 80 percent in 2023, their graduates swelled the ranks of higher education and contributed substantially to the nation's economy.

- When the nation was worried about the loss of manufacturing jobs in the 1950s and 1960s, particularly in the cities, their public schools stepped up to help initiate the federal Vocational Education Act in 1963.

As community development became the focus of the Gray Areas projects during the Kennedy administration, big-city schools were an important partner. When America needed to know whether the investments it was making in urban schools were paying off, big-city school systems stepped forward to initiate the Trial Urban District Assessment of the National Assessment of Educational Progress (NAEP). Superintendents from the nation's large urban school systems were the first to come out in favor of national academic standards as they were being developed, and they signed onto No Child Left Behind because they knew the power of accountability and results.

As school boards began to struggle under the weight of a divided public, the nation's urban school systems banded together to formulate new governance systems to provide stronger leadership in urban America. When the nation was locked in debate about the degree of testing that schools were doing, the nation's urban schools conducted and released the only inventory of national, state, and local assessments the country had ever seen.[9]

Year after year, the nation's urban public schools lift thousands of young people and provide hope for a better future. Take Yoseline Murrillo, a Dreamer who worked the peach fields of central California but graduated at the top of her class in the Fresno public schools and is now enrolled at UCLA. Or Boun Lod, a double amputee who came to the United States after being badly burned and disfigured in a house fire in her native Laos to graduate from the Guilford County Schools, who now attends Appalachian State College. Or Sean Russell, Jr., who lived in one of the poorest sections of Pittsburgh, Pennsylvania, who graduated from Westinghouse Academy and earned a Gates scholarship and enrolled at Stanford University as a bioengineering major. There are thousands of these examples.

In fact, the nation's urban school systems have graduated some of the most notable members of American society, including Martin Luther King,

Maya Angelou, Gloria Steinem, Warren Buffet, Ruth Bader Ginsburg, Thurgood Marshall, Anthony Kennedy, Elena Kagan, Arthur Ashe, Jonas Salk, Jesse Owens, Isaac Asimov, Quincy Jones, Simon and Garfunkel, Orville and Wilbur Wright, Muhammad Ali, Fred Rogers, Andy Warhol, Mitch McConnell, Oprah Winfrey, Michelle Obama, Jennifer Lopez, Dan Rather, Barbara Jordan, Spike Lee, Henry Kissinger, Marian Anderson, Colin Powell, Woody Allen, Norman Mailer, Ray Bradbury, and numerous Nobel Prize winners who have contributed immeasurably to the country's development, culture, scientific prowess, and well-being.

Indeed they have left their mark on the nation.

Skepticism Nonetheless

Still, critics claim that public schools did not do enough over the pandemic and that public education has failed to provide quality instruction and has lost the confidence of the citizenry. They cite as evidence the substantial drop in NAEP scores between 2019 and 2022, the decline in enrollment in traditional public schools, and poll results on the public's faith in their schools.

US Secretary of Education Miguel Cardona described the 2022 NAEP results as "appalling" and "unacceptable," while a noted critic from the Center for Educational Reform indicated that "this record plunge on NAEP scores is a continuation of bad education policy, pandemic or not. . . . This is academic malnourishment."[10]

Another skeptic characterized American education as unbearably bleak.[11] Staff at the Center on Reinventing Public Education (CRPE) went a step further and claimed that the prospects that public schools will make up for lost ground are dim, particularly if schools do not follow their suggested strategies.[12] At the beginning of the pandemic, Robin Lake from CRPE claimed, "Currently, there is no plan to prevent what could be long-lasting academic casualties. . . . Large urban districts, which serve the majority of economically disadvantaged children of color, are unprepared to provide rigorous and effective remote learning. . . . As a result, city children will fall further behind."[13]

Hearing criticism is routine for urban school leaders, and the condemnations were what some feared at the outset of the pandemic. But, in my opinion, some of the critiques were particularly ill timed. Our communities expected that we would lend a hand in managing the crisis during the pandemic, but instead of judging our performance in doing so, some people were judging us on expected test scores as the crisis was only beginning.

To be sure, NAEP scores nationally dropped by between three and eight scale score points between 2019 and 2022, while results among the big-city school districts held steady in eighth grade reading and reflected national declines in other grades and subjects. And enrollments in the big-city schools declined over the same period by about 7 percent. It is also true that charter schools and some private schools saw increased enrollment in their schools as public schools in the cities were shuttered.

But are the critics right about the significance and permanence of these declines and the lost public confidence in our schools? Time will tell, but data from the Brookings Institution suggest that part of the enrollment loss was the result of urban outmigration as people fled the higher infection rates that came with greater urban population density.[14]

In fact, there have been other times over the last fifty years when city populations and public school enrollments declined only to see participation bounce back to record levels. It is likely that public confidence in our schools has taken a hit, but early data suggest that the fall off may not be as severe nor as permanent as some might have imagined.

THE CENTRALITY OF URBAN EDUCATION

Public confidence in any of our institutions is a tricky issue. Trust in everything has waned over the decades, at least since Watergate. Schools are not immune from that distrust.

Still, a series of local focus groups in Cleveland conducted toward the end of the 2021–2022 school year by Triad Research found that school parents liked that the district regularly disinfected the buildings, gave out masks, disseminated laptops and Wi-Fi, and provided meal services. The provision of technology got particularly staunch support from parents who characterized the district's efforts as "the thing that kept it all from being a disaster." And a randomized survey of citizens across the city showed that the percentage who rated the public schools as good or fair had increased from 24 percent in June 2018 to 30 percent in May 2022, a period covering the pandemic. Ratings by parents with children in the district's schools were higher.

The truth is that people like sending their children to their neighborhood public schools. The latest national Phi Delta Kappa poll indicated that some 63 percent of public school parents give the public school in their community a grade of A or B.[15] A similar poll by Ipsos for National Public Radio on the heels of the pandemic in April 2022 found that more than eight in ten respondents thought schools had handled the pandemic well; some 76 percent of parents thought their child's schools did a good job of keeping them informed about their school's curriculum, including potentially controversial topics; and that an increasing number were seeing improvements in their child's academic progress, compared to 2021.[16] Still, some folks claimed that parents were simply ill informed.

Other than the professional critics of urban schools, did residents of the nation's major cities care about what their public schools did in this moment of crisis? One must think so, given the enthusiastic use of and participation in the services that schools provided. And they cared as the months dragged on and disagreements emerged about reopening buildings, requiring vaccines, and wearing masks. The numbers of people who showed up at school board meetings to voice their concerns were unprecedented. Those voices did not always agree with one another, and they were sometimes hostile and angry, but they cared enough about what their schools were doing to say what they wanted and needed.

The truth is that public schools in the nation's major cities are critical not only to the residents of these urban areas but also to the health of the nation. They are vital to the country's future. Over seven million students of the nation's fifty million are educated in the seventy-eight largest urban school systems in the country—a large enough number to affect the overall educational and economic wherewithal of the nation.

You should care how these public school systems perform because they produce our future leaders, determine the quality of our workforce, and shape the direction of our country, even if you do not have a child in one of these school systems or a child at all. And these schools are part of the nation's investment in its own future. To be sure, public education, particularly in the cities, has created an inimitable and diverse stew of citizenry that is the foundation of the nation's creativity and innovation, and its productivity is the engine of our national welfare.

John Adams, the nation's second president and a leading public school proponent, asserted, "There should not be a district of one mile square, without a school in it, not founded by a charitable individual, but maintained at the expense of the people themselves."[17] The nation's judiciary system, moreover, has treated our public schools with a certain reverence because of the unique role they play in creating a well-informed, voting citizenry.

Indeed, America's urban public schools have played a critical role in expanding and nourishing democracy, despite their sordid history in resisting racial integration. The public schools have worked to support new immigrants and enhance opportunities for racial minorities; students with disabilities; students of differing faiths, languages, and sexual orientations; and girls. This has contributed to our concept of nationhood—one that guarantees equal opportunity and justice for all.[18]

In an era of increasing national fragmentation and disinformation, you should care about the health, well-being, and improvement of a public institution that is meant to bind us together and keep us informed. You should care about how these institutions are doing. And you should care about why and how some public school systems perform better than others because there is so much misinformation about what works and because there are so many policy recommendations floated by so-called experts that simply do not work.

If we lose public schools or let public schools be substituted with a fragmentary and disconnected patchwork of independent schools, then we lose the collective ability to set instructional standards and hold schools accountable for meeting these standards. We also undermine the unifying identity of the country itself. Put another way by David Cleary, a senior staff aide to both US Senators Lamar Alexander and Richard Burr, "We don't have a common religion or race or ethnicity or ancestry in America, but we do have the public schools to create a common national identity."[19] He could not have been more on point.

Our public schools influence the nation in ways that everyone should care about. Our democratic system of government is grounded in a diversity of ideas. Democracy is not strengthened by the siloing of those ideas in separate and disconnected settings but by their discussion and reconciliation. Public schools are at the center of teaching people how to debate and grapple with their differences. Our schools are one of the few "town halls" we have as a nation, a shared space that helps create common values. Public education, then, particularly in the nation's cities, is the bedrock of whether our national ideals are real. And for our part, the "leaders of America's Great City Schools see a future where the nation cares for all children, expects their best, appreciates their diversity, invests in their futures, and welcomes their participation in the American dream."[20]

Finally, if you are not swayed by the centrality of public education to a healthy and functioning democracy, then you might be persuaded by the role that schools play in the economic wherewithal of our citizens and our nation. Decades of research, in fact, show that increased levels of education and higher national investment in education lead to better economic growth, higher salaries, greater workforce effectiveness, and higher gross domestic product. Among the most prominent was a study published in the European Economic Review using data on twenty-three countries from the International Assessment of Adult Competencies (PIAAC) that showed that a one-standard-deviation increase in numeracy skills was associated with an 18-percent wage increase among workers in their prime earning years.[21]

The vitality of our public schools is critical to the welfare of our country and democratic way of life. How well our schools do—both during a pandemic and in better times—is central to every one of us, whether you have a child in school or not.

LIVING UP TO OUR END OF THE BARGAIN

The questions at this point are about whether our schools are living up to our end of the bargain—pandemic aside. How are we doing? Have we improved? Are urban public school districts worth the money? Do urban public schools add educational value for urban students, or do they simply reflect or even perpetuate the economic and racial inequities seen across the country? Are they engines of upward mobility? Are they counterweights to economic inequality? Do the improvements accrue to student groups that have historically been left behind? Do they mitigate poverty and other barriers to any degree? Do urban schools do a better job with any of these things than other schools? Is public education in the big cities really the ticket out of poverty, the great leveler? Are public schools, as Horace Mann once claimed, "the great equalizer of the conditions of men, the balance wheel of the social machinery"?[22]

It is not likely that our schools can be both the tickets out of poverty and a reflection of that poverty at the same time. Either schools help people create brighter futures or they do not. Either schools help overcome poverty and other barriers, or they reflect those inequities. Either schools serve to perpetuate society's inequities, or they help overcome them. Either schools work to level the playing field, or they keep opportunity at bay. Either they add value to the nation, or they do not. They are either mirrors or windows of opportunity—not likely both.

There are pundits who have ready answers to these questions, of course, but many of those answers are grounded in politics or ideology or partial information. In the chapters that follow, we take up these questions about whether the public schools, particularly in our major cities, are living up to their end of the bargain by contributing to the nation's welfare and contributing to upward mobility.

In chapter 2, we look at the best evidence the nation provides to see if the prevailing narrative around urban public schools is correct. We use student-level data on the NAEP from 2003 through 2019 and trends between 2009 and 2019 because that ten-year period was when the largest number of big-city schools were participating in the urban component of the assessment. We also look at poverty levels along with language status, parental education, disability rates, literacy materials in the home, and race/ethnicity to see how they affect the answers to our questions since long-standing research indicates that these variables affect student outcomes. We predict statistically what student results would look like using these variables, and we compare those predictions against actual results over each administration of NAEP. In other words, we create a "value-added" measure or "district effect" with the difference between raw and adjusted NAEP scores to determine whether urban school districts were exceeding expectations and whether they were mitigating poverty and other factors to any degree. Were they producing enough "educational torque" to help students overcome the challenges they faced?

In chapter 3, we look at what urban schools nationally were doing to create the conditions by which improvement might be possible. We look at the strategies they put into place to help each other get better. Did it work?

In chapter 4, we examine what districts that were producing outsized effects or had shown some of the largest improvements were doing to get their gains. How did these districts make their improvements? What were some of the characteristics of high-performing or fast-improving systems? Were the changes these urban districts experienced informed by any accepted concepts or theories about how large organizations improve?

In chapter 5, we contrast the practices we saw among the faster-improving urban school districts, if we can find them, with those that did not see as much academic progress. How did these districts differ in what they were doing from the districts that were making progress? Where did they go off track? The lessons we learn from those comparisons should be useful in how we proceed.

In chapter 6, the reader gets to "listen in" on weekly calls that the nation's big-city school leaders and staff had during the global pandemic. You will "hear" what they discussed; the dilemmas they faced; the challenges they had; and how they banded together to get through one of the most difficult periods that public education has ever encountered.

In chapter 7, we examine the effects the global COVID-19 pandemic had on our urban public schools. How did the pandemic affect student achievement? What about enrollment, attendance, and other indicators? The reader will also see what some of the big-city school districts were doing with the federal funds they received to help with pandemic recovery and will look at some of the preliminary student achievement data that are emerging since the pandemic.

Finally, in chapter 8, we discuss some broad lessons about what we learned during the pandemic and reach some conclusions about why we saw progress in some places and not others before the pandemic. We ask how the successes and failures of urban education inform us about how to regain lost ground and what we need to do in the future. And we offer a dozen high-level recommendations for how urban public education can go well beyond the progress these schools saw before the pandemic.

What you will read in the upcoming chapters comes from the vantage point of the nation's urban public school practitioners. Those practitioners have paid close attention to the research and to the back-and-forth in the advocacy community. This is not a theoretical book. It is also not a book with a small number of heroes. Instead, it comes from people—lots of people—who run things, can analyze data, synthesize broad trends, and make sense of why their institutions work like they do. It also comes from people who are profoundly optimistic but who can ask tough questions about how change and improvement in our schools are best made.

Now—on the heels of the global pandemic that shuttered so many of our schools—is the time to ask these questions. Now is the time to be clear about what was working and not working in our schools, and what deserves to be rethought, reimagined, and redesigned. And now is the time for educational leaders to step back into their primary roles leading instructional improvement, rather than just managing crises. How we respond at this critical juncture will define our path to better schools and a stronger democracy when the country desperately needs both.

2

Are Urban Schools Capable of Improving?

We laid out a series of arguments in the last chapter about why you should care about the future of the nation's urban public schools.[1] We also ask several critical questions: Have urban schools improved? Do they add value? Which big-city school systems improved the most? Have the gains accrued to the groups that have historically been left behind?[2]

This chapter looks at the educational performance of students using the Large City Schools variable of the National Assessment of Educational Progress (NAEP), commonly known as "The Nation's Report Card."[3] This assessment is widely known and trusted as the best single indicator about how the nation's children are doing academically. (See the appendix for a discussion of the pros and cons of NAEP.)

Later in this chapter we look at the twenty-seven individual cities that are oversampled through the Trial Urban District Assessment (TUDA) of NAEP to produce city-specific scores. All TUDA districts are part of the Council of the Great City Schools, which includes seventy-eight of the nation's largest urban school systems.[4] (See the appendix.)

We also control reading and mathematics performance on the NAEP by statistically adjusting scores using background variables that research indicates correlate with student achievement: poverty levels, language status, parental education, disability rates, literacy materials in the home, and race/ethnicity.[5] (See the appendix for definitions of these variables.)

To answer the questions from the beginning of this chapter, I ask for the reader's patience as we wade through a lot of testing data and statistics. Your forbearance and careful reading will be worth the effort because you will emerge at the end with a fuller understanding of the progress that urban public schools made in the twenty years before the pandemic.

The first step in our analysis was to divide the NAEP sample into two distinct, mutually exclusive categories: students in Large City Schools (public only) and students in All Other Schools. Large City Schools refers to public school students, not districts, in jurisdictions with at least 250,000 people along with those in TUDA districts. The latter category, All Other Schools, includes all other students in the NAEP sample, minus the Large City Schools, including both public and private schools. Charter schools are in both categories.[6] We then looked at the demographic characteristics of students in the two categories and asked if they were different.

ARE URBAN SCHOOL CHILDREN DIFFERENT?

Our question here is this: Do Large City Schools serve a fundamentally different student body than All Other Schools, since research indicates that poverty and other factors affect student performance? To answer this, we used student demographic data collected by the National Center for Educational Statistics (NCES) on fourth and eighth graders as they were taking the national assessment.

The data show that Large City Schools had an aggregate fourth-grade enrollment in 2019 that was 24 percent Black, 44 percent Hispanic, and 19 percent White. The percentage of Black students in Large City Schools declined from 29 percent to 24 percent between 2009 and 2019, while Hispanic students increased slightly from 42 percent to 44 percent. The percentage of White students also declined.[7] (See the appendix for all data.)

By contrast, about 13 percent of fourth graders in All Other Schools were Black in 2019, approximately 23 percent were Hispanic, and about 53 percent were White. Between 2009 and 2019, the proportion of White students in All Other Schools declined, and the proportion of Hispanic students increased.

The NAEP data also showed that the percentage of fourth-grade students in Large City Schools who were eligible for free or reduced-price lunch (FRPL) in 2019—often referred to in this report as students from low-income families—was 68 percent, down slightly from 2009. The percentage of FRPL-eligible students in All Other Schools was 47 percent in 2019, an uptick from 43 percent in 2009. In other words, in 2019 the enrollment of FRPL students in Large City Schools was about 45 percent higher than in All Other Schools.

Interestingly, FRPL rates dipped between 2009 and 2019 in Large City Schools over the same period when rates in All Other Schools increased. We have taken these changes into account in our statistical analysis by using the racial, language, and FRPL rates in each NAEP testing year, because others have called attention to the changing demographics of some cities and what it might mean for school performance.[8]

In addition, NAEP data on fourth graders show that English language learners (ELLs) made up 20 percent of the enrollment in Large City Schools in 2019, the same as in 2009. The enrollment of ELLs in All Other Schools was about 10 percent in 2019, up slightly from 8 percent in 2009.

Finally, NAEP data in 2019 showed that 14 percent of Large City School fourth graders had an Individualized Education Plan (IEP),[9] about the same as All Other Schools. Both groups showed increases in their proportions of students with IEPs between 2009 and 2019 (i.e., 11 percent to 14 percent in Large City Schools and 12 percent to 14 percent in All Others). Our analysis did not include data on each category of disability.

Eighth-grade demographic data were similar to fourth-grade patterns. Black students made up approximately 24 percent of students in Large City Schools in 2019 and 12 percent of students in All Others. Both settings showed declines in the percentage of Black students between 2009 and 2019. In addition, Hispanic students made up approximately 45 percent of Large City Schools in 2019, compared to 22 percent in All Others. The percentage of Hispanic students in both settings increased between 2009 and 2019. White students made up about 19 percent of eighth-grade enrollments in

Large City Schools in 2019, compared with 55 percent of students in All Other Schools. The proportion of White students in both settings declined between 2009 and 2019.

At the eighth-grade level, the data also indicated that the portion of students who were FRPL eligible in 2019 was slightly lower than that at the fourth-grade level in both Large City Schools and All Others. About 66 percent of Large City School eighth graders were FRPL eligible in 2019, as were 43 percent in All Other Schools. In other words, eighth-grade students in Large City Schools were about 53 percent more likely to be from low-income families in 2019 than students in All Other Schools.

In addition, eighth-grade data indicate that the percentages of ELLs in Large City Schools grew from 12 percent to 13 percent between 2009 and 2019. And in All Other Schools, the percentages of ELLs moved from 5 percent to 6 percent during the same period.

The percentage of eighth-grade students with IEPs in Large City Schools ranged from 11 percent to 13 percent between 2009 and 2019. The enrollments in All Other Schools of eighth graders with IEPs ranged from 10 percent to 13 percent over the same period.

Finally, we examined the education levels of parents of students in Large City Schools and All Other Schools. The data on this variable were available from NAEP only for eighth graders. The results showed that the percentage of Large City School students' parents who did not finish high school was about 10 percent in 2019, compared to approximately 6 percent among parents with students in All Other Schools. About 43 percent of Large City School students' parents were college graduates in 2019, compared with 57 percent among parents with students in All Other Schools. In both settings, there were declines in the percentages of parents who did not finish high school and increases in the percentages of parents who were college graduates.

In sum, the NAEP data showed that the demographics of students in Large City Schools and All Other Schools were different from each other. Large City Schools tended to have more Black and Hispanic students than All Other Schools. In addition, Large City Schools were more likely to have higher enrollments of FRPL students and ELLs. Large City

Schools, moreover, tended to have larger percentages of parents who did not finish high school and lower percentages of parents who graduated from college than All Other Schools. The percentages of students with IEPs were similar in both settings, although there may be differences between the two types of schools in the types and severity of disabilities.

HOW DOES THE PERFORMANCE OF URBAN SCHOOLS COMPARE TO THAT OF OTHERS?

At this point, the question is whether student performance in urban public schools has improved. Have these schools gotten better? Do they add value? And can we tell which urban school districts have improved the most?

To answer questions about improvement, we compared NAEP reading and math scale scores of students in Large City Schools with those of students in All Other Schools between 2003 and 2019.[10] And to answer questions about whether urban school districts add value, we adjusted the NAEP scores by the variables we described earlier: race/ethnicity, IEP status, ELL status, parental education levels, literacy materials in the home, FRPL eligibility, and family incomes. This adjusted measure is what we use to determine whether schools add value and dampen the effects of poverty or whether schools simply reflect that poverty. We begin by looking at trends on unadjusted NAEP scores over time.

Trends on Raw Scale Scores: Large City Schools versus All Other Schools

The unadjusted NAEP scale scores demonstrate two trends. First, Large City Schools scored below All Other Schools every year between 2003 and 2019. And second, Large City Schools improved more than All Other Schools between 2003 and 2019, narrowing the gaps between the nation's urban schools and everyone else by between one-third and one-half, depending on grade and subject. (See figures 2.1 through 2.4.)

The graphs show NAEP unadjusted scores. They are reported on a 0-to-500 point scale, but each subject and grade is scaled somewhat differently and is not directly comparable. The X axis shows the year tested, and

Figure 2.1   Average scale scores on NAEP in fourth-grade mathematics, 2003–2019

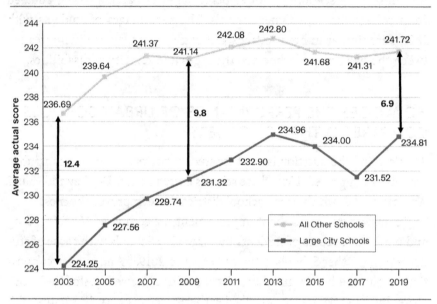

Figure 2.2   Average scale scores on NAEP in eighth-grade mathematics, 2003–2019

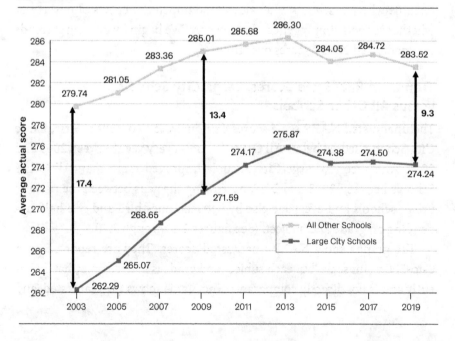

Figure 2.3   Average scale scores on NAEP fourth-grade reading, 2003–2019

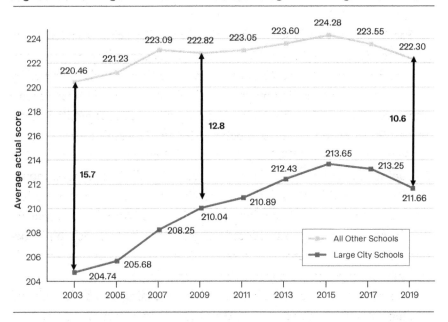

Figure 2.4   Average scale scores on NAEP eighth-grade reading, 2003–2019

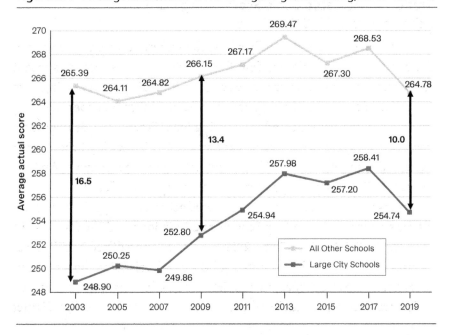

the Y axis shows the unadjusted scale scores. Most scores range from about 180 to around 320.

Specifically, the scale scores show that Large City Schools scored below All Other Schools by 12.4 to 17.4 points in 2003, depending on grade and subject. Between 2003 and 2009, however, Large City Schools improved by 3.9 to 9.3 points, depending on grade and subject, while All Other Schools improved 0.76 to 5.27 points, narrowing the gap between Large City Schools and All Other Schools in 2009 to between 9.8 and 13.4 scale score points.

Between 2009 and 2019, Large City Schools improved by another 1.62 to 3.49 points, depending on grade and subject, while All Other Schools moved from −1.49 to +0.58 points, further narrowing the gap to between 6.9 to 10.6 scale score points by 2019. In other words, the Large City Schools scored below the national average but reduced the gap with All Other Schools by between 32.5 and 46.6 percent between 2003 and 2019, depending on grade and subject. In general, the gaps between Large City Schools and All Other Schools narrowed more in mathematics than in reading, and both math and reading improved more between 2003 and 2009 than between 2009 and 2019.

Trends on Adjusted Scale Scores: Large City Schools versus All Other Schools

What happens if we statistically adjust the scores, however, according to the background variables we described previously? This section is meant to answer that and other related questions, including the following: Are Large City Schools performing above or below statistical expectations in reading and mathematics, after adjusting for differences in demographic characteristics? Do urban schools add value? Do Large City Schools do a better job at mitigating the effects of poverty than other schools? And are Large City Schools getting better at overcoming these effects?

To answer these questions, we compared actual NAEP performance levels for students in Large City Schools and individual TUDA districts[11] in 2009, 2011, 2013, 2015, 2017, and 2019 to adjusted or predicted NAEP scores in grades 4 and 8. We then adjusted All Other Schools using the same variables and compared actual and predicted scores for those two groups. The differences between actual and predicted scores, what we call a district effect or value-added measure, allow us to determine whether students in Large City Schools performed better than expected statistically and to compare their adjusted performance with students in All Other Schools. (A positive number suggests that the entity or jurisdiction is scoring higher than one would expect statistically given its demographic characteristics; a negative number suggests that the entity is scoring lower than one would expect statistically given its demographic characteristics. Zero is the point at which an entity scores what one would expect statistically.)

In addition, the results allow us to determine whether Large City Schools and All Other Schools were getting better over time at mitigating poverty and other variables that typically suppress performance.

Figures 2.5 through 2.8 show the results of the analyses. First, in 2019, the "value added" or "district effect"—that is, the difference between the actual

Figure 2.5 Trends in district effects[a] on NAEP fourth-grade mathematics by school type, 2009–2019

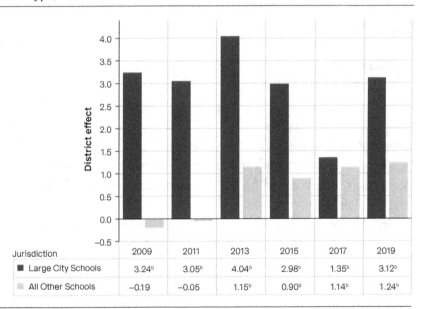

Jurisdiction	2009	2011	2013	2015	2017	2019
■ Large City Schools	3.24[b]	3.05[b]	4.04[b]	2.98[b]	1.35[b]	3.12[b]
All Other Schools	−0.19	−0.05	1.15[b]	0.90[b]	1.14[b]	1.24[b]

Note: Includes district-authorized charters, charters authorized by others, and independent charters.

[a] District effect is the difference between the actual district mean and the expected district mean.
[b] District effect is significantly different from zero at α < .05.

Figure 2.6 Trends in district effects[a] on NAEP eighth-grade mathematics by school type, 2009–2019

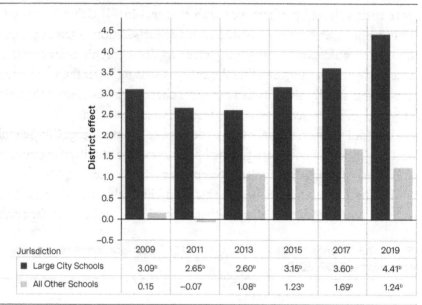

Jurisdiction	2009	2011	2013	2015	2017	2019
■ Large City Schools	3.09[b]	2.65[b]	2.60[b]	3.15[b]	3.60[b]	4.41[b]
▨ All Other Schools	0.15	–0.07	1.08[b]	1.23[b]	1.69[b]	1.24[b]

Note: Includes district-authorized charters, charters authorized by others, and independent charters.

[a] District effect is the difference between the actual district mean and the expected district mean.
[b] District effect is significantly different from zero at α < .05.

scale score and the adjusted score—was larger in the Large City Schools than statistical expectations in all four grade/subject combinations—fourth-grade reading, eighth-grade reading, fourth-grade mathematics, and eighth-grade mathematics.

In addition, the value added or district effects in Large City Schools was larger than expected every year between 2009 and 2019 in all four tested grades and subjects.

Second, we examined the differences between Large City Schools and All Others Schools in the value-added measure by year, grade, and subject. The results show that Large City Schools had larger district effects than All Other Schools in all four grade/subject combinations in every year between 2009 and 2019. In other words, the narrowing gap that we saw in

Figure 2.7 Trends in district effects[a] on NAEP fourth-grade reading by school type, 2009–2019

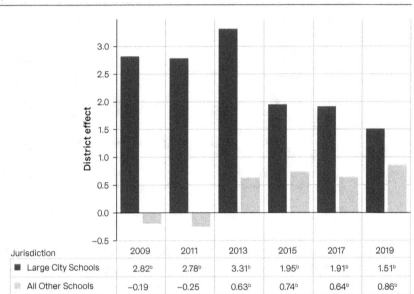

Jurisdiction	2009	2011	2013	2015	2017	2019
■ Large City Schools	2.82[b]	2.78[b]	3.31[b]	1.95[b]	1.91[b]	1.51[b]
All Other Schools	−0.19	−0.25	0.63[b]	0.74[b]	0.64[b]	0.86[b]

Note: Includes district-authorized charters, charters authorized by others, and independent charters.

[a] District effect is the difference between the actual district mean and the expected district mean.
[b] District effect is significantly different from zero at α < .05.

figures 2.1 through 2.4 was the result, in part, of Large City Schools producing an "effect" that was larger than All Others.

Third, the data show that district effects in Large City Schools did not change significantly between 2009 and 2019 in reading or mathematics in either grade, although the next section identifies some districts that improved their effects over time. On the other hand, All Other Schools showed small gains in their effects between 2009 and 2019 in most grade-subject combinations. Still, All Other School effects remained significantly below Large City School effects in 2019 in all grades and subjects.

In other words, Large City Schools had a district effect in 2019 in fourth-grade reading that was 1.8 times greater than All Other Schools; 5.6 times greater in eighth-grade reading; 2.5 times greater in fourth-grade mathematics; and 3.6 times greater in eighth-grade mathematics.

Figure 2.8   Trends in district effects[a] on NAEP eighth-grade reading by school type, 2009–2019

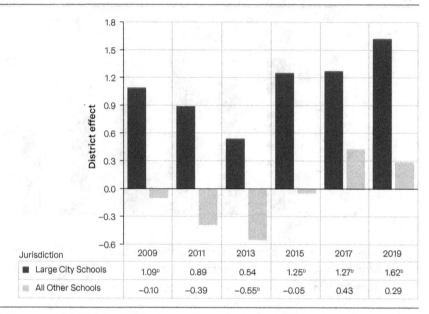

Jurisdiction	2009	2011	2013	2015	2017	2019
■ Large City Schools	1.09[b]	0.89	0.54	1.25[b]	1.27[b]	1.62[b]
▨ All Other Schools	−0.10	−0.39	−0.55[b]	−0.05	0.43	0.29

Note: Includes district-authorized charters, charters authorized by others, and independent charters.

[a] District effect is the difference between the actual district mean and the expected district mean.
[b] District effect is significantly different from zero at $\alpha < .05$.

City-by-City Results: Actual versus Expected (Adjusted) Performance

Our next research questions were as follows: Do some Large City School districts mitigate the effects of poverty better than other urban school districts? If so, which ones? Are some cities getting better over time? To find out, we use the TUDA portion of the NAEP, which oversamples students in twenty-seven major urban school districts to yield district level scores.

Tables 2.1 through 2.4 show the actual performance and the effect sizes of individual Large City School districts in 2019 in the order of their magnitude. (Jacob Cohen, the developer of the effect-size methodology, explains that an effect size of 0.8 or above should be considered large, 0.5 medium, and 0.2 small, but not all methodologists agree. For more

Table 2.1 Ranking of TUDA districts on fourth-grade mathematics scale scores, 2019 effect sizes, 2019 district effects, and trends in district effects

Scale scores, 2019	Effect sizes, 2019	Value-added or district effects, 2019	Changes in value-added or district effects, 2009–2019[a]
Charlotte (246)	Denver (1.66)	Miami-Dade County (14.90)[b]	D. C. (11.5)[c]
Miami-Dade County (246)	Boston (1.62)	Denver (14.05)[b]	Detroit (8.6)[c]
Duval County (244)	Miami-Dade County (1.38)	Dallas (12.51)[b]	Miami-Dade County (7.9)[c]
Austin (243)	D.C. (1.34)	Duval County (10.78)[b]	Chicago (7.0)[c]
Hillsborough County (242)	Fort Worth (1.30)	Fort Worth (10.42)[b]	Cleveland (6.5)[c]
All Other Schools (242)	Austin (1.29)	Boston (10.13)[b]	Fresno (3.0)
San Diego (240)	Dallas (1.25)	Austin (9.82)[b]	Atlanta (2.9)[c]
Guilford County (236)	Duval County (1.00)	Houston (9.29)[b]	All Other Schools (1.4)[c]
Clark County (235)	Charlotte (0.96)	Charlotte (8.91)[b]	Charlotte (0.1)
Dallas (235)	Houston (0.87)	Hillsborough County (7.87)[b]	Jefferson County (0.1)
Denver (235)	Atlanta (0.76)	D.C. (7.49)[b]	Large City Schools (−0.1)
D.C. (235)	Hillsborough County (0.71)	Atlanta (5.12)[b]	San Diego (−0.6)
Houston (235)	Cleveland (0.49)	Chicago (4.75)[b]	Austin (−1.6)
Large City Schools (235)	Guilford County (0.44)	Guilford County (3.49)[b]	Boston (−2.0)
Boston (234)	Chicago (0.39)	Large City Schools (3.12)[b]	Milwaukee (−3.7)[c]
Fort Worth (233)	Shelby County (0.29)	Cleveland (2.95)[b]	Houston (−4.1)[c]
Atlanta (232)	San Diego (0.28)	Shelby County (2.94)[b]	Los Angeles (−5.3)[c]
Chicago (232)	Large City Schools (0.16)	San Diego (2.64)[b]	Baltimore (−6.5)[c]

(continued)

Table 2.1 (*Continued*)

Scale scores, 2019	Effect sizes, 2019	Value-added or district effects, 2019	Changes in value-added or district effects, 2009–2019[a]
Jefferson County (232)	Clark County (0.09)	All Other Schools (1.24)[b]	Philadelphia (–7.5)[c]
New York City (231)	All Other Schools (0.07)	Clark County (1.00)	New York City (–11.2)[c]
Albuquerque (230)	New York City (0.02)	New York City (0.28)	
Shelby County (228)	Albuquerque (–0.09)	Albuquerque (–0.81)	
Fresno (224)	Jefferson County (–0.17)	Jefferson County (–1.61)	
Los Angeles (224)	Fresno (–0.40)	Fresno (–3.08)[b]	
Cleveland (218)	Baltimore (–0.56)	Baltimore (–4.84)[b]	
Philadelphia (217)	Los Angeles (–0.58)	Philadelphia (–6.97)[b]	
Baltimore (216)	Philadelphia (–0.62)	Milwaukee (–6.97)[b]	
Milwaukee (215)	Milwaukee (–0.79)	Los Angeles (–7.22)[b]	
Detroit (205)	Detroit (–1.37)	Detroit (–9.23)[b]	

[a] Only 18 urban school districts participated in TUDA in 2009.
[b] District effect is significantly different from zero.
[c] Difference in district effect between 2009 and 2019 is significant.

Table 2.2 Ranking of TUDA districts on eighth-grade mathematics scale scores, 2019 effect sizes, 2019 district effects, and trends in district effects

Scale scores, 2019	Effect sizes, 2019	Value-added or district effects, 2019	Change in value-added or district effects, 2009–2019[a]
Charlotte (288)	Boston (2.55)	Boston (17.63)[b]	D.C. (11.9)[c]
All Other Schools (284)	Houston (1.31)	Houston (12.01)[b]	Detroit (10.1)[c]
San Diego (283)	Dallas (1.27)	Dallas (11.87)[b]	Chicago (8.8)[c]
Austin (282)	Austin (1.06)	Chicago (11.40)[b]	Atlanta (4.0)[c]

Table 2.2 (*Continued*)

Scale scores, 2019	Effect sizes, 2019	Value-added or district effects, 2019	Change in value-added or district effects, 2009–2019[a]
Guilford County (280)	Charlotte (1.03)	Charlotte (10.50)[b]	Charlotte (4.0)[c]
Boston (279)	Chicago (0.86)	Austin (8.80)[b]	Jefferson County (3.8)[c]
Hillsborough County (276)	Atlanta (0.85)	Miami-Dade County (6.65)[b]	Miami-Dade County (3.7)[c]
Miami-Dade County (276)	Guilford County (0.68)	Atlanta (5.63)[b]	Milwaukee (1.4)
Chicago (275)	Fort Worth (0.63)	Guilford County (5.49)[b]	Large City Schools (1.3)
Denver (275)	D.C. (0.63)	New York City (5.49)[b]	All Other Schools (1.1)[c]
Duval County (274)	Cleveland (0.57)	Fort Worth (5.08)[b]	Boston (0.3)
Houston (274)	Miami-Dade County (0.56)	Large City Schools (4.41)[b]	Baltimore (–0.3)
Large City Schools (274)	Shelby County (0.42)	D.C. (4.10)[b]	Cleveland (–0.6)
Jefferson County (273)	Hillsborough County (0.32)	Cleveland (3.91)[b]	San Diego (–0.5)
New York City (273)	New York City (0.30)	Hillsborough County (3.87)[b]	Houston (–1.3)
Clark County (272)	Duval County (0.25)	Shelby County (3.68)[b]	New York City (–1.5)
D.C. (269)	San Diego (0.22)	Duval County (2.35)	Los Angeles (–3.2)[c]
Atlanta (268)	Large City Schools (0.18)	San Diego (1.86)	Fresno (–5.8)[c]
Albuquerque (267)	All Other Schools (0.06)	All Other Schools (1.24)[b]	Austin (–6.1)[c]
Fort Worth (265)	Jefferson County (-0.01)	Jefferson County (–0.12)	Philadelphia (–9.6)[c]
Shelby County (265)	Clark County (–0.14)	Clark County (–1.44)	
Dallas (264)	Baltimore (–0.27)	Baltimore (–2.34)	

(continued)

Table 2.2   *(Continued)*

Scale scores, 2019	Effect sizes, 2019	Value-added or district effects, 2019	Change in value-added or district effects, 2009–2019[a]
Los Angeles (261)	Philadelphia (–0.41)	Albuquerque (–3.68)[b]	
Philadelphia (256)	Albuquerque (–0.46)	Philadelphia (–4.67)[b]	
Baltimore (254)	Milwaukee (–0.56)	Detroit (–4.68)[b]	
Fresno (254)	Los Angeles (–0.59)	Milwaukee (–4.93)[b]	
Cleveland (253)	Detroit (–0.68)	Los Angeles (–7.39)[b]	
Milwaukee (252)	Fresno (–1.33)	Fresno (–10.86)[b]	
Detroit (244)			

[a] Only 18 urban school districts participated in TUDA in 2009.
[b] District effect is significantly different from zero.
[c] Difference in district effect between 2009 and 2019 is significant.

Table 2.3   Ranking of TUDA districts on fourth-grade reading scale scores, 2019 effect sizes, 2019 district effects, and trends in district effects

Scale scores, 2019	Effect sizes, 2019	Value-added or district effects, 2019	Change in value-added or district effects, 2009–2019[a]
Charlotte (225)	Denver (1.86)	Denver (18.97)[b]	D.C. (11.6)[c]
Miami-Dade County (225)	Boston (1.6)	Miami-Dade County (14.28)[b]	Cleveland (8.1)[c]
Hillsborough County (224)	D.C. (1.20)	Boston (12.60)[b]	San Diego (4.3)
San Diego (223)	Miami-Dade County (1.15)	Hillsborough County (10.07)[b]	Fresno (3.3)
Duval County (222)	Atlanta (0.88)	Duval County (7.88)[b]	Chicago (3.0)
All Other Schools (222)	Hillsborough County (0.77)	D.C. (7.62)[b]	Miami-Dade County (3.0)[c]

Table 2.3   *(Continued)*

Scale scores, 2019	Effect sizes, 2019	Value-added or district effects, 2019	Change in value-added or district effects, 2009–2019[a]
Guilford County (218)	Guilford County (0.68)	Atlanta (7.22)[b]	Atlanta (2.8)
Austin (217)	Duval County (0.66)	Charlotte (7.20)[b]	All Other Schools (1.1)[c]
Denver (217)	Charlotte (0.66)	San Diego (6.66)[b]	Philadelphia (0.4)
Clark County (216)	San Diego (0.62)	Guilford County (6.17)[b]	Detroit (0.1)
Atlanta (214)	Austin (0.60)	Austin (5.47)[b]	Boston (−0.2)
Boston (214)	Fort Worth (0.52)	Fort Worth (4.91)[b]	Charlotte (−0.7)
D.C. (214)	Cleveland (0.40)	Clark County (3.83)[b]	Large City Schools (−1.3)
Jefferson County (214)	Clark County (0.31)	Dallas (3.54)	Los Angeles (−3.3)[c]
New York City (212)	Dallas (0.28)	Cleveland (3.34)	Austin (−3.9)
Large City Schools (212)	Chicago (0.20)	New York City (3.20)[b]	Jefferson County (−4.2)[c]
Albuquerque (208)	New York City (0.19)	Chicago (2.71)[b]	Milwaukee (−4.7)[c]
Chicago (208)	Houston (0.08)	Large City Schools (1.51)[b]	Baltimore (−7.0)[c]
Los Angeles (205)	Large City Schools (0.07)	Houston (0.93)	Houston (−7.9)[c]
Shelby County (205)	All Other Schools (0.05)	All Other Schools (0.86)[b]	New York City (−9.3)[c]
Fort Worth (204)	Shelby County (−0.07)	Shelby County (−0.71)	
Fresno (204)	Jefferson County (−0.09)	Jefferson County (−0.89)	
Houston (204)	Albuquerque (−0.16)	Fresno (−1.39)	
Dallas (203)	Fresno (−0.16)	Albuquerque (−1.56)	

(continued)

Table 2.3   (*Continued*)

Scale scores, 2019	Effect sizes, 2019	Value-added or district effects, 2019	Change in value-added or district effects, 2009–2019[a]
Philadelphia (197)	Los Angeles (–0.37)	Los Angeles (–4.94)[b]	
Cleveland (196)	Philadelphia (–0.49)	Philadelphia (–6.02)[b]	
Baltimore (193)	Baltimore (–0.68)	Baltimore (–7.24)[b]	
Milwaukee (190)	Milwaukee (–1.04)	Milwaukee (–10.89)[b]	
Detroit (183)	Detroit (–1.42)	Detroit (–11.19)[b]	

[a] Only 18 urban school districts participated in TUDA in 2009.
[b] District effect is significantly different from zero.
[c] Difference in district effect between 2009 and 2019 is significant.

Table 2.4 Ranking of TUDA districts on eighth-grade reading scale scores, 2019 effect sizes, 2019 district effects, and trends on district effects

Scale scores 2019	Effect sizes 2019	Value-added or district effects 2019	Change in value-added or district effects, 2009–2019[a]
San Diego (266)	Boston (1.51)	Boston (11.36)[b]	D.C. (7.3)[c]
All Other Schools (265)	Atlanta (0.90)	Miami-Dade County (6.70)[b]	Detroit (5.0)[c]
Miami-Dade County (262)	Cleveland (0.86)	Cleveland (6.42)[b]	San Diego (3.5)
Charlotte (261)	Dallas (0.62)	Atlanta (6.41)[b]	Cleveland (3.0)
Hillsborough County (261)	Miami-Dade County (0.56)	Dallas (5.62)[b]	Jefferson County (1.8)
Duval County (258)	Hillsborough County (0.42)	Hillsborough County (5.12)[b]	New York City (1.7)
Guilford County (258)	Chicago (0.33)	Chicago (4.22)[b]	Atlanta (1.6)
Jefferson County (258)	Duval County (0.27)	New York City (3.86)[b]	Boston (1.6)

Table 2.4 (Continued)

Scale scores 2019	Effect sizes 2019	Value-added or district effects 2019	Change in value-added or district effects, 2009–2019[a]
Austin (257)	San Diego (0.27)	San Diego (2.58)	Large City Schools (0.5)
Boston (257)	D.C. (0.24)	Duval County (2.52)[b]	Chicago (0.4)
Denver (257)	Charlotte (0.22)	Houston (2.29)	All Other Schools (0.4)
Clark County (256)	New York City (0.22)	Charlotte (2.13)	Miami-Dade County (−0.2)
Atlanta (255)	Houston (0.22)	Shelby County (1.93)	Milwaukee (−0.3)
Large City Schools (255)	Shelby County (0.21)	D.C. (1.62)	Charlotte (−0.3)
New York City (254)	Atlanta (0.19)	Large City Schools (1.62)[b]	Baltimore (−0.8)
Chicago (253)	Guilford County (0.10)	Austin (1.55)	Fresno (−1.8)
D.C. (251)	Jefferson County (0.09)	Guilford County (0.78)	Houston (−2.2)
Albuquerque (249)	Large City Schools (0.07)	Jefferson County (0.75)	Los Angeles (−4.4)[c]
Houston (249)	All Other Schools (0.01)	All Other Schools (0.29)	Austin (−5.2)[c]
Shelby County (249)	Clark County (0.00)	Clark County (0.03)	Philadelphia (−5.4)[c]
Los Angeles (248)	Austin (−0.08)	Baltimore (−0.65)	
Fort Worth (243)	Fort Worth (−0.22)	Fort Worth (−1.88)	
Philadelphia (243)	Milwaukee (−0.22)	Milwaukee (−2.06)	
Cleveland (242)	Philadelphia (−0.28)	Philadelphia (−2.99)[b]	
Dallas (242)	Los Angeles (−0.34)	Los Angeles (−3.93)[b]	
Fresno (242)	Detroit (−0.55)	Detroit (−3.98)[b]	

(continued)

Table 2.4   *(Continued)*

Scale scores 2019	Effect sizes 2019	Value-added or district effects 2019	Change in value-added or district effects, 2009–2019[a]
Baltimore (241)	Albuquerque (–0.68)	Albuquerque (–5.32)[b]	
Milwaukee (240)	Fresno (–0.74)	Fresno (–6.50)[b]	
Detroit (232)			

[a] Only 18 urban school districts participated in TUDA in 2009.
[b] District effect is significantly different from zero.
[c] Difference in district effect between 2009 and 2019 is significant.

information, see endnote.[12]) The tables also show the Large City School value-added or district effects and the effects in All Other Schools. And the tables rank *changes* in the value added or district effects between 2009 and 2019.[13] Note that not all participating TUDA districts are shown in the far-right column, which presents trends in value-added scores between 2009 and 2019.[14]

Please note that effect sizes as developed by Cohen are not the same thing as the district effects or value-added measure.

The data show that individual cities had considerable variation in their results in 2019. For instance, cities ranged in their district effects in *fourth-grade mathematics* from +14.90 in Miami-Dade County to –9.23 in Detroit (table 2.1). Overall, seventeen of twenty-seven cities (Atlanta, Austin, Boston, Charlotte-Mecklenburg, Chicago, Cleveland, Dallas, Denver, the District of Columbia, Duval County, Fort Worth, Guilford County, Hillsborough County, Houston, Miami-Dade County, San Diego, and Shelby County) posted statistically significant positive district effects in 2019, while six had statistically significant negative district effects.

Next, table 2.2 shows data on individual cities in *eighth-grade mathematics*. City effects varied from +17.63 in Boston to –10.86 in Fresno in 2019. Some fifteen of twenty-six cities[15] (Atlanta, Austin, Boston, Charlotte-Mecklenburg, Chicago, Cleveland, Dallas, the District of

Columbia, Fort Worth, Guilford County, Hillsborough County, Houston, Miami-Dade County, New York City, and Shelby County) had statistically significant positive district effects in 2019 while six had statistically significant negative district effects.

In *fourth-grade reading* (table 2.3), individual district effects ranged from +18.97 in Denver to –11.19 in Detroit in 2019. Overall, fifteen of twenty-seven cities (Atlanta, Austin, Boston, Charlotte-Mecklenburg, Chicago, Clark County, Denver, the District of Columbia, Duval County, Fort Worth, Guilford County, Hillsborough County, Miami-Dade County, New York City, and San Diego) had statistically significant positive district effects in 2019, while five had statistically significant negative district effects.

In *eighth-grade reading* (table 2.4), individual cities varied from +11.36 in Boston to −6.50 in Fresno in 2019. Overall, nine of twenty-six cities (Atlanta, Boston, Chicago, Cleveland, Dallas, Duval County, Hillsborough County, Miami-Dade County, and New York City) had statistically significant positive district effects in 2019, while five had statistically significant negative effects.

City-by-City Trends

The previous tables and graphs were meant to answer questions about whether Large City Schools were mitigating the effects of poverty, language, and other demographic variables to any degree. That is, were Large City School districts producing an effect in 2019 that was greater than one would expect given their demographic characteristics? Did they add value? In this section, we look at individual city trends in value-added effects between 2009 and 2019. (See the far-right column of tables 2.1 through 2.4.)

In *fourth-grade mathematics*, eighteen of the twenty-seven districts have trend lines that extend from 2009 to 2019, and six of these districts show significantly larger district effects in 2019 than they did in 2009: the District of Columbia, Detroit, Miami-Dade County, Chicago, Cleveland, and Atlanta (table 2.1). Three districts were notable for having gone from below statistical expectations in 2009 (i.e., the zero line) to above statistical expectations in 2019: Chicago, Cleveland, and the District of Columbia.

In eighth-grade mathematics, eighteen of the twenty-seven districts have trend lines that extend from 2009 to 2019, and seven of these districts show significantly larger district effects in 2019 than they did in 2009: the District of Columbia, Detroit, Chicago, Atlanta, Charlotte-Mecklenburg, Jefferson County, and Miami-Dade County (table 2.2). Notably, the District of Columbia went from below statistical expectations in 2009 (i.e., the zero line) to above statistical expectations in 2019.

In fourth-grade reading, eighteen of the twenty-seven districts have trend lines that extend from 2009 to 2019, and three of these districts show significantly larger district effects in 2019 than they did in 2009: the District of Columbia, Cleveland, and Miami-Dade County (table 2.3). Again, the District of Columbia went from below statistical expectations in 2009 (i.e., the zero line) to above statistical expectations in 2019.

Finally, *in eighth-grade reading,* eighteen of the twenty-seven districts have trend lines that extend from 2009 to 2019, and two of these districts show significantly larger district effects in 2019 than they did in 2009: the District of Columbia and Detroit (table 2.4). No district moved from significantly below zero to significantly above zero during the ten-year period in eighth-grade reading.

Overall, these were notable gains for several districts. The districts that posted significant district effects in all four grade/subject combinations in 2019 included Boston, Miami-Dade County, Hillsborough County, Atlanta, and Chicago. Several others had significant district effects in 2019 in three of four grade/subject combinations: Dallas, Cleveland, New York City, Duval County, Fort Worth, Charlotte-Mecklenburg, the District of Columbia, Austin, and Guilford County.

In addition, between 2009 and 2019, districts that showed significantly larger effects over the period in at least two grade/subject combinations included the District of Columbia, Detroit, Miami-Dade County, Chicago, Cleveland, and Atlanta. The District of Columbia posted the largest increases of any TUDA district in all four grade/subject combinations, including moving from below statistical expectations to above statistical expectations in three of four grade/subject combinations. (See table 2.5.)

Table 2.5 Districts with multiple district effects in 2019 by grade/subject combination and districts with at least two significant trends between 2009 and 2019

Value added or district effects in all four grade/subject combinations in 2019	Value added or district effects in three grade/subject combinations in 2019	Value added or district effects in at least two grade/subject combinations from 2009 to 2019
Boston	Dallas	District of Columbia
Miami-Dade County	Cleveland	Detroit
Hillsborough County	New York City	Miami-Dade County
Atlanta	Duval County	Chicago
Chicago	Fort Worth	Cleveland
	Charlotte-Mecklenburg	Atlanta
	District of Columbia	
	Austin	
	Guilford County	

Progress of Critical Student Groups

The next question involves the progress or lack thereof of student groups that historically have been underserved. We look at these data in two ways: we look at the difference between performance for each group between 2003 and 2019, and we look at changes in the gaps among groups. Here we use the national public sample for comparison rather than the All Other Schools category.

While many of the results depend on the group, the grade, and the subject we are looking at, a pattern across groups does emerge. Looking at the score changes—and gaps—depicted in the tables below, it becomes clear that Large City Schools saw progress among their most critical student groups in most subjects and grade levels, but their achievement gaps remained stubbornly persistent.

- For instance, Large City School **African American** students, most of whom were also from low-income families, made substantial progress on NAEP in fourth-grade math and reading and eighth-grade math between 2003 and 2019.[16] Yet, at the same time, White students in the Large City Schools were also making progress at about the same rate, leaving the gaps between White and African American students in 2019 about the same as they were in 2003. (See table 2.6.)

- Between 2003 and 2019, fourth- and eighth-grade **Hispanic** students in the Large City Schools improved their NAEP reading and math scores across the board. But this progress was about the same as that made by White and African American students between 2003 and 2019, leaving substantial gaps between White and Hispanic Large City School students. (See table 2.7.)

Table 2.6 Change in NAEP math and reading scores among Large City School African American students and change in gaps, 2003–2019

	4th-grade math	8th-grade math	4th-grade reading	8th-grade reading
Scale score in 2003	211.9	247.3	193.0	240.7
Gap with Whites	30.8	38.1	33.3	27.5
Scale score in 2019	221.3	258.4	199.5	241.2
Gap with Whites	30.5	37.8	32.0	33.2
Change in scale score, 2003–2019	+9.3*	+11.1*	+6.5*	+0.5

* Change is significant at $p < .05$.

Table 2.7 Change in NAEP math and reading scores among Large City School Hispanic students and change in gaps, 2003–2019

	4th-grade math	8th-grade math	4th-grade reading	8th-grade reading
Scale score in 2003	219.2	255.6	197.4	240.7
Gap with Whites	23.5	29.8	28.9	27.5
Scale score in 2019	229.8	266.4	205.3	249.0
Gap with Whites	22.0	29.8	26.2	25.4
Change in scale score, 2003–2019	+10.6*	+10.9*	+7.9*	+8.3*

* Change is significant at $p < .05$.

- Progress among **low-income** and non-low-income students mirrored the trends of African American and Hispanic students. (See table 2.8.) Students from low-income families in Large City Schools made considerable progress in all areas between 2003 and 2019. There was a tendency, however, for the gaps between low-income and non-low-income students in Large City Schools to widen somewhat over the period.
- The progress of **ELLs** was trickier to assess because this group is defined by their English language proficiency. Still, the group made significant progress between 2003 and 2019, while the difference between ELLs and non-ELLs tended to widen somewhat over the study period (table 2.9).

Table 2.8 Change in NAEP math and reading scores among Large City School students from low-income families and change in gaps, 2003–2019

	4th-grade math	8th-grade math	4th-grade reading	8th-grade reading
Scale score in 2003	217.1	252.4	196.4	241.0
Gap with non-low-income	23.3	26.7	26.7	22.4
Scale score in 2019	226.7	263.9	202.5	245.8
Gap with non-low-income	25.5	30.8	28.8	26.7
Change in scale score, 2003–2019	+9.6*	+11.5*	+6.1*	+4.8*

* Change is significant at $p < .05$.

Table 2.9 Change in NAEP math and reading scores among Large City School English language learners and change in gaps, 2003–2019

	4th-grade math	8th-grade math	4th-grade reading	8th-grade reading
Scale score in 2003	211.0	237.6	184.3	215.1
Gap with non-ELLs	16.1	27.6	24.3	37.5
Scale score in 2019	219.3	242.9	188.2	219.9
Gap with non-ELLs	19.4	36.1	29.3	40.3
Change in scale score, 2003–2019	+8.3*	+5.4	+3.9*	+4.9

* Change is significant at $p < .05$.

Table 2.10 Change in NAEP math and reading scores among Large City School students with disabilities and change in gaps, 2003–2019

	4th-grade math	8th-grade math	4th-grade reading	8th-grade reading
Scale score in 2003	204.1	228.7	174.8	211.9
Gap with students without disabilities	22.0	37.4	32.6	41.0
Scale score in 2019	207.6	239.0	176.2	220.1
Gap with students without disabilities	31.6	40.7	41.4	39.9
Change in scale score, 2003–2019	+3.5*	+10.3*	+1.4	+8.2*

* Change is significant at $p<.05$.

- The patterns were different among **students with disabilities**. There were gains in most subjects and grades among Large City School students with disabilities. And the gaps with students without disabilities widened in some but not all cases (table 2.10). For instance, fourth-grade math scores among students with disabilities appeared to improve from 2003 to 2019, while gaps with students without disabilities grew over the same period. In the eighth grade, math scores among students with disabilities improved from 2003 to 2019, but the gap between the two groups widened slightly. In reading, fourth-grade students with disabilities saw marginal improvement between 2003 and 2019. Reading scores among eighth graders also improved, while the gap between the two groups stayed about the same.

We also looked at trends among **students in the 90th percentile** and **those at the 10th percentile** in NAEP math scores to see which groups, if any, showed progress and to compare those trends with the same groups in the national public sample of NAEP. (See tables 2.11 and 2.12.) Specifically, we examined students in all subjects and grades, comparing the national sample with the Large City School sample.[17]

Table 2.11 Change in NAEP math scores among Large City School students in the 90th and 10th percentiles and change in gaps, 2003–2019

	4th graders at 90th percentile 2003	8th graders at 90th percentile 2019	4th graders at 10th percentile 2003	8th graders at 10th percentile 2019
Scale score in 2003	262.3	310.7	185.8	213.6
Gap with national sample	7.4	10.6	10.6	14.9
Scale score in 2019	276.7	328.1	191.7	222.2
Gap with national sample	2.8	4.3	6.5	7.5
Change in scale score, 2003–2019	+14.4*	+17.4*	+5.9*	+8.6*

* Change is significant at $p < .05$.

Table 2.12 Change in NAEP reading scores among Large City School students in the 90th and 10th percentiles and change in gaps, 2002–2019

	4th graders at 90th percentile 2003	8th graders at 90th percentile 2019	4th graders at 10th percentile 2003	8th graders at 10th percentile 2019
Scale score in 2002	249.9	294.9	153.5	204.0
Gap with national sample	11.1	8.5	15.1	14.7
Scale score in 2019	260.3	303.0	157.8	201.7
Gap with national sample	5.2	4.9	9.1	9.8
Change in scale score, 2002–2019	+10.4*	+8.1*	+4.3*	–2.3

* Change is significant at $p < .05$.

Math

- At the **90th percentile** in fourth-grade math, we saw substantial improvements among students in the national sample, while students in the Large City Schools who scored in the 90th percentile improved even more. The result was that students in the 90th percentile in the Large City Schools narrowed the gap with students in the 90th percentile nationwide between 2003 and 2019.

- The pattern was similar in eighth-grade math. Among students in the national sample who scored at the **90th percentile**, NAEP scores improved from 2003 to 2019. At the same time, Large City School students who scored at the 90th percentile improved by a larger margin, meaning that the gap between the students in the 90th percentile in the national sample and the Large City Schools narrowed.
- At the other end of the continuum, that is, fourth graders in the **10th percentile** in the national sample saw nominal gains in math scores between 2003 and 2019, while students in the 10th percentile in the Large City School sample improved significantly, meaning that the gap between the two groups narrowed.
- Among eighth graders at the **10th percentile** in math, students in the national public sample showed little to no improvement between 2003 and 2019, while eighth graders in the Large City Schools who scored at the 10th percentile showed significant improvement, narrowing the gap between the lowest performing students in the national and Large City School samples.

Reading

- The patterns were similar in reading. The improvement of both fourth and eighth graders at the **90th percentile** in reading in the Large City Schools outpaced those at the 90th percentile in the national public sample, narrowing the gap between the two groups between 2002 and 2019.
- At the lower end of the scale, fourth students at the **10th percentile** in the national sample saw a slight decline in performance, while students at the 10th percentile in the Large City Schools saw a gain, again narrowing gaps between the two groups. But at the eighth-grade level, students in both the national sample and in the Large City Schools in the 10th percentile lost ground, although city students lost less and the gap between the two narrowed somewhat.

Finally, we looked at individual Large City School systems whose progress was summarized in tables 2.1 to 2.4 to see how they did with these varying student groups. The data for 2019 suggest that if a fourth grader were African American and from a family of low income, they would be scoring above the national averages for this group in math and reading if they were attending school in Miami-Dade County, Duval Couty (Jacksonville), Charlotte-Mecklenburg, Hillsborough County (Tampa), Guilford County, or Boston. An eighth grader who was African American and low income would be outscoring their same-race and income peers across the nation in math and reading in Charlotte-Mecklenburg, Chicago, Boston, Duval County, Miami-Dade County, and Shelby County.

It is worth noting that Chicago, the District of Columbia, and Miami-Dade County showed substantial gains among African American students who were also from families of low income. In each case, their improvements outstripped any other jurisdiction's gains for this group. The list of cities where Hispanic students who were also from families with low income would be scoring above their racial and economic peers nationally would be similar.

It is clear from the NAEP evidence that each of the main demographic groups that populate the nation's urban public schools made substantial progress between 2003 and 2019. At the same time, little overall headway was made in narrowing achievement gaps, suggesting an overall improvement in the quality of instruction but little effect from any targeted efforts that might have moved some of these groups at a faster rate.

We should remember that these gaps are the result of long-standing inequities in what is provided to each group by the schools themselves and by external forces. In addition, the intersections of poverty and race, language, and disability are fraught in the urban context because of their scale and history.[18]

Graduation and Other Indicators

In addition to NAEP data collected every two years by the NCES, the Council of the Great City Schools has been collecting data on other academic indicators since 2015–2016. Table 2.13 shows trend data from 2015–2016 through 2019–2020 on five secondary-grade academic indicators for districts that are part of the organization. Data are reported in medians,

Table 2.13 Trends on various academic indicators for the Great City Schools

	2015–2016	2016–2017	2017–2018	2018–2019	2019–2020
Four-year cohort graduation rate[a]	79%	81%	81%	83%	85.6%
Percentage of 9th graders who failed 1 or more core course(s)	32%	30%	29%	32%	23.6%
Percentage of students who completed Algebra I by end of grade 9	70%	75%	73%	73%	75.7%
Percentage of secondary students who took 1 or more AP courses	21%	22%	23%	25%	25%
Percentage of all AP exam scores that were 3 or higher	38%	42%	44%	45%	51.1%

[a] Brian Garcia, Chester Holland, Akisha Osei Sarfo, and Ray Hart, *Academic Key Performance Indicators* (revised report) (Washington, DC: Council of the Great City Schools, November 2023).

that is, half the districts were above, and half were below the reported percentages.

The data, which covered half the period discussed earlier in this chapter, shows steady improvement in the four-year cohort graduation rate, the percentage of ninth graders who failed one or more core courses, and the percentage of students who had successfully completed Algebra I by the end of ninth grade. These latter two indicators are strong predictors of high school graduation. In addition, the percentage of Great City School students who took one or more AP courses and who scored a three or higher on the AP exam, enough to earn college credit, also improved.

Return on Investment

The NAEP performance data indicate that fourth- and eighth-grade student outcomes in reading and mathematics have improved in the Large City Schools over the years. The data also indicate that these urban schools and school systems were adding value to expected outcomes, exceeding the value added by All Other Schools, and narrowing the gap with the nation.

One of the questions we asked in this chapter is whether urban public schools are also seeing a return on investment (ROI) that is comparable to the return from public education in general. So, are they?

Generally, ROI is a measure of gains compared to costs and is used to evaluate the efficiency of an investment. Here we measure the educational gains in terms of NAEP eighth-grade math scores and then compare these gains to the added spending that is associated with them.

We look at the growth in NAEP scores between 2009 and 2019, like we did earlier in this chapter, and we measure it against the change in current per pupil expenditures over that same period, adjusted for numbers of students from low-income families, English language learners, and students with disabilities.

We look solely at the eighteen TUDA districts that took the assessment between 2009 and 2019 rather than using the Large City Schools variable of NAEP because calculating an accurate expenditure value for the Large City Schools would be difficult. We compare the results to public schools nationwide after adjusting them on the same variables. For the economists and statisticians in the room, the formulas for the analysis were as follows:

$$TUDA = \frac{\left(NAEP_{2019}^{TUDA} - NAEP_{2009}^{TUDA}\right)}{\left(APPE_{2019}^{TUDA} - APPE_{2009}^{TUDA}\right)} \qquad US = \frac{\left(NAEP_{2019}^{US} - NAEP_{2009}^{US}\right)}{\left(APPE_{2019}^{US} - APPE_{2009}^{US}\right)}$$

The average per-pupil expenditure (APPE) is the current expenditure of each TUDA district and the nation, divided by the enrollment of each district and the nation, weighted by their numbers of students from low-income families (0.19), English language learners (0.22), and students with disabilities (0.30).[19] Expenditure data and student demographic data are from the Common Core of Data provided by NCES.

For our eighteen TUDA districts, eighth-grade math scores increased by 0.05 standard deviations between 2009 and 2019. When we compare that to scores from public school students across the nation over the same period, we find that the national public scores actually *fell* by 0.02 standard deviations. The TUDA districts increased spending per pupil by $4,816.35 over the same time, while the average for all public schools increased by $4,205.74—but the TUDA districts clearly got more from this added spending as seen by the gains in achievement.

One might think that the ROI in urban schools would not be as great as in public education overall, but our analysis shows that continued investments in large urban school districts might be expected from this period to yield the same if not greater returns in performance as all other public school districts.

Research indicates that there are large economic returns when skills measured by NAEP scores improve. The United States rewards skills as measured by test scores more than almost any other developed country.[20] These high rewards for skills reflect the fact that the US economy is dynamic, and individuals must be prepared to learn new tasks over their lifetimes. Thus, the gains in scores seen in TUDA districts suggest strong economic returns to the investments made in TUDA schools.

WHAT DOES IT ALL MEAN?

In this chapter, we ask whether urban public schools are holding up their end of the bargain. Are they improving? Are they overcoming or mitigating to any extent the many factors that often dampen student achievement? Do they add value? Are they a force for upward mobility? Are they a good return on investment?

What we found is that Large City Schools score below national averages, but they have improved, and they have improved faster than All Other Schools. Consequently, they narrowed the performance gap with the nation by a substantial margin. The results also showed that urban public schools outperformed expectations. They scored higher than what one would predict statistically, given their differing demographics. Consequently, they do add value over and above what All Other Schools in the aggregate produce. And the results mean that tens of thousands more urban school students were reading and doing math at proficient levels in 2019 than in 2003.

There were also a substantial number of urban school districts that not only scored higher than expected but have also gotten better at adding value over time. The data, moreover, showed substantial progress by many of urban education's historically underserved groups but no improvement in achievement gaps. Still, there were a handful of urban school districts that narrowed some of their achievement gaps and serve as models for others.

Finally, we took a brief look at the ROI that urban schools produce for their students. We found that these urban school systems produced a return that was comparable to the nation's overall investment in public education.

The questions we raised in this chapter and in chapter 1 involved whether urban public schools could improve. The answer is yes. The improvements were sometimes uneven and inconsistent. No one would claim that the gains are sufficient, but one thing is clear: the assertion by some that these districts are not capable of improvement or have not improved is wrong. Some might argue that improvement occurred because of changes in demographics, but we know that not to be true because we accounted for that in our adjustments. NAEP patterns like the ones we saw in this chapter do not happen by accident or coincidence. Changes like these occur only because people made them happen.

In the next chapters, we will look at how some of these Large City School districts, which produced outsized effects, beat the odds between 2009 and 2019 and improved more than other districts. We will then contrast them with districts that did not make as much progress. Finally, we will discuss what these districts can teach us as public education moves forward from the pandemic.

3

Architects of Our Own Improvement

The evidence in the last chapter showed that the nation's large city public schools made substantial progress on NAEP between 2009 and 2019. The period before that (2003 to 2009) also showed that the large cities made significant gains, even faster gains in fact than during the 2009–2019 period. All told, the two-decade story about urban public schools is one of mostly steady improvement, although scores wobbled a bit between 2013 and 2019. More important, big-city schools improved faster than the rest of the country and were able to cut the gap with everyone else by substantial margins.

Are urban schools capable of improvement? Yes. Did they improve? Yes. Do urban schools provide value and produce a reasonable return on investment? Yes. In this chapter, I ask a new set of questions about why and how traditional urban public schools made progress. Over this and the next two chapters, I tell the story in two parts: how urban schools banded together at the national level and what they did to improve at the local level.

I know there will still be questions despite having presented strong evidence. Were these improvements the result of demographic changes? No, we adjusted the data each testing cycle by fluctuations in English language learners (ELLs), students with disabilities, students from low-income families, and students of color. Were the results because of increased competition from charters, homeschooling, and other schools? Maybe, but the effects were irregular and small. What about the standards? Were the gains because of the new reading and math standards? Possibly, but the evidence was circumstantial and uneven, and the gains may have been stronger before the standards were launched. Were they the result of the *No Child Left Behind Act* of 2001 (NCLB)? Perhaps, since the onset of accountability appeared to spur the upward movement in test scores. Were the gains the result of happenstance? No, changes of this magnitude and consistency are never coincidental. Somebody or something must galvanize them.

To be sure, there were many things that happened during those twenty years or so that contributed to the improvement of urban public education. The rise of multiple philanthropies providing support for education; numerous new consulting organizations to offer technical assistance; stronger research on what worked; public pressure to improve; better data; more pre-kindergarten participation; and other factors all played a role.

In addition to these helpful developments, however, was one other factor that few people give much attention to: the commitment and determination of urban school district leaders and staff to improve.

Many institutions, large and small, struggle with change and the need to overhaul traditional practices and structures to meet the evolving demands of their constituents. Critics often contend that urban public education is particularly resistant to change and improvement. To be sure, there have been numerous instances when big-city school leaders stood in the way of progress: for example, resistance to desegregation in some cities.

But, over the last several decades, urban school leaders across the country were often in the forefront of efforts to reform and improve their institutions. They understood the public's dissatisfaction; they appreciated parental feedback more than people thought; and they often got into the field to make a positive difference in the lives of children who were too often left behind. Few of these big-city school leaders got into the work to perpetuate mediocrity. Many of the urban school superintendents, in fact, came from neighborhoods that had historically been ignored and, as students, they were sometimes ignored themselves. These leaders were often willing to rethink instructional approaches and operational processes, and they were willing to be held accountable for results. The truth is that public schools in the nation's large urban centers have been more open to novel approaches, ideas, and progress than they are given credit for.

I base this assessment on the forty-seven years I spent working with and then leading the association that represents the nation's largest urban public school districts, the Council of the Great City Schools. Its board of directors is composed of the superintendent and one school board member, usually the president of the board, from each of its (currently) seventy-eight member districts. I had an up close and often personal look at what was going on behind the scenes, why the schools made the headway they did, and why some faltered.

What is different about this association of urban school systems, in addition to its unusual structure that includes both the governance and management sides of the institution, is that urban school leaders use their organization to articulate a broad goal of improvement in urban education and to devise a series of wide-ranging strategies that will spur them forward. Unlike many other membership organizations, the Council does not exist to prop up, defend, or apologize for its members.

On the contrary, its mission is to represent and drive improvement—to serve as a critical friend and help districts do the demanding work of getting better on behalf of their students. The membership defined its mission and wanted it that way, even when it made things more difficult for them in the short term.

AN ALLIANCE FOR IMPROVEMENT

I joined the Council of the Great City Schools in 1977, Jimmy Carter's first year as president. It was also the year that *Roots* started its smash run on television, *Star Wars* opened, Elvis Presley died, and the first Apple computers went on sale. Over those decades, I have known hundreds, maybe thousands, of school board members and superintendents in urban America, and I can say with confidence that these local leaders were among the finest, most dedicated public servants that any nation could produce. That does not mean that they all did good things, all the time. Some got into trouble along the way, and some took their eyes off the ball, but most got into the field aspiring to do big, important things for children and for the nation's well-being.

These people included Richard Green, chancellor of the New York City schools; Sid Marland and Richard Wallace, superintendents from Pittsburgh; Constance Clayton from Philadelphia; Arthur Jefferson and Sam Brownell from Detroit; Alonzo Crim and Benjamin Mays from Atlanta; Tom Payzant and Carol Johnson from Boston; Carol Comeau from Anchorage; Norbert Schuermann from Omaha, and so many others who not only were giants in their respective communities but banded together in an alliance to address the challenges that US urban public schools were facing.

These leaders first started meeting together as big-city school systems in 1956, at the urging of Chicago school board president Sargent Shriver—who would go on to form the Peace Corps with his brother-in-law, John F. Kennedy—and Chicago superintendent Ben Willis, who would be on the wrong side of history in resisting the desegregation of the city's schools.[1] Originally named the Great City Schools Improvement Studies, the initial group of twelve big-city school systems focused mostly on the changing demographics of the big cities, the bureaucratic functioning of their districts, and the loss of industrial jobs in US urban areas. While much of their efforts contributed to the intellectual foundations of this country's work in public education and the federal government's involvement in the field, it is unclear whether it directly improved educational or instructional quality in urban school classrooms nationwide, as the name of the group implied.

We must admit, as well, that at the time, the nation's expectations for what students might learn and be able to do were being lowered erroneously because of stereotyped ideas about what a diverse student body could accomplish. In fact, these sinking expectations would do enormous damage to the academic outcomes of students, particularly in our urban public schools.

It was also during this period, between 1954 and 1957, when the nation was convulsed by some of the most momentous events in its history. The US Supreme Court overturned de jure segregation in *Brown v. Board of Education*. Emmitt Till was murdered. Rosa Parks remained on her Montgomery bus. Levittown-type housing in the suburbs made up 75 percent of all new housing starts. The nation's big cities first started losing population. The Interstate Highway bill was signed into law. One hundred members of Congress signed the Southern Manifesto, opposing *Brown v. Board of Education*. President Eisenhower sent the 101st airborne into Little Rock to desegregate Central High School. Sputnik was launched. And Milton Friedman proposed the idea of private school vouchers.[2]

These watershed years seeded many of the challenges the nation's urban public schools would face in the years ahead. Unfortunately, it is lost to history how significantly the tumultuous events of that period shaped the thinking of Shriver and Willis in calling together the nation's twelve largest city school systems, but people who remember the period report that urban school leaders at the time knew that the ground was shifting under them.

On the heels of the forced busing battles of the 1970s, urban public education began to be viewed as too bureaucratic, too organizationally inept, and too politically self-interested to warrant the public's waning confidence. It was also not clear that public school leaders and staff could rustle up the will to get better. The call to arms report, *A Nation at Risk*, which was published in 1983, was as much about our urban public schools as it was about public education more broadly.[3] And it was much of this dissatisfaction with urban public education that led to calls for systemic reform, site-based management, school choice, and so on.

Along with its members, the Council of the Great City Schools fell on hard times in the 1970s and early 1980s when the organization became more recognizable as an "old boys club" dedicated to the care and feeding of its high-profile membership than to the needs of its students. The seemingly innocuous event that triggered it to change occurred in July 1988, when a group of male superintendents from the big cities walked, with their golf clubs, out of a presentation by Philadelphia superintendent Constance

Clayton. The outrage that ensued was personal, but it crystallized for a new generation of rebel leaders that standards had slipped, the organization had lost its way, and the group was incapable of improving or meeting the public's demands for greater results or accountability.

Clayton; Richard Wallace, superintendent from Pittsburgh; Joseph Fernandez, chancellor of New York City; Forest Rieke, Portland school board president; and others were at the forefront of efforts over the next several years to overhaul the organization and turn it into a force that could respond to the rising public pressure for improvement and results.

Everyone on staff, including me, was fired in late 1991, but several weeks later I received a call from Clayton, telling me that I had been rehired as the group's executive director with explicit instructions to "remake the organization." She never asked whether I had found another job in the interim.

Over the subsequent months in 1992, the executive committee and the board of directors of the organization were revamped, and the group developed three broad goals for the nation's urban public schools that remain today: teach all children to the highest standards; strengthen urban school district governance, leadership, and management; and bolster confidence in the nation's big-city public schools.

It was the first goal, however, that suggested something different was happening in urban education. Reform around instruction had been in the air at least since the mid-1980s, when Anthony Alvarado's work in District 2 of New York City garnered so much attention. And it was this focus on getting better that galvanized an emerging cadre of big-city school educators.

It was also clear to the group that no one was riding to our rescue. We did not want to wait for the organizational ambulances anyway. We wanted to be instruments of our own improvement. We were determined to control our destinies and the fate of urban education itself. It was a choice between playing offense or defense. We were determined to make things better.

From then on, the organization focused on one thing: improvement—real improvement. This improvement centered around student achievement, in particular, but it also included our own governance and operations. It was an orientation that differed markedly from what the organization had done before and anything any other national education membership organization had tried to do, before or since.

The same orientation around continuous improvement was also sweeping through the business community at the time. Peter Senge's learning organization,[4] Deming's Total Quality Management,[5] Malcolm Baldridge's performance excellence,[6] Jim Collins' *Good to Great*,[7] *Six Sigma*,[8] and so many other theories of organizational transformation emerged in the 1970s, 1980s, and early 1990s. All of it was based on the premise that organizations could improve and learn from what they were doing and that transformational leadership could be taught and developed.

Senge, in particular, was clear about learning organizations being places where people continually expanded their capacity to meet the goals they set. This meant building a vision, cultivating systems thinking, identifying connections among elements of a system, supporting expertise, and cultivating collaborative learning. Many argued at the time about whether these approaches were appropriate for public education, but the air was thick with reform and improvement.

The imperative behind these seminal theories, a rising tide of school reform reports following *A Nation at Risk*, and the research of Ron Edmonds[9] gave rise to what came to be known as *improvement science* and its application to the education field.

Edmonds was especially important in the evolution of urban education with his five characteristics of effective urban schools: strong administrative leadership, high expectations, an orderly atmosphere, basic skills acquisition as a school's primary purpose, and frequent monitoring of student progress. Following Edmonds, it was Tony Bryk from Chicago and Paul LeMahieu from Pittsburgh, two veterans of urban education, who applied what was being written about learning organizations and improvement to schools.[10] Specifically, they wanted to know what we were trying to accomplish, how would we know whether a change was an actual improvement, and what changes would result in improvement.

Urban educators, for their part, understood by the early 1990s that the public was demanding improvement. Everybody wanted it. Urban school leaders knew that the public was not satisfied with their schools, and it was the impetus for Clayton, Wallace, Fernandez, Rieke, and others in the Council's leadership to revamp the organization. Urban school leaders started to develop their own goals around improvement and learn the power of systems thinking through the work of school superintendents Rod Paige in Houston and Eric Smith in Charlotte-Mecklenburg. But urban education lacked almost everything else that Bryk, Edmonds, Senge, and others said was necessary to be effective and get better.

To create what it lacked and to spur the improvement urban education leaders—and the public—wanted, the alliance of big-city school educators either initiated or played a leading role over the next several years in a series of activities to help its members advance. A casual conversation with David Hornbeck, then the superintendent of the Philadelphia school district, helped kick-start our efforts. He said to me over dinner one night in 1998, "Why don't you figure out why some of us are making progress and some of us aren't? It would help us a lot." It was the question that framed our improvement efforts going forward and is central to this book.

What we did at the national level, over the subsequent years, bore a striking resemblance to improvement science, although we never used that term. We did not follow all its principles, but what we did was consistent with the framework. We defined goals around high standards; we thought through what we would need to do at a national level to accomplish the goal for our members; we thought systemically; we figured out how to help each other; we rustled up the resources to make the gains possible; and we developed the data we needed to determine whether we were making progress.[11]

The effort even had something akin to Bryk's "networked improvement communities" or something we called Strategic Support Teams. Our work did not have the deliberate cohesion of improvement science, and we did not pursue it in the same sequence, but the efforts had the same purposes, and the components locked together to form a clear improvement strategy. Its elements included goals, standards, curriculum, professional development, data, resources, research, and technical assistance.

Supporting High Standards and Quality Instruction

In 2010 the Council, for instance, came out in favor of the Common Core State Standards, the first national membership group to do so. Urban school leaders did not initiate or write the standards. The National Governors' Association, the Council of Chief State School Officers, ACHIEVE, and Student Achievement Partners did that. What urban schools did, however, was to back the writers as they began their work. We reviewed numerous drafts during the development of the standards, and we backed them in an open letter to the public that was individually signed by the Council's superintendents. The importance of this was picked up by the *New York Times* as evidence that the new benchmarks had considerable political backing and a viable future in the places that most needed improvement, urban public schools.[12] Andres Alonzo, superintendent of the Baltimore City Public Schools punctuated our support by making an impassioned statement in favor of the standards at their release in suburban Atlanta in 2010.[13]

The nation's big-city schools backed the standards, because they understood that low expectations had done enormous harm historically to America's urban children. And they were determined to reverse course. It was this backing of the standards that sent signals to the press and the public that urban schools were in favor of raising, not lowering, standards as they were attempting to improve. The urban school move also created a sense of ownership and direction among urban school leaders that they used to overhaul their instructional systems once the standards were released. They convened training sessions on the standards, developed implementation materials and videos, and released public service announcements to boost public support, which were viewed hundreds of millions of times across the nation.

The big-city school group also developed guides translating the standards into high-quality curricula and guidance on how to build professional development around them. The group wrote grade-by-grade parent brochures on the standards in multiple languages, criteria for assessing instructional materials against the standards, rubrics for implementing the standards, and tips for using the standards with English language learners and students with disabilities.

The organization went on to develop a Professional Learning Platform (PLT), based on the standards, with videos of teachers working with struggling readers and ELLs, and we initiated a first-of-its-kind materials-buying cartel using the joint purchasing power of the nation's big-city school systems to encourage publishers to produce better materials around the standards. Critics of the standards would later argue that they made no difference,[14] but we will see in chapter 4 how critical they were in revamping the instructional programs in some of the nation's fastest-improving urban public school systems.

But it was not just the standards that the nation's urban schools used in their determination to improve. In 2010 and 2012, the group initiated a damning set of reports on itself, under the banner of a "Call for Change," that focused explicitly on the academic performance of African American males and Hispanic students. These reports led the group to pledge, with President Obama in 2014, to improve learning conditions for these students, an effort that became part of Obama's My Brothers' Keeper initiative.

The Council also expanded its improvement agenda to focus on strengthening school board governance and leadership by initiating and helping to design the Accelerating Board Capacity Institute at Harvard University and seeding what became the "student outcomes focused" governance model that is now being applied in big-city schools across the country. It then founded the Aspiring Urban School Superintendents Institute to enhance the skills of aspiring big-city school leaders.

Creating the Data to Gauge Our Progress

The group also supported its commitment to improving student achievement with data to gauge our progress and determine what was working. Where the data did not exist, the organization created it. We released the *National Urban Education Goals: Baseline Indicators* in 1992 that presented the first racially disaggregated data on urban schools nationally;[15] published annual *Beating the Odds* reports on the reading and math performance of urban students on state assessments from the late 1990s through 2008;[16] agreed to take President Clinton's Voluntary National Tests (VNT) in 1997; and initiated the Trial Urban District Assessment (TUDA) of NAEP in 2000.

This latter action was a surprise to a sizable number of people, because, at the time, voluntary participation by the states in NAEP was rapidly waning. Looking for new customers, the National Assessment Governing Board, which oversaw NAEP, commissioned the National Academy of Education to make recommendations on how to boost participation. The Academy concluded that the nation's urban schools were not likely to participate, but they failed to ask us if we were interested. When I testified before the governing board at its fall meeting in 2000, I volunteered the first set of urban school districts for what became TUDA.[17] I knew I could fulfill this offer because I was able to convince fifteen big-city school districts to participate in the VNT just three years before. I then worked with Peggy Carr from NCES to develop the Large City Schools variable that you see in this book. The governing board accepted my offer, and over time the initiative grew to include twenty-seven major urban school systems that gave us the data to know whether we were getting better.

I told the governing board at the time, and repeated it publicly every time NAEP results were released, that we were doing this because we wanted to know if our efforts and the efforts of others were producing results in urban education; we wanted to be able to compare ourselves with others with the same problems; and we wanted to be able to figure out what reforms were working and which ones were not.

Later, we would successfully advocate before the National Assessment Governing Board to bring its NAEP math framework into closer alignment with the college and career standards, because we were convinced that some of the fall-off in scores after 2013 was because the test was not measuring what schools were teaching.[18]

In 2005 the organization went on to develop its own educational performance management system—the only one of its kind in the nation—of key performance indicators (KPI)[19] to keep regular tabs on operations city-by-city. The system has over four hundred non-instructional indicators at this point in the areas of cash management, compensation, financial management, management, food services, maintenance and operations, transportation, human resources, and information technology that are gathered and reported back to the membership each year. The group followed these annual reports in 2014 with academic KPIs on pre-kindergarten participation rates, NAEP results, ninth-grade course failures, algebra I completion rates, grades, Advanced Placement participation and test scores, attendance, discipline indicators, and graduation rates—some of which the reader saw in chapter 2.

Knowing that data itself was insufficient, the organization used these new performance systems to study which systems were improving the most and why some urban school systems made faster academic progress than others—just like Hornbeck suggested. We published the first such report in 2002—*Foundations for Success: Case Studies of How Urban School Systems Improve Student Achievement*—comparing the practices of improving urban school systems with those of districts that were not showing as much progress.[20] We followed that report with three others: *Succeeding with English Language Learners: Lessons Learned from the Great City Schools*,[21] *Pieces of the Puzzle: Factors in the Improvement of Urban School Districts on the National Assessment of Educational Progress* in 2011,[22] and *Mirrors or Windows: How Well Do Large City Public Schools Overcome the Effects of Poverty and Other Barriers?* in 2021,[23] which formed the basis for this book.

In addition to using this approach of studying why some urban districts made faster academic progress than others, we used it to improve noninstructional operations and save money. The effort was picked up in Rick Hess's book, *Stretching the School Dollar*,[24] and was described in numerous articles. We studied why the operational indicators were better in some places than others and did case studies on effective practices behind the KPIs on such disparate areas as grants management,[25] accounts payable,[26] and procurement.[27] We published the districts that were in the top quartile on each indicator, and we synthesized lessons learned on how the districts organized themselves; their leadership and management structures; financial operations; business support systems; human resources and personnel management; and information technology.[28]

We accompanied these studies with other analyses meant to inform or spur student outcomes in the big cities. Examples included major studies of turnaround schools, testing practices, COVID-19 guidance (see the appendix), and other policies. And we worked with Russ Whitehurst and the Institutes of Education Sciences to imbed senior researchers into our urban school systems to answer critical questions about our improvement that the research community was not addressing on its own.

To make sure the standards and research were being applied on the ground, the Council initiated a technical assistance function to review organizational, instructional, and operational practices of member districts and to develop blueprints for improvement. Districts like Richmond, Boston, Cleveland, Detroit, the District of Columbia, Kansas City (MO), and others that followed the blueprints often saw substantial gains. We conducted over 350 of these Strategic Support Teams, as we called them, in 65 major city school districts between 1998 and 2021—and they continue to this day.

Getting the Resources We Needed

Finally, the Council did everything we could to help build out the architecture of federal elementary and secondary education programming by working with legislators and Congressional staff on such efforts as the Magnet Schools of America program, E-Rate, the dropout prevention act, the Urban Schools of America (USA) bill, and the Thurgood Marshall Plan for Urban Schools. Some of these efforts proved successful; others did not, but the organization was aggressively pushing new legislation on Capitol Hill over the years to create as much backing as we could with federal lawmakers for the efforts we were making to improve urban education.

We also worked with Congressional leaders and staff to retarget federal aid provided through the Vocational Education Act, Title I, Title II, and Title III on school districts with high numbers and percentages of students from low-income families—an effort that is worthy of its own book. Our purpose was to garner for urban schools the resources they needed to carry out the improvements we were espousing. The targeting of federal program dollars now adds some $1.0 billion a year to the budgets of the nation's big-city schools.

The effort started when we advocated for the full count of children who qualified for Aid to Families with Dependent Children in the Title I formula during the 1977–1978 reauthorization of the Elementary and Secondary Education Act and continued in our partnership with Congressman George Miller (D-CA) in 1983 to target federal Vocational Education Act funding on the poorest districts. Our relationships with Senator Pell, Congressman Gus Hawkins, Bill Ford, Dale Kildee, Bill Goodling, and others were pivotal to our success during this period. I remember, as well, sitting for hours in the Library of Congress, surrounded by Census documents and a handheld Texas Instruments calculator, during the 1987–1988 reauthorization, to work out a new Title I concentration grant formula that exists to this day. We were able to convince Senator Tom Eagleton (D-MO) and Senator Robert Stafford to target 50 percent of funding under the original Title II math and science program. And Jeff Simering and Manish Naik, from the Council's staff, worked with Senator Kennedy (D-MA) and others in the House during the NCLB authorization to turn the old Title VII discretionary grant program into the current, targeted Title III formula grant and boost funding for English language learners.

The additional aid has played a major role—along with sharper targeting of state aid over the decades—in boosting our results and narrowing the funding gaps between low-income and wealthier schools nationwide, documented by Adam Tyner in his piece for the Fordham Institute, "Think Again. Is Education Funding in America Still Unequal?"[29] Inequities still exist but they are not what they used to be.

Moreover, we backed NCLB—the only national education group to do so—because we wanted to signal to the public that the nation's urban school leaders were not afraid of results or accountability for them. The major civil rights groups followed, as did many of the national conservative organizations, but the other education groups either took no position or opposed the legislation. They were shocked at what we did, in fact, but the move garnered us new friends and some grudging respect. We knew the legislation was not likely to work as advertised, but we thought it more important to underscore our commitment to higher achievement and accountability than to quibble over the legislation's poorly calibrated particulars. Besides, the legislation comported with our improvement agenda, and supporting it was simply the right thing for us to do.

The improvement agenda and the strategies to carry it out were developed and implemented over time, but they were all deliberate and meant to fit together. Not everything worked, of course, and the Council was not the only organization working on urban school district improvement during this period.

Nonetheless, the leadership of urban school superintendents and school board members along with their partnership with the Council of the Great City Schools around a unified vision of improvement was among the strongest, most consistent, and long-standing forces on behalf of urban public education's betterment during this period. Having a network of peer districts working together around how to improve and a critical friend like the Council to define a direction and build momentum and support helped spur at least part of the Large City School gains that we saw in chapter 2.

Of special importance in these improvement efforts, however, were the Strategic Support Teams or technical assistance teams mentioned earlier. These were what many people would think of as audits, except that we spent more time and effort crafting recommendations, proposals, and solutions to what we saw than we did to discerning what had gone wrong. There are lots of folks who were critics of urban public education, but few who knew how to improve what they were criticizing. We did not want to be among those people. Our Strategic Support Teams were our answer.

The Power of Peer-to-Peer Support

The Council started its Strategic Support Teams in 1998 after Congress authorized a federal control board in 1995 to govern the District of Columbia and its schools. Julius Becton, a former Army General who was named to take over the schools, had stepped down in 1998 as superintendent of the D.C. public schools on the heels of a damning report on the school district's finances by the city's then-CFO, Anthony Williams. When Becton resigned, he famously said, "I have been through World War II, Korea, and Vietnam, but I have never been through anything like this."

Arlene Ackerman, Becton's chief academic officer, took his place. Ackerman and the control board asked me if the Council could review the school system and make recommendations on how to improve it. The Council had never done anything like this before, but her request was quickly followed by a similar invitation from John Stanford, the Seattle superintendent and former Army friend and colleague of Becton's.

In a phone call with Ray Cortines, who had been superintendent of the Los Angeles Unified School District and the San Francisco schools, Chancellor of the New York City Public Schools, and US Department of Education official—and friend—I mentioned what we had been asked to do. He casually said, "Why don't you round up some of your buddies and help them out?" Not wanting to seem like an idiot, I did not ask him what he meant. But, in the shower the next day, I put the pieces together. I decided to start calling some the best superintendents and line officers from our member districts to see if they would be willing to examine one of their fellow urban school systems and provide ideas on how they could improve. Everyone said yes, and all volunteered to do the work *gratis*.

After months of fact finding, interviews, and site visits, we issued our report to the D.C. control board and to the superintendent, and we followed it up in short order with reviews of Cleveland and Buffalo.

When we started, however, we received considerable pushback from some of our members. I remember James Williams, who was the superintendent of the Dayton Public Schools and later the superintendent of the Buffalo Public Schools, telling me that he would oppose my efforts to provide technical assistance to the districts, because it might make superintendents look like they did not know what they were doing.

In a meeting after the first several of these Strategic Support Teams, Becky Montgomery, a school board member in St. Paul, and Cliff Janey, superintendent of the Rochester, New York, Public Schools, both officers of the Council at the time, told me, "We don't care how much china you break as long as you are fair and accurate, but you better be both."

It was one of many hurdles we had to overcome to get the cities to realize their own vision, but the Council's leadership realized the potential and backed us and each other completely. The nation's urban school leaders also understood that their joint efforts under the aegis of the Council was a strategy that was likely be successful because we knew that we would not abandon each other.

Ultimately, the hundreds of reports we produced proved to be invaluable not only because of the detail behind them but because we spent so much time developing strategies with each review on how the districts could get better. Over time, as we produced reports on scores of cities and their instructional programs and operations, it became clear that the initiative would also provide unique professional development for anyone participating on the review teams. Boston superintendent Tom Payzant once remarked that, "It was the best professional development any of my team ever received."

At this point, it is critical to reiterate that these technical assistance teams were composed of practitioners from urban school systems that were making headway in the areas we were reviewing—based on the data systems we were developing. Great City Schools staff organized and coordinated the teams, but the practitioners were what made the teams effective and expert. We did not use consultants, researchers, advocates, or commentators, although a good many of those individuals, including members of the press, requested that they participate.

The important thing about these teams was that they involved urban educators helping other urban educators hundreds of times over decades. We called it "Cities Helping Cities." The approach also built a sense of group ownership among urban educators in each other's welfare and success. We were in this together.

Most importantly, the big-city school systems readily consumed the reports, whether they were the subject of the reviews or not, because they wanted to learn what their colleagues were proposing. They understood it gave them the keys to improvement that they could not get consistently anywhere else. The districts lined up for the reviews as we completed more of them, in spite of the resulting bad headlines that often made people squirm.

The approach, however, allowed the districts to work directly with talented and experienced practitioners from other major urban school districts with established track records. The recommendations coming from the teams had validity because the individuals who developed them had faced many of the same problems. In addition, using senior urban school practitioners was often faster, less expensive, and more expert than retaining a private firm. And the reports generated through the process were often more hard-hitting than what school systems would get from hiring a consultant who might pull their punches because they wanted repeat business. We did not care about repeat business; we cared about improving urban education.

One might think that these reviews would not be tough on districts that were voluntary members of the urban school organization. But we were always clear that if any district did not want the unvarnished truth from their peers, the district should not ask for it.

The results were often not pretty. District staff were sometimes fired because of our findings. Some districts were taken over by their states because of what we found. Some people went to jail, and many ugly newspaper headlines were generated.

A case in point involved the Birmingham public schools in Alabama. The Birmingham schools have gotten much better over the years, but there was a time when they were struggling badly. In this case, the school board asked us to conduct a high-level review of the system's organizational structure, financial allocations, and broad operational efficiencies. Bob Carlson, the Council's director of management, led the team through our typical process of reviewing data, interviewing staff members, examining organizational charts and other documents, drafting a preliminary report for the superintendent's review, and conducting a confidential debriefing.

It was not long after the debriefing that the superintendent began calling me, asking for changes in the report. We were always happy to correct errors, but this was different. He wanted us to alter our findings. We did not waver, and we filed the final report. The board president asked us to present our findings and recommendations at a public meeting, something we often did.[30] In January 2008 I traveled to Birmingham to summarize the report for the school board. The board meeting room overflowed with numerous television cameras and a large crowd of interested citizens.

During the presentation, I noticed the superintendent and his staff walking through the audience, passing out copies of the report. I thought little of it. After questions from the board, a gentleman from the audience came up to me and said he had difficulty following my presentation using the document that staff had handed out. Assuming that my presentation had not been clear, I apologized and wrapped up the evening.

As I was leaving, I mentioned to the superintendent that we would post our report on the Council's website later that evening. To my surprise, he was adamant that posting the report was unnecessary. I ignored his protests, however. The next day, I received an email from the superintendent asking me to take down the report from our website, claiming that the public would not understand it.[31]

Sometime over the next several days, a sharp-eyed citizen who had been at the presentation went to our website, downloaded the report, and realized it was not the same report that was handed out during our presentation. The person called the reporter at the *Birmingham News* who had already run an initial story. Our report had been substantially altered, and the findings had been deleted. Page numbers were out of order, and the typeface did not match the original document.[32] I was shocked.

I gave the reporter a copy of the official version. She told me that not only had the superintendent handed out a falsified version of our report but he had leaked the altered report to the newspaper several days beforehand. Both of us were furious. The next day, the paper ran a front-page story with the headline, "BIRMINGHAM SCHOOLS HID THE BAD NEWS: REPORT CRITICAL OF SYSTEM ALTERED."[33] The board suspended the superintendent and eventually allowed him to resign. It was a good example of drama that sometimes went on behind the scenes as we did these reviews.

The truth was that the reports coming from these reviews were hard-hitting and exacting, but that is what the members asked for and expected because they wanted to improve. At the same time, we learned a great deal about why some districts did not make the progress they wanted. We also used what we were learning in the field with the research we did on which districts were making the most progress to learn broader lessons about what worked in urban education. There was always a reason a district was not getting traction under its strategies because progress or lack thereof was never accidental. It was the result of what adults were either doing or not doing on behalf of kids.

Among all the benefits to conducting the reviews, the process allowed us to know what we know. It gave us a ringside seat to what the districts were doing, the strategies they were using, and the results they were getting. It also allowed us to conduct the kinds of analysis the reader will find in chapters 4 and 5 about why some districts made more headway than others. Our teams worked in scores of big-city school systems, interviewed thousands of teachers and staff, and observed thousands of classrooms of all types—over the years. In many ways, this process was like detective work, in which we collected evidence and tried to figure out which pieces mattered in moving the needle on student achievement.

Almost none of these steps to help each other improve received much public or press attention, except when our negative findings confirmed some stereotype about what was wrong with urban public education. Almost everyone missed the larger purpose of the work, which was to improve. It became clear to us that most of the positive press that urban schools got over the period was typically generated by third parties after they had finished a contractual arrangement with one or more of our cities and issued a press release about themselves. It felt to us that people assumed urban educators could not possibly have played a role in their own improvement. But they were wrong; urban educators were architects of their own progress.

The upward trajectory of outcomes that we saw in chapter 2 was not a surprise to us or the districts. In many ways, the improvements were the result of deliberate, purposeful, and often coordinated action by dedicated individuals who knew what they were doing and wanted to learn how to do the work better.

In my forty-seven years affiliated with the Great City Schools, I have seen real commitment and extraordinary effort by tens of thousands of dedicated urban educators who were working to make things right for the nation's big-city schoolchildren. Most of it was accomplished amid considerable rhetoric about the incapability of urban education to change or to improve. But the evidence suggests that urban educators, working in alliance with one another, could change, and they could get better at teaching children and operating their systems.

It does not mean that all these people got everything right all the time or that urban education is getting the results that both critics and champions of our efforts want. It also does not mean that our path was smooth and even: far from it. There were actors along the way who were more interested in themselves than the kids. There were some folks who really did not know what they were doing. And there were many hurdles along the way.

It was also true that our own efforts were not adequate, and they did not have universal effects on all urban school systems across the country. Not everyone was wide awake and not everyone responded to our efforts with the same enthusiasm or dedication. And there is still considerable work to do, especially after the pandemic.

But when we asked the question in chapter 2 about whether urban public schools and school districts can change for the better, then the answer is most certainly yes. The gains we saw were not an anomaly, they were not a one-off. They were the result, at least in part, of urban educators, as a collective, being there for each other around an agenda of improvement in ways that no one else was or could be. It was urban educators working to control the destinies of their own institutions, rather than waiting for someone else to save them.

By 1997 we began noticing that about 40 percent of urban school districts were showing slight gains on state reading and math exams. It gave us the confidence to volunteer that year for President Clinton's Voluntary National Tests, initiate our technical assistance teams in 1998 and the Trial Urban District Assessment of NAEP in 2000, endorse NCLB in 2001, institute our performance management system in 2005, and back the Common Core State Standards in 2010. It also suggested that we were on the right track and that we should buckle down harder on our efforts to improve.

The combination of initiatives appeared to have made a difference. The Council of the Great City Schools had reinvented itself not just to represent its members like other national organizations do but to lead them toward a future where we were doing better for our students. Urban school leaders had recreated an organization that would serve them and their children better than what existed previously.

The effort did not follow all the steps that are now articulated in improvement science, to be sure, but the gist of the work was the same. We were not only trying to get better; we were getting better at getting better.

At the same time, we were pushing at the national level to improve urban public education, local leaders who were part of the national effort were emerging with the same commitments and determination. For the most part, that commitment had always been there, but now there was better research on what worked, better data systems to assess student needs and progress, more consistent experience in the field about what was producing results, stronger materials, higher standards, more funding, and a joint mission built around improving that everyone could rally around.

In chapter 4 we look at some of the districts identified in chapter 2 as making disproportionate gains in reading and math. We will discuss what the leaders and staff of these systems did to achieve these gains. We will follow that with contrasting their practices with those in districts that did not make as much progress.

4

What Worked?

Chapter 2 showed that urban public schools can make substantial progress in student achievement and did so between 2003 and 2019. And it showed that the progress was greater than in schools at large across the United States. In addition, the data demonstrated that some major urban school systems made more progress than others.

This leads us to the main questions we ask in this chapter: How did some urban school districts make progress? What worked? How were they able to mitigate barriers and improve student achievement? Were there strategies these districts used that could inform what other major urban school systems do, particularly as they recover from the pandemic?[1]

To help answer these questions, the Council of the Great City Schools looked at several other studies that attempted to discern why and how school districts improve. Most of the available literature, however, involves single districts, or the studies do not compare successful and unsuccessful districts. Examples of recent works include Tony Bryk's study of Chicago,[2] Rick Hess's look at San Diego,[3] Charles Kerchner's examination of Los Angeles,[4] and Michael Pitts' study of Atlanta.[5]

Several other studies look at multiple districts, but they do not always look at major urban school systems, draw broad lessons across districts, or contrast them with less successful districts. This is not to discount how groundbreaking these studies were, including seminal works such as Mark Tucker's look at high-performing, mostly nonurban, districts;[6] Don McAdams and Dan Katzir's case studies of governance systems in multiple urban and suburban districts;[7] Julie Marsh's research on three unnamed urban districts that partnered with the Institute for Learning to implement NCLB;[8] Karen Chenoweth's study of four small school systems and their attempts to restructure their instructional programming;[9] Paul Cobb's eight-year study of unnamed school systems and their efforts to build greater instructional coherence;[10] the Childress, Elmore, Grossman, and Moore-Johnson study of multiple urban school systems and how they compare with various private-sector companies;[11] Heather Zavadsky's look at five Broad Prize winners;[12] the Susan Moore-Johnson study of five districts and their search for systemic cohesion;[13] and the Organization for Economic Cooperation and Development (OECD) and McKinsey studies of strong school systems across the globe.[14]

These important studies tell us a great deal about urban public schools and school districts. The research on multiple systems, in particular, informs us about the importance of governance, leadership, coherence, alignment, curriculum, professional development, data-based decision-making, and various operating systems. In undertaking our own study, we hoped to add to our understanding of urban school system improvement by examining from a practitioner's perspective a series of big-city school systems that had shown improvement on a common, single assessment and then contrasting them on the same dimensions with urban school systems that did not show as much improvement.

METHODOLOGY

To answer the questions we posed, the Council of the Great City Schools embarked on an effort to better understand the practices that might have driven higher levels of performance and student growth seen before the pandemic. Between May 2018 and February 2019, a project team from the organization visited six districts: the Boston Public Schools, Chicago

Public Schools, the Dallas Independent School District, the District of Columbia Public Schools, Miami-Dade County Public Schools, and the San Diego Unified School District. We chose each district for slightly different reasons, but all of them demonstrated results on NAEP that were above statistical expectations or results that showed substantial improvements between 2009 and 2019, after adjusting for student demographics. The reasons for picking each district include the following.

- Boston demonstrated consistent results in fourth- and eighth-grade reading and mathematics that were well above statistical expectations in all areas in 2017 and 2019. In addition, the district was above statistical expectations in every grade, subject, and year between 2009 and 2019.
- Chicago also showed reading and mathematics results in fourth and eighth grades that were above statistical expectations in 2017 and 2019. Moreover, Chicago was one of only a handful of districts that showed gains in at least two grade/subject combinations, and it was one of the few districts showing gains between 2009 and 2019 that went from below expectations to above in at least one area.
- Dallas showed reading and mathematics results that were above statistical expectations in three of four grade/subject combinations, and it produced a district effect that was well above its scale scores in all grades and subjects. (Remember, a district effect is the difference between what a district scored on the NAEP and what was expected statistically.)
- The District of Columbia had a district effect in 2017 and 2019 that was above statistical expectations in three of four grade/subject combinations. Moreover, the district improved its district effects by more than any other district in all four subject/grade combinations during the ten-year period. In addition, it went from below expectations to above expectations between 2009 and 2019 in three out of four grade-subject combinations—the only city to do so.
- Miami-Dade County also showed results that were above expectations in fourth- and eighth-grade reading and mathematics in 2017 and 2019

and in most years over the ten-year period. Moreover, the district demonstrated some of the largest overall gains in both subjects and grades over the study period.

- San Diego posted results that were above statistical expectations in two of four grade/subject combinations in 2019: fourth-grade mathematics and fourth-grade reading.

We might have picked other districts as well. For instance, Denver could have been included because of its overall positive effects in fourth-grade reading and mathematics. Unfortunately, it only had results over two testing cycles, and we could not calculate a district effect in eighth grade because no student questionnaire data were submitted. Cleveland or Atlanta might have also been chosen because of their improvements. And the research team was convinced that Detroit was a district to watch in the future.

In each case, our analysis started with the results each district was getting and worked backward to see what they were doing to produce those results, rather than gathering program implementation data and working forward to the results. In this way, the analysis was purposely "output" focused rather than "input" oriented. The approach allowed us to better gauge why the results looked like they did, particularly as we compared and contrasted practices across systems.

In addition, the team studied two "counterfactual" districts, which I will discuss in chapter 5. We selected these districts based on their chronically low achievement and tepid progress. During the review, we noted clear contrasts between these districts and the other six districts that had shown improvement. These contrasts were both striking and potentially informative for other districts seeking to make systemic improvements in teaching and learning.

During the site visits to each district, the project team interviewed the superintendent, school board members, chief academic officer, director of research and assessment, director of professional development, and head of district turnaround efforts, as well as focus groups of varying sizes of curriculum staff and content area experts, instructional coaches and other school support staff, principal supervisors, principals, teachers, parents, and community members.

We reviewed organizational charts, strategic plans, professional development plans, curriculum documents, and core instructional materials and interventions. In some districts, we also visited schools and classrooms, and debriefed school and district leaders following our walk-throughs. Finally, the team analyzed an extensive array of data on each district, in addition to the NAEP data, to better understand the nature and extent of district performance.

Readers should keep in mind that the descriptions of each district are accurate as of the time of our site visits. District programs, strategies, and priorities may have evolved or radically changed since then.

In addition to the six case study districts, we include brief descriptions of several other districts that have made progress over the years.

While the six case study districts had different demographic, political, and financial contexts and varying histories of reform, they had common features and practices that appeared to be connected to their progress in student performance.

HOW DID THEY IMPROVE?

As we saw in chapter 3, the Great City Schools were increasingly focused on improving student achievement over the years. The efforts of the group did not explicitly follow the tenets of any one improvement theory, but they shared many elements in common with improvement science. We set broad goals, adopted standards, developed data and used it to gauge progress, and deployed fellow practitioners in an effort to improve big-city public schools and understand how to get better faster.

The overall framework for improvement science was developed by Anthony Bryk and his colleagues at the Carnegie Foundation for the Advancement of Teaching.[15] Fundamentally, it is a problem-solving approach centered on continuous inquiry and learning. A core principle of the methodology is that a system's improvement is a result of its design and operation, rather than individual effort or programs.[16] Ultimately, the approach helps organizations build a shared understanding of how their systems work, what actions need to be taken to improve, and how to create an organizational culture of continuous improvement.

Bryk and his team concluded, after many years working in and researching urban school systems, that these systems were often slow to change because they were infected with a case of "solutionitis." That is, they gravitated toward initiatives and programs that were easy and quick to implement. Districts, in Bryk's contention, were more focused on program adoption than outcomes improvement. This reorientation began to change in the 1990s as advocates began to call for a fundamental shift in education from "inputs" to "outcomes."

As improvement science became further developed, it organized around six core principles. First, make the work problem specific. Second, focus on work processes rather than programs. Third, look at the system producing the outcomes and ask why it is producing the outcomes it is. Fourth, understand that we cannot improve what we do not measure. Fifth, use a process of continuous inquiry to drive improvement. And sixth, make use of networks of experts to inform the work.[17]

The six districts that we examine did not explicitly use improvement science to guide their reforms—except Chicago—but what they did and why they did it was broadly like what improvement science espoused. Leaders aspired to improve their systems; they set specific outcome goals for improvement; they reformed their systems rather than implementing more programs; they used data to gauge what was working; and they participated in a variety of networks to inform and bolster their improvements. They also focused continuously on how to improve and were not sidetracked strategically by other crises or problems.

Chicago, on the other hand, did use the tenets of improvement science more explicitly. In addition to goal setting, systemic thinking, and use of data, the district followed Bryk's planning steps and cycles of continuous improvement. Two studies of Janice Jackson's efforts in Chicago, in fact, found that she effectively "re-cultured" the district's central office and its work to spur continuous improvement by articulating a vision for system reform, reframing how power worked in the system, bolstering organizational norms around professional learning and continuous improvement, encouraging shared leadership, partnering with others, and modeling the leadership practices she wanted.[18]

Interestingly, how these six districts initiated their reforms differed one to another. The reforms were not always prompted by the same things. It is worth noting that an unusual number of the leaders in the six districts were heading schools in their own hometowns or birth places: Janice Jackson in Chicago, Tom Payzant in Boston, Michael Hinojosa in Dallas, and Cindy Marten in San Diego. Each leader cited those origins as providing a particularly personal incentive for improving their systems. Otherwise, reforms were triggered differently from city to city.

Research on school systems across the globe by Mona Mourshed, Chinezi Chijioke, and Michael Barber found that reform and improvement were often ignited by at least two of the following three things: a political or economic crisis, a critical report, or the energy and expertise of a new leader.[19] You will see some combination of these three things in each of the districts I describe in this chapter.

The financial and economic meltdown experienced by the country in 2008 and 2009 prompted budget cuts in Miami-Dade County, which allowed Alberto Carvahlo to initiate instructional reforms that spurred substantial gains in achievement. The mayoral takeover of the District of Columbia public schools by Mayor Adrian Fenty, whose playbook was modeled after New York City mayor Michael Bloomberg and chancellor Joel Klein, triggered school reforms in the capital city. The embarrassment of being tagged the "worst school system in America" by US Secretary of Education Bill Bennett spurred Chicago into action. The desire of the San Diego school board to improve student achievement prompted it to hire Cindy Marten, who was achieving substantial gains as principal of Central Elementary School.

And it was clear to Michael Hinojosa, a charismatic leader who was born in Mexico and raised by parents with only a third-grade education and whose sons graduated from Harvard and Princeton, that Dallas had given up on its public schools. He desperately wanted to change that. He used a curriculum audit to launch "Dallas Achieves" and started the work with a series of questions for his staff: What is your main expectation? What would you do first? What would make Dallas the best? Who were the most respected people on staff? Who are the most critical external stakeholders to ensure our success?

What each of the leaders in these six systems had was motivation, expertise, and the wherewithal to make the changes they envisioned.

It was also clear that the school leaders used disparate levers to start their reforms. In each case, they seized on an area that needed particular attention or that provided a special opportunity to begin their reforms rather than trying to do everything at once. Michelle Rhee started her reforms in D.C. with the school district's human capital system—an area she had special expertise in. Kaya Henderson took the next steps with those reforms by leveraging the district's instructional program, the Common Core Standards, and the community. In Boston, Tom Payzant started with math instruction. In Miami, Carvahlo leveraged his financial situation to standardize the instructional program. Marten began with the San Diego School District's organizational structure and the Common Core Standards. And Janice Jackson built on the reforms of her predecessors in Chicago to leverage the instructional leadership skills of her network leaders and principals along with implementing the Common Core.

Improvements in urban school systems often start with system leaders taking their opportunities for reform where they find them, but these improving urban school systems also shared many common features in their improvement efforts.

STRONG AND STABLE LEADERSHIP FOCUSED ON INSTRUCTION

Leadership, particularly at the superintendent level, was the primary factor among the urban school districts that were making substantial headway in student achievement. To achieve major improvements in student outcomes, big-city school leaders had to be relentlessly focused on instructional gains if they stood any chance of moving the needle on student achievement. If they lost focus or got distracted by a crisis of any length, they were likely to lose momentum on their improvement efforts. We saw this single-mindedness in every one of the districts that saw gains in how their children were doing. If they ever moved off an improvement agenda, it was for short periods, and they returned as quickly as possible to the business at hand.

The relative stability of leadership was also a key factor in the progress these districts made before the pandemic. At a time of increasing leadership turnover in urban districts, the relatively long tenures of superintendents in districts such as Miami, where Alberto Carvalho was superintendent from 2008 to 2022, and San Diego, where Cindy Marten served as superintendent from 2013 until her appointment as Deputy Secretary of Education in 2021, enabled these districts to pursue a consistent and sustained reform and improvement agenda over years.

In Dallas, Superintendent Michael Hinojosa's first term spanned six years, from 2005 to 2011. Coming on the heels of a string of relatively short-lived leaders, this period was referred to by staff as a time of "instructional healing," in which the district was able to refocus its attention on teaching and learning and find the momentum necessary to drive instructional reform. When Hinojosa then returned to Dallas as superintendent in 2015, after the tenure of Mike Miles, his historical knowledge of the district enabled him to quickly regain momentum, build on Miles's progress, and continue moving the work forward. Staff in the district now commonly refer to his first and second terms as "Hinojosa 1.0" and "Hinojosa 2.0."

We also saw that strong, long-standing leaders can affect a district for years. In Boston, staff still cite the impact of Tom Payzant's eleven years as superintendent, and the culture of shared accountability that he and his successor Carol Johnson built. Kaya Henderson also served five years as chancellor of the District of Columbia Public Schools and three years as deputy chancellor before that under Michelle Rhee, and the capacity they built has lasted well beyond their tenures.

Moreover, many of the districts benefited from the stability of their curriculum and instruction leaders. The tenures of Janice Jackson, chief academic officer and then chief executive officer of the Chicago Public Schools; Brian Pick, chief academic officer in the D.C. Public Schools (DCPS); Marie

Izquierdo, long-time chief academic officer of the Miami-Dade County Public Schools; Ivonne Durant and Denise Collier, chief academic officers in Dallas; and Linda Davenport, mathematics director of the Boston Public Schools, serve as examples. The longevity of their instructional leadership allowed these districts to maintain a consistent and expert instructional approach, even when there were transitions at the top of the districts.

It is important to note, however, that it was not simply the *stability* of leadership that yielded academic improvements in these cities, because one can find TUDA districts in our analysis where superintendent tenures were relatively long and student achievement did not improve. Leaders in districts that did improve, on the other hand, brought strength, primacy, and focus to their instructional programming for a sustained period. In other words, they used their long tenures to focus on improving student outcomes.

In fact, districts like the District of Columbia, Chicago, and Boston showed us that progress can be maintained and even accelerated despite leadership churn if a district sustains its focus on instruction and retains its broad instructional strategy.[20] In D.C., the district was both consistent and intentional in sequencing its reforms, even while personnel changed. The focus of the district's initial reform efforts was human capital, accountability, and building an effective teacher corps. Leaders initiated a department of human capital led by Jason Kamras that replaced the largely transactional personnel system with a department focused on recruitment, selection, onboarding, induction, professional development, career ladders, and the exiting of staff. They renegotiated the teachers' union contract that overhauled hiring, tenure and seniority, pay-for-performance, and the teacher evaluation system. This also helped create an overall environment where there was a perceived "brain gain"—talented people coming into the district because they saw an opportunity to turn around a once-failing system.

Rhee's deputy and then successor Kaya Henderson expanded on this teacher-centered reform agenda when it had weeded out many of its weakest teachers and staff. The next step was to further enhance the capacity of the remaining personnel by equipping them with the necessary curricular resources, guidance, and professional learning. Over the Henderson years, this focus expanded with school-based structures, new materials, and the content expertise necessary to help teachers effectively implement the district's new curricular resources. In other words, each subsequent leader approached the district's past efforts and successes as an important foundation for their own work, all the while remaining focused on what was needed to further improve instruction.

Chicago offers a similar story in sustaining and advancing its reforms across multiple superintendents. Paul Vallas started many of Chicago's instructional reforms in 1995 after Richard Daley convinced the state legislature to place the district under his control. Vallas initiated direct and scripted instruction, along with an emphasis on fixing the city's dilapidated school facilities. Arne Duncan followed with an emphasis on academic improvement, choice schools, freshman on-track performance, and graduation. A series of CEOs followed between 2009 and 2017 when Janice Jackson took over—Ron Huberman, Terry Mazany, Jean-Claude Brizard, Barbara Byrd-Bennett, Jesse Ruiz, and Forrest Claypool—but they all built on top of their predecessors in emphasizing instructional quality, good data, community support, and high standards rather than starting over with new agendas.

This idea of strong leadership focused on quality instruction prompted another big-picture observation. In some districts, the board of education was a full partner with the administration in improving district instruction, while in other places school boards appeared to add little value. Where they were partners in the work, the board and the superintendent were largely on the same page about the district's instructional vision and theory of action and provided effective oversight and accountability for meeting the system's academic goals. Boston, Chicago, and San Diego were good examples. In other cases, school boards were too focused on their own internal divisions to accelerate (or even impact) the administration's work to boost student outcomes. In these instances, the boards can take credit for hiring effective CEOs but get little credit for the academic gains that those superintendents and their staff attained.

Similarly, there were districts showing positive effects that were under the aegis of their mayors and others that were not. The data show that what city and district leaders did to improve the overall quality of instruction made a greater difference than the governance structure of the school systems per se.

Finally, in each of the districts we visited, strong, instruction-focused leadership was nurtured not only at the central office but throughout the organization with the empowerment and support of principals and principal supervisors. In fact, several of the case-study districts reported that their instructional visions and theories of action were built, in part, around *school leaders as levers of change* who had a common understanding of the district's improvement strategy. As conduits between the district and schools, principal supervisors and principals were increasingly seen as critical to the success of this approach.

For example, when asked about factors driving district progress in Chicago, staff who were interviewed cited the "genuine principal leadership" in the district. But the district took a more strategic approach than just deploying strong school leaders and hoping for district transformation. Principals and their local school councils were empowered to make decisions that were right for their communities—a situation that has been in place in Chicago since the late 1980s—but the district ensured via its network chiefs that principals were sufficiently supported, coached, and held accountable for academic results. In other words, Chicago used its network structure and principal supervisors to realign its organizational structure around the instructional focus it wanted to achieve system wide.

Area superintendents in San Diego also described a strong hands-on relationship with principals, meeting with them regularly to review school-wide progress and help determine goals. In our interviews with the district leadership team, they told us that they believed it was the support and oversight structure of the school system that allowed for their site-based approach to work (a dynamic that does not always work in other districts).

Importantly, to ensure that principal supervisors were equipped to effectively advance school leadership and capacity in this way, their roles were explicitly redefined around instruction. Whereas in previous years principal supervisors or regional superintendents oversaw a host of administrative and operational matters, these districts took multiple steps (including narrowing spans of control, rewriting supervisor job descriptions, reallocating

operational responsibilities to other staff or offices, and providing professional development) that fundamentally refocused their work with schools
and principals around bolstering instructional effectiveness. In addition to
Chicago and San Diego, Dallas, Miami, and the District of Columbia, all did
this to some extent.

The organizational structure of the six districts often looked very different from system to system, but it was how district leaders aligned the
elements of the organization—goals, standards, curriculum, materials, personnel, reporting lines, professional development, and assessments—
around the improvements that made all the difference. It was not the boxes
on the chart that mattered so much; it was the system and its workflows
that mattered.

In every case, leaders of these districts pursued a change management strategy that redefined the culture and direction of their systems
in ways that showed staff that their institutions could be more successful
for children and rallied people around a common goal at an achievable
speed.

HIGH STANDARDS AND COMMON INSTRUCTIONAL GUIDANCE AND SUPPORT

It also was apparent from our site visits that rigorous academic standards
and high-quality curriculum played an important role in the improvement
of the districts we examined. And as much as anything, it was the clarity
and shared understanding of a district's teaching and learning expectations
that mattered as much as the standards and curriculum.

Implementing and Supporting the Standards

For instance, the leadership of the Chicago and the District of Columbia
public schools used the introduction of the Common Core State Standards in 2010 to rethink and refocus their entire academic program. This
was also at least partially the case with the Miami-Dade County schools.
Chicago, the District of Columbia, and San Diego were among the first
local school systems in the nation to adopt and implement the Common

Core State Standards and were aggressive in the rollout process, planning and implementing the standards at scale from the outset.

What the standards did for the districts was at once profound and hard to detect from the outside. In a 2017 interview with Chicago CEO Janice Jackson, she summed up the value of the standards by asserting, "They redefined the instructional direction of the district."[21] The standards essentially allowed the districts to level-set. They defined direction, raised expectations, anchored the curriculum, created coherence and alignment, focused professional development, built capacity, suggested what to assess, and drove continuous improvement. And the standards and their communication to the workforce allowed the districts to do the work with their own teachers rather than consultants.

Moreover, each of these districts was particularly good at setting academic goals that defined their priorities and direction. In some cases, this goal setting was done by the school board and superintendent jointly, which we would recommend; sometimes the goals were more explicitly owned by the superintendent and senior staff. Sometimes the goals were overarching and systemic, and in other cases they were granular and focused on narrower areas of improvement. Either way, these goals provided direction and set priorities for the system and its people. And, in some cases, they were the basis for the district's accountability systems.

This practice of setting academic goals, communicating the rationale and meaning of them, and better articulating what districts expected from their instructional programs was at the heart of their standards-based reforms. Each district we visited clearly communicated those expectations at each grade level, including what high-quality instruction and student work should look like. This was true regardless of whether they formally adopted the new college and career-ready standards or used a common district curriculum. For example, while San Diego did not have a traditional district-wide curriculum, they did lay out "critical concepts" they expected teachers to cover at each grade level and subject, and the district worked with schools to develop units of study based on the standards to ensure that this common understanding was employed in every classroom. In addition, they reinforced this understanding through their professional learning communities (PLCs).

In another case, Miami-Dade County Public Schools provided teachers with detailed, standards-aligned pacing guides embedded with links to relevant instructional materials and resources. "*What* our children are going to learn is non-negotiable," explained an instructional leader in the district. But while the content was determined by the district, the "how" was left up to the classroom teacher, with more guidance provided for teachers who needed it. The district also provided a curated set of options in terms of instructional materials. This not only helped ensure the use of high-quality, vetted materials but also allowed the district to better support schools in using these materials. As one district staff member pointed out, "We can't support at scale a cornucopia of materials."

Similarly, to drive instructional coherence and consistency in Dallas, the central office released instructional units every six weeks called Six Weeks at a Glance (SWAG). In addition to clearly laying out instructional expectations across core subjects, the district released them six weeks *in advance* to allow teachers lead time to prepare. These units were accompanied by professional development sessions that were voluntary but heavily attended to provide teachers a chance to dive into an upcoming unit, experience a modeled strategy, collaborate, and plan. Teachers also worked with each SWAG unit in their PLCs and had access to on-site coaching and an online bank of videos of teachers piloting the lessons in other classrooms.

Moreover, the district carefully monitored implementation through school and classroom visits, during which district leaders looked at whether teachers were following the scope and sequence, what texts they had selected, and what strategies they were using with students. Since all district curriculum resources were online, lead staff members also had access to analytics that told them who was using the materials, what they were using, and which resources were used the most. The district also fielded a user survey with every unit and used the results to further refine their guidance and support.

In the District of Columbia, the unifying vision for instructional quality was referred to as "instructional oneness." It started in earnest with Kaya Henderson's work to learn from what its teacher evaluation data was telling leaders about their most effective teachers. The district provided principals and teachers with a clear picture—and exemplars—of what high-quality instruction should look like. Teachers reported getting more guidance than ever before. The teachers the Council team interviewed explained that in the past there had been a revolving door of textbooks and initiatives, with little support or direction from the central office. Now, with the advent of IMPACT (the accountability system), LEAP (Learning together to Advance our Practice), the district's teacher leadership development initiative), and resources such as an instructional video bank, they felt they better understood the district's expectations and how to meet them.

At the time of our visit, D.C. was in the process of moving even closer toward a centralized or standardized set of instructional expectations. In addition to a unified curriculum, which was built by the district's most effective teachers around the new standards, there was at least one required unit of study in each content area per quarter and exemplars in each content area. As one instructional leader explained, while there was a shared district curriculum before, it looked drastically different from classroom to classroom and school to school. The district was therefore addressing this unevenness by ramping up the amount and content-specificity of its support for teachers. At the same time, the district was aligning its professional development, materials, and assessment system with the new standards—and simultaneously implementing more music, art, dance, library, field trip, Advanced Placement, and physical education opportunities to spur more student engagement and attendance.

Chicago was also moving toward a universal district curriculum, although schools were able to opt out if they could show that they were producing results. Like some of the other case study districts, Chicago provided schools with a curated set of instructional materials to choose from and the guidance they needed in selecting appropriate grade-level materials. The district also created a "Knowledge Center"—an online clearinghouse with thousands of resources. Unlike other online databases we have encountered, the district vetted the materials that were posted to the Knowledge Center, ensuring that they were high quality and aligned to the standards.

This norming of instructional expectations, resources, and guidance was described in more than one district as "autonomy with guardrails" rather than "one size fits all." It was based on the general acknowledgment that, while pure site-based autonomy may work in some high-performing districts with elevated capacity and experienced staff, it does not work for all districts and schools—and it does not always work every time that significant, systemic academic improvement is needed.

This meant, particularly in lower-performing urban school systems, there needed to be greater definition, specificity, and support, as well as a norming of standards and instructional expectations across all schools to ensure uniformly higher quality and greater equity with the highly mobile student body found in most big-city schools. At the same time, many districts granted autonomy to principals based on performance. Dallas, for example, defined its instructional approach as "managed instruction with earned empowerment." Chicago's and Miami's theories of action were similar. Our research suggests that it works much more reliably for low-performing urban school systems than other approaches.

Moreover, although it is referred to here as "norming" or "centralization," this standardization of instructional expectations was often described by central office staff as the district becoming more service oriented. These central office staffers believed it led to greater support for schools since staff needed to provide technical assistance on a smaller number of things. In other words, empowerment without support, resources, and clear communication of district expectations will not drive growth.

In San Diego, this service orientation led the superintendent to dismantle the two-sided structure of the system—operations versus academics—in favor of a design that put principals at the center of the work. Marten called this reform as "leading from the middle." She and her chief of staff acted as the chief academic officer, and she reoriented the district around improving classroom instruction. The district also phased out its system-wide formative assessments in lieu of school-driven tests, a strategy that worked in San Diego because of the overarching use of the standards and the strength of their PLCs. The message this structure was designed to convey was that everyone's chief responsibility was to support schools, principals, and teachers—and the quality of instruction.

Our interviews and data analysis also suggested that there was a distinctive "state effect" in places like Massachusetts, Florida, Texas, and North

Carolina. Boston was a clear beneficiary of the state's historically ambitious standards in addition to its own local efforts. This also was the case in Miami, Hillsborough County, Orange County, Duval County, and Pinellas County. On the other hand, Dallas and other Texas cities did not formally adopt the academic standards that other states were putting into place, but they did make it clear what they wanted taught across their systems.

Controversy Around the Standards

There has been considerable controversy around the role that the Common Core State Standards played in improving student achievement. Tom Loveless, for instance, an analyst at the Brookings Institution, concluded that they had been a "failure."[22] An analysis by Michael Cohen, however, the former head of ACHIEVE, concluded that the thin effects Loveless and other researchers were seeing were because they were looking in the wrong place.[23] One would want to see the effects of broad educational policies show up at the state level, which was where they looked. However, it is hard to find them at the state level when those effects are really the result of multiple local school systems that have implemented those policies at differing times and with varying degrees of fidelity. It is at the local level where you want to look for the impact of reforms like the Common Core. And it was at the local level where we found them.

Finally, the effects of the standards were likely dampened by the misalignment of the standards and NAEP, particularly in mathematics. That is, concepts being tested by NAEP were not always assessed in the same order or depth as outlined in the standards. A study by Enis Dogan for the National Center for Educational Statistics, for instance, found that the misalignment cost TUDA districts an average of 2.42 scale score points in fourth-grade math in 2019 and 1.39 points in eighth-grade math.[24] (See the appendix.)

The big-city school systems were more likely to put the new standards into place because they backed a strategy they saw as reversing the low expectations that many had of their urban children. The importance of the standards to urban schools was that they bolstered expectations, defined quality, and created the fulcrum around which the districts could provide instructional cohesion and aligned materials, professional development, and assessments. While it was true that the standards, by themselves, would not raise achievement levels, few practitioners who knew what they were doing thought that they would. Aligned support systems around the standards were needed to drive student achievement. And that is how many of these districts achieved the gains they did.

Teacher and Leader Quality

The strength of teachers and principals was another defining feature across the six districts and was the result of intentional human capital strategies on the part of district leaders to boost the capacity of schools to make instructional improvements. In Boston, for example, relatively high teacher pay contributed to both the high quality of teachers and low teacher turnover. In addition, the policy of mutual consent hiring (phased in around 2010) allowed school leaders more choices in selecting teachers, and it is credited with creating better matches between teachers and schools.

In the District of Columbia, the first phase of the district's reform efforts was largely a human capital strategy, whereby weak teachers were removed, and effective or potentially effective teachers were identified using the district's evaluation system, IMPACT. More than any other district, except Dallas and Miami, D.C.'s efforts to differentiate effective from lesser-effective staff and improve the quality of its workforce was one of its most effective reform strategies.

The Chicago Public Schools pivoted toward a leadership development focus early in its reform efforts. One of the most significant changes they made was to introduce a layer of screening in addition to state certification to determine suitable principal candidates, who were then selected by parents and communities as part of the school-based governance system the district had. This screening process has evolved over time, but it has remained a rigorous undertaking that requires candidates to present a portfolio of work, complete a written exam, and participate in a set of interviews in which they are asked to respond to various scenarios and leadership challenges. According to district staff, this process has successfully raised the quality of the candidate pool, and it has enabled the district to imbed district-defined expectations, competencies, and beliefs about what makes a strong school leader into the selection process.

Similarly, in its human capital work, Miami-Dade County first focused on strengthening its principal ranks and finding school leaders that reflected the district's priorities. The district also placed a special focus on the staffing and leadership of fragile schools. In the early phases of their reform work, the district identified effective teachers using a value-added measure charting progress over three to five years and then recruited those teachers to work at struggling schools. They also moved other teachers out of high-needs sites, sometimes involuntarily.

Dallas's pay-for-performance model—the Teacher Excellence Initiative—also focused on identifying the most effective teachers and paying them significantly more to work in high-need schools, the district's Accelerating Campus Excellence (ACE) schools. Moreover, the district mounted a system-wide effort to identify and deploy bilingual teachers as it built out its dual language model across the system.

Research by the National Council on Teacher Quality found that teacher evaluation systems, when implemented effectively, could benefit teachers and students alike.[25] They examined teacher evaluation systems in Dallas, Denver, the District of Columbia, and Newark, along with two states, and found that these evaluation systems resulted in more even distribution of teaching talent, higher pay for teachers, better retention of the best teachers, and greater improvement.

In addition to these strategies, many of the districts we visited focused on the development of teachers and future leaders. The District of Columbia partnered with outside organizations such as Relay Graduate School to support teacher candidate residencies, while Chicago established the Chicago Leadership Collaborative, a partnership between the district and leading principal development programs to create a pipeline of highly qualified leaders to meet the district's needs. Other districts, such as San Diego, offered mentors to new principals, as well as providing teachers and vice principals with opportunities for growth and leadership.

In fact, Chicago's early focus on growing the leadership capacity of school and network leaders has endowed them with a deep leadership "bench"—evidenced by the fact that the district's former CEO, CAO, and many other chief positions were filled internally with instructional staff who had risen through the ranks and brought a wealth of expertise and experience at multiple organizational levels to their roles.

PROFESSIONAL DEVELOPMENT AND OTHER CAPACITY-BUILDING MEASURES

In addition to high standards, standardized curricular guidance, and human capital strategies, the six case study districts employed a variety of other strategies aimed at school-based instructional capacity building. One can see this in the reorientation of the role of principal supervisors, as well as the widespread use of teacher leaders, school-based instructional leadership teams, building and network-level instructional coaches, and PLCs in the districts we visited.

School-based support structures such as instructional leadership teams and PLCs exist in many districts around the country. However, it was the level of intentionality and focus that really set these six districts apart. In Chicago, teachers described a transition during which they began getting clearer signals from the central office that school-level instructional team meetings mattered, and schools became more accountable for the selection, capacity building, and support of their teacher leaders. Chicago also employed PLCs and professional learning summits after they adopted the Common Core to train and then deploy teacher leaders to bring that expertise back to their buildings.

Miami-Dade County, meanwhile, hosted yearly Synergy Summer Institutes, weeklong professional development courses attended by teams of school staff. The institute was designed to provide these teams with the opportunity to study data together, reflect on current practices, identify the essential practices that should be sustained or enhanced during the upcoming school year, and take part in strategic planning to ensure continuous improvement at their school sites.

San Diego and Dallas had the most well-articulated PLCs we saw, which were closely monitored and supported by the district. In fact, in

San Diego, PLCs appeared to have affected the whole culture of the school system and were cited by district and school staff alike as perhaps the most crucial factor driving the district's progress. As in Chicago, the evolution of PLCs was the result of intentional guidance and messaging from the central office. One principal described the evolution of PLCs at her site from conversations about evaluation to sessions that were now devoted to collaborative problem solving, providing her with an invaluable opportunity to work and learn alongside her teachers. According to district and school leaders, this structure helped the district drill down on Tier 1 core instruction and its effectiveness.

Of course, just having PLCs in place was not enough to achieve instructional growth. Without clear guidance on what the district's expectations were for the time spent in PLCs and training on how to effectively lead collaborative, content-driven work sessions, PLCs in other systems often amounted to glorified "bull sessions" rather than meaningful opportunities to improve teachers' instructional practice and build capacity.

Another unique and even counterintuitive strategy that served to build school capacity in San Diego was the district's requirement that schools develop their own formative assessments. In past years when there was a district-mandated interim assessment, staff found that teachers would give the tests but not necessarily use the data. So, while this process took a lot of schools' time to develop, they acknowledged that the process of designing assessments built not only expertise but ownership of formative assessment data where it was needed most. Of course, there were numerous guardrails in place. Area superintendents, for example, met with principals quarterly to review school-wide progress and help determine goals, and teachers received support in developing formative assessments through school-based instructional leadership teams, PLCs, and meetings with area leadership. The downside was that the district did not have the benefit of system-wide assessment results over the course of the school year, but leadership concluded that its regular school and classroom monitoring gave them the information they needed.

In the District of Columbia, LEAP was another good example of a district strategy for building school-based instructional capacity. Through a weekly cycle of professional development in small, site-based, content-specific professional learning communities (LEAP Teams) led by content experts (LEAP Leaders), the district developed on-the-ground expertise in teaching the district's Common Core–aligned curriculum.

In Dallas, meanwhile, principals and teachers cited the value of school-based support staff and structures such as Campus Instructional Coaches and Campus Instructional Leadership Teams (CILT) made up of principals, assistant principals, and core teachers. And while coaches and school-based instructional leadership teams were certainly not unique to this district, it was the level of support and structure that sets this district's practices apart. The CILT teams in Dallas received intensive, content-specific training from the academic department six times a year to ensure that they were prepared to lead learning at their respective campuses. Meanwhile, a corps of Instructional Lead Coaches served as the "coaches of coaches," providing ongoing professional development and support for the campus-based coaches to ensure that the support that they provided to teachers was consistent and aligned to the district's vision for high-quality instruction.

Ultimately, the success of these capacity-building efforts was grounded in a common vision for instructional excellence, a clear set of expectations of what students should know and at what level of depth, and implementation that created ownership and buy-in among principals and teachers.

ACTING AT SCALE

Another similarity we observed across the faster-improving districts was a shared belief that system-wide results could only come from system-wide change. Rollouts of reform initiatives, curricular materials, and programming (including implementation of college- and career-readiness standards) were undertaken at scale in many—if not all—of these districts.

In Miami-Dade County, Superintendent Alberto Carvalho explained that he does not believe in pilots. His strategy for district-wide reform instead involved spending a lot of time planning and researching, but then acting at scale to remove all vestiges of past practice. "If you want improvement at scale, act at scale," he told the Council team. "The only way to overcome the gravitational pull of the *status quo* is to execute forcefully."

Of course, acting at scale took on many different forms from district to district. In Miami-Dade County, they phased in instructional reforms and new academic standards by grade level, but leaders did so across all schools at the same time. In Chicago, the rollout of the district's new literacy program was executed across the board, while in mathematics they adopted a grade six through eight "bridge."

Importantly, the Council team concluded after visiting these districts that it was not only the scale of the work that determined their district-wide success but the level of coherence, alignment, and support for these rollouts that made the biggest impact. In this way, instructional reform initiatives adopted district wide benefited from the shared focus and effort of staff working together toward common goals and expectations. This unifying instructional vision was critical in places like the District of Columbia as they rolled out their initiatives. Similarly, in Boston, the rollout of a new concept-rich core mathematics program in 2000 was undergirded by a unifying instructional philosophy and sustained support, professional development, and oversight for implementation over several years. In contrast, as noted in a 2011 Council report, *Pieces of the Puzzle*, the district's reading reforms did not benefit from the unanimity of approach we saw in mathematics. In fact, most schools chose their own reading programs at the time.[26]

ACCOUNTABILITY AND COLLABORATION

The rollout of accountability systems—starting with the superintendent—was cited as a key lever for change across the six districts we examined. The IMPACT system in the District of Columbia was the centerpiece of its human capital strategy. In addition to helping identify effective and ineffective teachers, this practice of holding everyone—including principals, assistant principals, and instructional coaches—accountable for student growth reportedly helped to focus everyone on the primary goal of supporting instruction and building an overall culture of responsibility. The program was not necessarily popular with the teachers' organization, but we think it was central to the district's ability to boost student outcomes.

In Dallas, which was a national pioneer at the local level in the use of value-added data, growth indices played a key role in driving shared accountability for student results. Like IMPACT, these measures were controversial at first as they provided a quantitative measure of teacher effectiveness based on student achievement data. However, over time they became more accepted since they compared students in each classroom to other similar classrooms and students in the district. The classroom and school effectiveness indices are now used in the district's evaluation instruments for teachers and principals, as well as in the district's pay-for-performance initiative (the Teacher Excellence Initiative [TEI]).

Similarly, the school accountability system in Chicago was among the first factors cited by school leaders and staff in the district's progress. Interviewees reported that the evaluation tools for both teachers and principals took a deep look at what was happening in classrooms through regular walk-throughs, and they measured success in terms of student growth on the district's interim assessments. These evaluation tools in turn helped to standardize the work of teachers and create clear expectations for instruction across schools. In fact, everyone in the district was evaluated in some way on student growth, and this helped build a sense of direction and shared responsibility for student progress.

Interestingly, this culture of accountability has come hand-in-hand with increased collaboration in some places. Leaders and staff in several of the sites the Council team visited discussed an intentional shift from competition to teamwork as accountability became a more shared phenomena—a shift that could be seen in everything from how principal supervisors worked together with the curriculum department and other central office departments to the practice of connecting principals and teachers across schools. In Chicago, for example, staff reported that collegiality had improved drastically—despite several teacher strikes and tense relations with the union. Personnel saw the vertical and horizontal exchange of information increase dramatically and a shift toward more inclusive, cross-functional strategic planning.

This service orientation has, in turn, nurtured an environment of sharing lessons learned and resources across schools. The network chiefs (Chicago's principal supervisors) saw it as part of their job to create opportunities for collaboration and to promote cross-pollination between schools and networks. The Council team heard the same thing in the District of Columbia, where instructional superintendents saw the systemic sharing of lessons learned and effective practices as a key part of their role, describing themselves as "facilitators of the learning principals do with one another."

In fact, the Council team observed that principal supervisors were a key mechanism by which many districts helped further accountability, communication, and collaboration district wide. Despite differences in organizational structure from district to district, principal supervisors allowed districts to communicate system-wide standards, instructional expectations, and priorities while helping to identify which school sites required additional support and what opportunities existed for sharing effective practices.

In all, accountability was being redefined in these districts away from the more mechanistic, administrative accountability that one saw under *No Child Left Behind* toward one that was oriented around a shared culture of responsibility for improving student outcomes.

CHALLENGES AS OPPORTUNITIES

One interesting characteristic was the resilience and resourcefulness that these six districts demonstrated in the face of change, challenge, or adversity. What was striking in each case was that leaders saw an emerging challenge as an opportunity either to make changes or to introduce reforms. Conversely, they did not let a budding crisis permanently divert their attention from their main priority of improving achievement. In other words, they did not shift into crisis management mode but retained their focus on instructional improvement despite external circumstances.

In Miami-Dade County, for example, the economic crisis of 2008–2009, which resulted in budget cuts of over a billion dollars, was credited by district leaders as having "opened the door" to a wave of instructional and operational reforms, including greater centralization of curricular guidance and resources to save on costs and support schools in the most effective and efficient manner. In Dallas, superintendent Hinojosa used the same economic downturn to right-size district staff. In both cases, the challenges were met with a determination to turn a "sow's ear into a silk purse" and avoid getting off track.

This ability to respond constructively to new circumstances could be seen clearly, as well, in the districts' responses not only to a crisis but to a new situation: the adoption of new, rigorous academic standards. Districts such as Boston, Chicago, Miami, and the District of Columbia, for example, were not tentative or reluctant when the standards were released; they were among the earliest adopters. San Diego even petitioned for a waiver from the California Standards Test so that they could phase-in the Common-Core-aligned Smarter Balanced Assessment Consortium test ahead of other districts in the state.

Instructional leaders and staff at each site talked about seizing the opportunity provided by the standards to advance instructional coherence across their systems. While some of these districts were already underway in their instructional improvement efforts, the introduction of college- and career-readiness standards helped these districts connect the work of supporting higher-quality instruction to assessment and evaluation.

The chief academic officers and curriculum leaders we spoke with also cited the value of shared learning as staff unpacked and implemented the instructional shifts that the standards prescribed. In fact, the process of adopting the standards was often described as "evening out" the support provided to teachers and principals across networks, as everyone worked to get onto the "same page." In other words, these districts were seeing change as an opportunity, not a burden.

In each school district we visited, the successful implementation of college- and career-readiness standards was dependent on communications and close collaboration between the school management structure, the curriculum staff, teachers, and leaders at the central office. These districts worked cross-functionally to support implementation through multipronged strategies involving professional development, curriculum guidance and materials, instructional reviews, data reporting, and teacher and principal evaluations.

Of course, standards have not always led to student gains in other districts. In one district leader's opinion this was because there was often not enough investment of time, effort, and resources in the implementation process. Progress, in other words, was not a function of declared alignment to rigorous standards but of alignment in practice, which required sustained monitoring, support, and leadership focus to ensure that instructional changes made at the systems level reached the classrooms.

SUPPORT FOR STRUGGLING SCHOOLS AND STUDENTS

Some districts may have also seen gains in part because of an explicit emphasis on supporting struggling students, English language learners, students living in poverty, and students with disabilities. In Chicago, the district's implementation of multitiered systems of support (MTSS) and its use of student-level data to inform its instructional strategies were factors in their progress. In Miami, principals reported becoming more deliberate in reaching struggling students, as well as increasingly using disaggregated data and on-track indicators along with strategies, interventions, and supports based on understanding how different students learn and what student work should look like.

The San Diego Unified School District developed a particularly robust focus on individual students and student work. This was the result of a district-wide effort undertaken several years ago to study the experiences of struggling students and identify what it revealed about their instructional and support needs. In school and classroom walk-throughs and in their professional learning communities, teachers and administrators dedicated a significant part of their time to discussing individual students, looking at student work, focusing on grade-level instruction, and using school-level data to design lesson plans around the specific needs of the lowest-performing students in each classroom. What they did not do was lower standards or overemphasize remedial work.

The Council team found that districts varied considerably in their approach to struggling schools and school turnaround efforts. The District of Columbia schools, for example, did not articulate a clear school turnaround strategy as part of their efforts to improve, although it did replace most of its principals with individuals recruited from other school systems that had a record of improvement. The district's main objective instead focused on programming and instruction system wide—along with an explicit effort targeted to Black male students, who were showing special academic needs.

In contrast, Dallas, a district with some of the highest concentrations of students in extreme poverty, had a particularly strong focus on equitable resource allocation. The district used an "intensity of poverty" index based on census block data to identify schools with particularly high needs, looking at not only poverty but generational poverty. A common sentiment echoed in interviews with staff was that "schools that need more should get more—in time, treasure, talent." This could be seen in the district's emphasis on ensuring that struggling schools serving high numbers of students from low-income families, Black students, and English language learners received increased levels of campus-based support, additional resources, and effective teachers and principals.

A primary example of this resource allocation strategy in Dallas was the district's Accelerating Campus Excellence (ACE) initiative, a strategy that Michael Hinojosa borrowed from the Charlotte-Mecklenburg school district. The ACE initiative targeted the district's historically failing schools—that is, those with five years or more of not meeting state accountability requirements—and provided them with additional resources that included strategic staffing (paying the most effective teachers to work at these schools via the district's pay-for-performance model, TEI); prescriptive, data-driven instructional practices; increased monitoring and feedback; enhanced social emotional learning; extended learning time; and investments in school and classroom upgrades.

The district also instituted a series of "transformation schools" to create more racially and economically diverse settings in which students could learn. These transformation schools are not only proving to be successful academically but also draw thousands more applications than there are seats.

In addition to this school-based strategy, Dallas implemented a robust effort to improve the academic performance of its Black students, particularly its male students. The effort included a combination of early childhood participation, staff diversification, strategic partnerships, single-gender schools, an African American studies program, mentoring, and enhanced instruction, along with other initiatives. In fact, the Dallas school board held the superintendent explicitly accountable on his annual evaluation for progress with these students.

In San Diego, meanwhile, the district identified its highest-needs schools as "focus schools." Oversight for these schools was distributed evenly across principal supervisors: each one had six focus schools. Although district staff reported that focus schools had the same level of autonomy as other sites, they also reported spending more time at these schools, conducting more classroom walk-throughs, and working intensely with them to ensure that the district's "critical concepts" were covered at each grade level.

Miami also cited its focus on "fragile" schools—and the alignment of resources to meet student needs at these sites—as one of the main pillars of its district improvement strategy. In addition to deploying the most effective teachers and leaders to these schools, the district directed greater support and resources to these sites.

Moreover, Miami employed the unique strategy of pairing its support for struggling schools with its school choice initiative. Seventy-two percent of Miami-Dade County students were involved in a choice program of some sort, and students had over one thousand choice options. Their approach, as described to the Council team, was to support struggling schools by increasing student engagement using niche programming. In other words, these schools and programs were designed specifically to appeal to parents, students, and communities, and district staff referred to this strategy as "demand-driven reform and innovation."

Like Miami-Dade County, Dallas used choice schools and programs to meet the needs of struggling schools, as well as to incentivize parents to remain in the district. There were waitlists at each of the district's twenty-five P-TECH (Pathways to Technology Early College High School) and ECHS (Early College/Collegiate High Schools) campuses, and the district offered a range of other choice options, including over fifty two-way dual-language schools and over thirty magnet school programs. Both Dallas and Miami were able to provide extensive choice options without fracturing the cohesion of their core instructional programs by maintaining a uniform districtwide curriculum and assessment system while varying the delivery system or program emphasis from school to school.

Miami also focused efforts on its Black male students in a way that was like both Dallas and the District of Columbia. And the Boston schools strengthened their instruction for English language learners after a 2010 settlement with the Department of Justice.

Most of the districts used strong data systems to identify their struggling schools and students. Data systems and use of that data were particularly strong in Dallas, Miami, and Chicago but were less robust in Boston, San Diego, and the District of Columbia—but they were strong enough. Overall, the data systems in most urban school districts are comparatively strong, so much so that they did not seem to distinguish between districts that showed substantial improvement and ones that did not, since we saw comparatively strong research and data functions in one of the counterfactual districts that we describe in chapter 5. The difference was in how the districts used the data to drive results.

COMMUNITY INVESTMENT AND ENGAGEMENT

Finally, a notable feature of school districts that were improving was the active engagement and investment of community organizations, educational groups, foundations, businesses, and local colleges and universities—particularly in Boston, Chicago, Miami, and the District of Columbia.

The Boston Public Schools benefited from having a high concentration of educational institutions located in and near the city. School and district staff alike cited investments made in after-school and summer enrichment opportunities as a crucial factor in students' progress and sustained achievement. One district leader estimated that about 80 percent of Boston students had benefited from some sort of outside investment. This high concentration of colleges and universities in the city also meant a plethora of training programs and residencies for teachers.

In Chicago there were similar investments in after-school activities and programs for kids. In addition, the school district's relationship with the University of Chicago Consortium on School Research ensured that district staff and leadership had access to a wealth of data on district schools and was cited as a key factor in helping the district sustain its commitment to its new accountability system, which was initially met with both internal and external resistance.

Miami had an impressive array of community partners that the system relied on to provide support. The district arranged for hundreds of organizations and companies to provide summer internships for students, including offerings ranging from the American Dental Center to the Miami Arts and Academics Youth Summer Camp. The Miami-Dade County Public Schools also had a vast array of other community partners like the First National Bank of South Miami, American Airlines, and the Mexican American Council to provide support services.

While these partnerships and investments were critical sources of support and resources for city schoolchildren, it was equally important that these districts were intentional about the investments made in—and on behalf of—their schools by these partners. Programs were vetted to ensure that they were consistent with district objectives and approaches, and staff dedicated time and focus to coordinating and connecting these investments so that schools were not overwhelmed with redundant programming or mixed messaging on district instructional priorities.

In the District of Columbia, chancellor Kaya Henderson built on her predecessor's reforms to begin her "Hopes and Dreams Campaign" in 2011. This was not like the efforts of other big-city school systems that worked to develop community partnerships. This campaign was designed to build public support of the city's schools. District leaders asked people what they wanted in their school system. What do you want for your children? What should your schools look like? From the feedback from over ten thousand people, Henderson drafted a strategic plan and returned it to the community, asking the question, "Is this what you meant?" The last version, "A Capital Commitment," had five goals, around which leaders were confident that they had the public's backing.

The public engagement in the District of Columbia was comprehensive, long lasting, and effective—so much so that the system's need to close schools in 2013 was accomplished without a whimper. Enrollment began to increase, and results began to accumulate. Once Henderson and her teachers finished building a new system-wide curriculum, they took it to perspective partners across the city and asked, "What are you doing that aligns with what we're doing?" The effort was called "City as Our Classroom," and it gave the district a three-legged stool on which to perch its reforms: human capital, standards and curriculum, and community engagement.

In Dallas, the district kept many of its schools open until 6:00 p.m. to provide tutoring, social services, and food, and it relied on various nonprofit organizations throughout the city to provide the resources. Dallas, like the other districts, also used their partnerships to provide mentoring, internships, summer jobs, site visits, and the like for district students.

Each of these school systems also used the Strategic Support Teams from the Council of the Great City Schools to get external feedback on their improvement efforts from other big-city public school systems that had faced some of the same challenges.

These six urban school systems also had environments or "ecosystems" that helped them along the way. Miami and Dallas had substantial community support that built off the popularity of their school superintendents. Hinojosa dealt with community skepticism and indifference when he started his reforms, but he nurtured a city of "believers" as he began to produce results. Much of the same dynamic existed for Carvahlo in Miami.

Henderson faced a more mixed situation in the District of Columbia, where the teachers' union was opposed to the new teacher accountability system but cooperated on other actions. In addition, the D.C. city council and the wealthier wards of the city were consistent critics. Nevertheless,

Henderson's popularity, energy, transparency, and results won her allies with the media, business community, and parent groups.[27] And Janice Jackson had strong allies in Chicago with the school board, the mayor, her school principals, business leaders, the philanthropic community, and local universities but faced continuing headaches from the teachers' union and the press.[28] An excellent description of Chicago's ecosystem and history of reform can be found in Bryk's recent book, *How a City Learned to Improve Its Schools*.[29]

As I said at the beginning of this chapter, there were other urban school systems beyond the six described here that showed gains during this period. And what they were doing was often similar to the six districts described above. The Council did not always conduct formal case studies of them like we did of these six, but we did less-formal reviews of various aspects of their programming over the years. We include them here to augment the improvement efforts that were described earlier. Denver, Kansas City (MO), Detroit, Atlanta, and Cleveland, for instance, showed substantial improvement over the years. And cities like Long Beach and St. Paul have also posted substantial improvements.

Atlanta was a particularly interesting case because its improvements came alongside a major cheating scandal that obfuscated the reforms and improvements that were happening at around the same time. (The scandal involved several schools around 2010, where personnel were found to have altered state test scores. NAEP scores were not implicated.) Beverly Hall led the Atlanta Public Schools from 1999 to 2010, after having served in similar leadership roles in Newark, New Jersey, and Queens, New York. An expert in student achievement and what drove it, Hall granted flexibility to schools in Atlanta but with a twist.

Instead of giving schools full flexibility over their instructional program, like one sees in some places, Hall gave the schools a choice of programs that she had preapproved—Success for All, Direct Instruction, Modern Red School House, Move It Math, Co-Nect, and International Baccalaureate—some of the programs that were espoused as part of the Comprehensive School Reform Models that were funded by the federal government.

The research on the effectiveness of these programs was mixed, but what Beverly Hall did to make them work was to assign resolute instructional staff from the central office who had been specially trained on each model to provide technical assistance and professional development to schools that had chosen them. The models were paired with regular assessments and stiff accountability for progress. The result was flexibility with guardrails and strong accountability that Meria Carstarphen and others built on over the succeeding years.

Cleveland was another district that looked like it was improving by granting school autonomy, but chief executive officer Eric Gordon, who had been appointed to the top job in June 2011 after having served briefly as the district's chief academic officer, found a way to improve instruction across the board and provide a flexible system at the same time. He proved to be a savvy operator, having grown up in poverty and concluded that it was the adults who were the problem in improving the school system—not the kids.

The Cleveland schools found themselves in a challenging position as Gordon was taking the reins of the district. The US Supreme Court had approved the city's private school voucher plan in 2002.[30] The rise in charter schools in the city and the budding appetite for choice that emerged with the high court ruling made it clear that city leaders needed to take bold action to salvage their school system.

Mayor Frank Jackson went to the state and convinced the legislature to hold off on a proposed takeover, while city leaders crafted a game plan. He then assembled a task force that included Gordon, business leaders, the unions, charters, philanthropists, and others to fashion a set of reforms that would speak to the community's growing appetite for choice and the state's need for progress. The result was the Cleveland Plan that Gordon and others took back to the state. The state approved the blueprint in 2012.

The plan stated that "Cleveland must transition from a traditional, single-source school district to a new system of district and charter schools that are held to the highest standards and work in partnership to create dramatic student achievement gains for every child. The plan is built upon growing the number of excellent schools in Cleveland, regardless of provider, and giving these schools autonomy over staff and budgets in exchange for high accountability for performance."[31]

What Gordon did was to provide full flexibility to his schools in terms of budgeting, hiring, and some materials, but he was an early adopter of the Common Core State Standards and used them to galvanize his instructional reforms. He overhauled the district's scope and sequence documents around the standards and gave schools a choice of several standards-based instructional programs—like what Hall had done in Atlanta. And he did everything he could to build the community's trust.

As time went on, he began to question the effectiveness of the commercial products the district had purchased, but he stuck with the standards and played the "long-game" in trying to improve instructional practices inside his flexible strategy.[32] Ultimately, Gordon pulled off an educational black-belt maneuver that provided flexibility but led to substantial improvements in reading and math. But it took time.

Denver's turnaround began with the improbable tenure of superintendent Michael Bennet, now US Senator from Colorado. Bennet replaced Gerry Wartgow, who stabilized the district after years of upheaval and turnover, developed a strategic plan (the Denver Plan) with many of the proposals that the Council of the Great City Schools made after a 2005–2006 review of the district's instructional program and ELL initiatives.[33] With Bennet was a well-respected school board, led by Teresa Pena; a skilled chief academic officer, Jaime Aquino, who is now superintendent of the San Antonio public schools; Susana Cordova, who was director of literacy and later Denver superintendent; and Brad Jupp, who led an innovative teacher evaluation initiative that added substantially to the district's gains and who later became advisor to US Secretary of Education Arne Duncan. It was a powerhouse team.

When Bennet left Denver for Washington, he was replaced by Tom Boasberg, Bennet's chief operating officer and childhood friend, who doubled down on many of the reforms his predecessor put into place. In 2014, when the Council returned for another look at the system's efforts to improve student performance, it found a much-improved program.[34] A sense of urgency to improve instructionally characterized the district's work;

new college and career-readiness standards had been put into place; materials that did not align with the standards were dispensed with; academic expectations were incorporated into principals' evaluations; resources were redeployed to schools that needed them most; teacher effectiveness coaches were put into place; math and ELA scope and sequence documents were developed that were in alignment with the standards; new interim assessments were implemented; and many other reforms meant to improve student achievement anchored the district's work. By 2019 Denver saw some of the most substantial gains on NAEP of any of the participating cities.[35]

Kansas City (MO) was another major urban school system that saw significant improvements over the years, but the improvement was not linear. The school district lost its state accreditation in 2001 when Benjamin Demps Jr. was superintendent. Shortly afterward, the school board, led by David Smith, head of the local Boys & Girls Clubs, brought in Bernard Taylor, who lasted about five years but who did not produce the kinds of gains the community wanted. The Council of the Great City Schools was asked to come in during the last year of the Taylor administration to review the district's academic program and noninstructional operations, but after Taylor left, the system brought in Anthony Amato and then Mark Bedell to head its system.

Bedell asked the Council, once again, to review the district's academic, financial, and operational programs, and he paid close attention. Over the six years he was superintendent, Bedell elevated expectations for student achievement, strengthened district curriculum, boosted school district quality, and aligned instruction with state standards. He strengthened instructional content and foundational skills in the early grades, increased the number of reading and math coaches, stepped up the quality of the district's professional development, identified needed interventions, created instructional walk-through and monitoring procedures, consolidated accountability documents to provide clearer expectations, improved academic department coordination, reoriented the work of principal supervisors around instruction, and increased the numbers of Advanced Placement courses and certified teachers. And the district partnered with the local business community, foundations, and community organizations to re-build trust and collaboration.

Most important, the district, under Bedell's leadership, strengthened its accountability structure by having the superintendent evaluated each year by the school board on a series of metrics that tracked district progress on goals that it had set under the strategic plan. The system saw significant gains in student outcomes by 2020, when I wrote the state superintendent arguing that the system's progress was sufficient to regrant its accreditation.[36] The state did so in 2021.

Detroit, like Kansas City, also improved, but the path was anything but smooth. From 1999 through 2005 and again from 2009 through 2016, Detroit's public school system was overseen by a series of state-appointed financial managers. The system waxed and waned over these periods as student performance would increase for a bit and finances would appear to stabilize before every positive trend reversed itself in one new set of leaders and scandals after another. In 2016, however, the Michigan legislature created the Detroit Public School Community District to replace the original Detroit Public Schools and reinstalled an elected school board. The board hired Nikolai Vitti, a Detroit native and superintendent of the Duval County (Jacksonville) schools in Florida. He had also apprenticed under Alberto Carvahlo in Miami.

Vitti moved quickly to reverse the downward slide in student performance by implementing the Common Core State Standards for the first time in the district, training principals and teachers on their implementation, developing new curriculum aligned with the standards, implementing new data systems to drive instructional interventions for students who were behind, providing professional development, and setting up instructional monitoring systems district wide.[37] By 2019 the district saw sizable gains in reading and mathematics scores on the NAEP.

DISCUSSION

None of the districts that we have seen improve over the years did things in the same way. Each one of them devised their strategies in ways that fit their contexts. But what was common across all of them was that they used the college and career ready standards to anchor and direct their reforms. They aligned the elements of their systems around instructional improvement. They strengthened the capacity of their people to provide higher-quality instruction. They were clear about what they expected to be taught—not how. And they emphasized a shared culture of responsibility for student outcomes. All of them improved the quality of their classroom instruction. That was the key.

The leaders of these districts made it clear that it was important to know what problems they were trying to solve. They knew that using precanned solutions in search of a problem or failing to be strategic about which few problems they would tackle was a losing proposition. The tactics these districts used were wildly different, but their broader strategies devoted to moving their systems in service of better classroom instruction—rather than simply adopting new programs—were similar. Finally, all used elements of continuous improvement and regular monitoring of that improvement to drive themselves forward.

In chapter 5, we look at a set of urban school districts that did not show the same improvements and will compare their practices along the same dimensions that we observed in these faster-improving urban school systems.

5

What Did Not Work?

In chapter 4, I described actions by districts that made substantial progress. In this chapter, I look at the same dimensions in two districts that were not making as much progress.[1] I also supplement what we found in these two districts with examples from other districts that were not getting the results they wanted.

As part of our analysis, the Council of Great City Schools looked at the literature for research that would compare the practices of improving and not improving urban school systems on the same dimensions. While there are numerous studies and articles on the failures of urban public education on one factor or another, we did not many find studies, other than our own, that systematically compared the two sets of districts on the same dimensions. I hope this chapter and chapter 4 will help close the gap in our understanding of why these systems got different results.

METHODOLOGY

The Council picked two large urban school systems that were not making substantial academic progress and then contrasted them with those that were either high performing or making significant progress. We used two criteria for selecting the districts: they were low performing on NAEP or other measures, and they were not making much academic progress on it or other assessments.

The first counterfactual district that we examined—the Jackson Public Schools in Jackson, Mississippi—did not participate in the Trial Urban District Assessment (TUDA) of NAEP, but we were able to convert state assessment results into NAEP metrics. We conducted a series of site visits to the district in 2017 to help them while they were going through a transition in superintendents. Since that time, the school district hired a new superintendent, Errick Greene, who implemented many of the Council's recommendations and improved the district's performance substantially. They still have many challenges, but they have made significant progress under Greene's tenure. Nonetheless, during the period we were there, the team noted clear contrasts with districts that were making progress—most notably in the areas of instructional focus, capacity building, and accountability.

The second counterfactual district was the School District of Philadelphia. This district did participate in TUDA and was a far larger urban school system than Jackson. Like in Jackson, the Council team, which I was on, interviewed scores of administrators, instructional leaders, area superintendents, principals, teachers, community members, and others early in 2020. We also visited schools and sat in on scores of classes, and we reviewed an extensive number of documents, including the curriculum and other instructional and professional development tools. Finally, we analyzed a considerable amount of data beyond NAEP to better understand student outcomes.[2]

We looked at these counterfactual districts on the same dimensions that we looked at when examining the work of the faster-improving urban districts to make sure we were comparing apples to apples. If the practices were different, we could have more confidence that we were looking at something that could help explain why these districts were getting different results. And it would help us differentiate why some districts made academic progress and others did not. It also could help us weed out extraneous variables that had little discernible effect on student outcomes. We supplemented these comparisons with examples of weak practices that we saw over many years of conducting our Strategic Support Teams. Again, the descriptions were accurate at the time of our visits but may not reflect what the districts are doing currently.

WHAT WENT WRONG?

As we conducted many of these reviews, it was interesting to us that the districts, which were having trouble getting any traction under their instructional reforms, often thought they were doing what worked. Many times they believed they were doing what the faster-improving districts were doing. In fact, it was quite common for us to hear from these district leaders that they were pursuing best practices.

Sometimes what districts were doing looked like the right thing at the surface level. It often required someone from the outside to look at the details to ascertain how their practices differed from ones that were producing better results in similar school systems.

Often these districts had goals, but these goals were not necessarily built around student achievement nor were they measured and tracked. They often adopted standards but did not necessarily implement them with the same force that improving districts did. They almost always had curriculum, but it was usually not specific enough to guide teachers on what was expected. They typically had professional development, but it was focused on the wrong things. They often had instructional coaches or professional learning communities, but they were either poorly trained or deployed. Further, they often had regular assessment systems, but these systems were not always well aligned to what they thought they were teaching or the data were not regularly used to drive improvements.

In contrast to districts that were making real improvements in student outcomes, it was also clear that these districts were not fundamentally focused on instructional improvement or achievement. They sometimes had the outward appearance of emphasizing better instruction, but the details showed misaligned or weak instructional practice. Instead, they were too often focused on managing crises, cutting budgets, handling political problems, squabbling over who to hire, fixating on contracts, or any number of other issues that distracted them from what schools were established for: teaching children. In some cases, school leaders were simply not expected to improve outcomes for students. They were hired to do something else. In each of these situations, the lack of focus on student achievement resulted in the predictable. The district did not improve academically to the extent they wanted.

The Philadelphia district had periods over the years when it did focus on academic improvement. That was certainly the case when Constance Clayton ran the school system between 1982 and 1993, and there were attempts to improve the district's instructional program afterward. The state's financial oversight of the district, however, kept pulling the system's attention away from student outcomes. And this lasted for years.

Unlike the situation in Miami-Dade County, which leveraged its financial crisis to overhaul its instructional program, Philadelphia's financial crisis remained the state's focus and the district's efforts for a considerable period, so much so that it did not get around to student achievement for a long time.

The situation was more extreme in Jackson, where the school system lacked both the focus and expertise to improve student outcomes. For a considerable period after 1969, when the district was desegregated, the district struggled with declining enrollment and sinking standards. Until recently, the system simply did not have the expertise needed to improve student outcomes. In both Philadelphia and Jackson, efforts to improve student outcomes were short lived and unconvincing.

When all was said and done, there was little evidence that these systems paid much attention to continuous academic improvement in the ways that the improving districts did. Unlike Chicago, Miami, Dallas, and the District of Columbia, which had explicit mechanisms in place to set and monitor academic goals, adapt and unpack standards, align their organizational and instructional systems, build staff capacity, overhaul systemic procedures and routines that were not serving student outcomes, and regularly monitor the impact of change, the districts showing less improvement simply did not have the pieces in place whereby they could understand why they were not getting the gains they wanted. They did not learn from the fact that they were not improving, until it became painfully obvious. In both cases, it was hard-hitting reviews of Jackson and Philadelphia that helped galvanize a re-orientation of the systems around better student achievement.

GAPS IN LEADERSHIP

When the Council team visited the Jackson schools in 2017, the school dis-trict was on the cusp of being taken over by the state, but an agreement between the governor and the mayor to work together on the capitol city's improvement prevented the seizure at the last minute. The mayor had ap-pointed a new school board with well-regarded members and an excellent chair, Jeanne Middleton-Hairston. Still, they were new in their positions and new to governing a large urban school system in a way that would drive its academic performance. The acting superintendent, at the time, Fred-drick Murray, was struggling with how to meet the board's new sense of urgency, focusing instead on reorganizing the central office staff. Unfor-tunately, the reorganization was mostly unrelated to what it would take to align the system's people and resources for better results.

Philadelphia's situation was different. The school system had been under the thumb of a skeptical and sometimes hostile state legislature for years after then-school superintendent David Hornbeck threatened to close the city's schools if the state did not pony up the funds to keep the dis-trict running. The state essentially seized the district and appointed a five-member School Reform Commission (SRC), which governed the sys-tem between 2001 and 2018, with three members appointed by the gover-nor and two by the mayor.

When Bill Hite became superintendent in 2012, he faced a projected $1.0 billion deficit, the specter of having to close schools, and an aging physical infrastructure. When he departed the district in 2022, he had expertly addressed many of the district's financial challenges, but neither he nor the SRC had much time to deal with student achievement, which had moved upward over the decade by only a handful of points.

When we made our site visits to Philadelphia in 2020, we conducted a review of SRC meetings between 2016 and 2018 and school board sessions between July 2018 and December 2019. Over the last two years of the SRC's existence, the governing body addressed issues of budget and finance, contracts, and charter schools (the district is the chartering authority for the city's charter schools) more than any other topics. Issues involving how students were doing academically in the school system rarely made the SRC's agendas.

In fact, when the Council of the Great City Schools conducted a survey in 2016 of how much time its school boards devoted to student achievement, Philadelphia ranked forty-three of fifty-one responding cities. Under the first year and a half of the new school board, meeting agendas were devoted mostly to contracts, personnel, and various board policies. Not until the sublimely talented school board president Joyce Wilkerson and its popular superintendent, Bill Hite, realized that this focus was getting the district nowhere did the system start to reorient its work around student outcomes.

Unfortunately, that same 2016 survey found that Philadelphia and Jackson were not alone in their school boards devoting little attention to student learning. About 56 percent of school boards responded that they spent between 0 and 10 percent of their time monitoring student achievement outcomes.

We saw many examples of urban school boards over the years that did not pay much attention to how kids were doing. A prominent example was the Detroit public schools in 2008.[3] Then-superintendent Connie Calloway asked the Council to conduct an assessment of the system's instructional, financial, and operating procedures. Pedro Martinez, the chief financial officer of the Chicago Public Schools at the time and now CEO of the Chicago schools, and I made the presentation before the school board and a packed audience of community members and press. As we got into our report, school board members began chanting in unison, "Liar, liar, liar." Not only did they pay little attention to student achievement, they did not want to hear about it.

We saw similar inattention to student outcomes when we reviewed the Pittsburgh Public Schools in 2016. While board members often got along, they spent almost no time on student achievement, preferring to devote their attention to the superintendent's personnel hires and operational details that were better left to the administration. The school board had no clear direction or theory of action, no measurable system-wide goals, no way of evaluating itself, and no regular time during its meetings when the members discussed student achievement.

We found much the same things when we went to Minneapolis, Milwaukee, Columbus, and other cities over the years. A. J. Crabill tells many such stories in his well-received book, *Great on Their Behalf: Why School Boards Fail, How Yours Can Become Effective*.[4] In it, he looks at sample school board agendas to see how much time and attention is devoted to how children are doing academically.

A variation on these examples involves school board members who attend conferences and return to propose that their districts try something they heard at one of the sessions. This is surprisingly common. For instance, in Anchorage a school board member attended a state school boards association meeting and heard a presentation from the Pawtucket Regional School District in Massachusetts on its reading program. Despite the fact that Pawtucket had an enrollment that was only 5 percent of Anchorage's, a poverty rate that was less than half of Anchorage's, profoundly different demographics, and reading performance that had not improved over the last three years, the school board invited Pawtucket to present its reading program publicly. The school board then asked the Anchorage superintendent about implementing the reforms in Alaska's biggest district.

On the face of it, this might sound like a board trying to make helpful suggestions to their superintendent, but it puts superintendents in the difficult position of saying to their bosses, "This is really not a very good idea for this district." In this case, who is held accountable if reading scores do not increase?

We take three things away from these examples. One, a district can have strong and stable leadership for an extended period, but if that leadership is not focused on student outcomes, achievement is not likely to improve much. Stability in the job is important when achievement is the focus of that longevity, but a long tenure by itself will not produce better student outcomes. Two, having both the board and the superintendent focused on higher student achievement in complementary ways is ideal—and is more likely to produce results—but producing better results can occur without the board, if they do not get in the way. What does not work is when no one in leadership—neither the board nor the superintendent—pays attention to achievement or makes it secondary to other priorities. The public notices and students suffer. And three, having boards overstepping their roles and expertise is a recipe for dysfunction. It is not leadership; it is a failure of leadership.

CURRICULAR AND INSTRUCTIONAL INCOHERENCE

Unlike the clear instructional vision and strategic reforms we saw in districts that were making progress, the two counterfactual districts lacked a coherent strategy or working theory of action for improving student achievement district wide. Although Jackson had a document that it considered to be a strategic plan, we saw little evidence that it drove the academic work of the district. During the initial visit, staff members we interviewed could not describe what the district's strategy was for improving academic performance. Several years before, the district had disbanded its curriculum department in favor of outsourcing its instructional and assessment leadership to a local consulting firm, leaving the district with little way to build its own capacity or modify its instructional approach.

Jackson also lacked a focus on improving its Tier 1 or regular class-time instruction that we saw in districts that were making progress. Instead, the district was focused disproportionately on interventions with its lowest 25 percent of students. These interventions, however, were ill defined and differentially applied from school to school. And the interventions were not evaluated for effectiveness. This focus on the lowest 25 percent was to garner extra state accountability points. But, in doing so, the district was missing an important segment of students—those between the lowest 25 percent and proficiency. So, even as an intervention strategy, it was falling short of moving schools out of "failing" status. Moreover, it was ignoring basic instruction for everyone else. Consequently, the district did not see the overall progress that it might have.

This lack of attention to the overall quality of its instructional program was also showing up in its Advanced Placement results. The district had Advanced Placement courses in all its high schools (a good thing), but few students scored a three or above on the AP exams. In fact, if one discounts Murrah High School, then over 97 percent of all AP test takers in the district scored a "1" on the AP exam, the lowest possible score. This suggested that AP course content was not actually being provided in these classes or that students had not been adequately prepared in previous years to handle the complexity and rigor of AP coursework—or both.

On the surface, the district had things like "learning walks" to monitor classroom instruction—like we see in other districts—but, in Jackson, they were focused more on observing student engagement, classroom climate, and whether teachers were following procedures than on the content, rigor, and alignment of instruction. In other words, the district was monitoring the wrong things. In addition, no one at the central office appeared to use the results of the walk-throughs from school-to-school to inform broader patterns of student needs or to improve district-wide strategies.

The lack of coherence in Jackson's strategy was further evidenced by the fact that district network leaders each used a distinct set of strategies and plans for improving student achievement based on only their individual expertise and experience. There is nothing wrong with using different strategies in varying areas of a city, but none of it in Jackson was based on the needs of students in those areas—and no analyses were done on what the effects of those multiple strategies were. The result was that the district had little leverage over its own improvement and no alignment in what it was doing. In other words, everyone was aiming in different directions and no targets were being hit.

Finally, there were no district-wide resources or tools to guide administrators or teachers on the level of instructional rigor or the quality of student work expected by the district in specific grade levels and content areas. Nothing specified what good teaching looked like or what students could be expected to know or do because of the district's instruction.

The second counterfactual district—Philadelphia—had similar issues, although not as severe. Here, the district had a curriculum that was grounded in multiple and sometimes inconsistent textbooks that the system or its schools had purchased rather than a curriculum grounded in the standards. In addition, it meant that the district's curriculum was inconsistently aligned with the state's standards, and materials purchased by the schools were not always vetted for consistency with the standards.

The curriculum itself contained pacing guides, instructional units, and lesson plans—all the things one would want to see, but they differed from text to text, meaning that what students studied depended, in part, on which texts their schools had selected. For instance, students using one textbook in one school might be studying ratios, proportions, and percents, while others in the same course in another school using a different textbook might be solving equations and inequalities. In addition, guidance on each text often differed in its specificity and expectations for student work. Guidance emphasized coverage page by page in some schools, while stressing conceptual understanding in others.

At the same time, the platform on which the curriculum sat had supplemental materials but no explanations for teachers about what gaps in the curriculum they were meant to fill or how they could best be used. Moreover, we found interventions in Philadelphia for students who might be falling behind, but little guidance on when the interventions should be used, under what conditions, or for how long, which resulted in teachers sometimes using intervention materials as core instructional tools.

The comeuppance was that the system had little ability to drive improvement district wide, create instructional cohesion within or across grades, or align materials, professional development, technical assistance, or assessments in the way that the faster-improving districts were doing.

Finally, like in Jackson, Philadelphia lacked a clear set of instructional expectations or a theory of action about how it expected to raise student performance. Instead, the task of improving student achievement was left mostly to the district's networks. Some of them, in fact, did an excellent job, but the strategy was not system wide.

Many of these circumstances in Jackson and Philadelphia were like what we saw in other major cities, including ones that later made substantial progress in student achievement. When we first reviewed the instructional program in the District of Columbia in 2007, for instance, we found standards that stacked up well against other states—for its time—but an instructional program that was defined at the individual school level with varying degrees of quality. When we reviewed the instructional program in Cincinnati in 2004, like Jackson, we found that it had dismantled its curriculum department, figuring that it could either buy what it wanted or contract for the expertise it needed.

Periodically, we saw districts that thought they could purchase improvement off the shelf. They were good examples of what Bryk termed as being fixated on "solutionitis." We saw a good illustration of why that does not work when we noticed that Boston and Cleveland were using the same commercial math program (Everyday Math) in the mid-2000s but were getting different results. It is important to use materials that are of high quality and aligned with the standards, but the materials must be accompanied by other strategies and supports if they are to make a meaningful difference in student achievement. By themselves, the materials will not raise achievement any more than the standards by themselves will. The Little Rock schools were another example of this: they had purchased high-quality materials, but the quality of classroom instruction was low because of the lack of training on how to use the materials.

Instead, quality materials must be accompanied with strategies and professional development for teachers so that they know how concepts are built over time in the curriculum, where ideas that students find most difficult are likely to occur, and how to address those difficulties and common misperceptions.

The instructional programs of districts that were struggling to gain momentum often had fundamental problems that hampered their ability to get better results for students. Before the Common Core State Standards were released in 2010, for instance, we often found instructional guidance in districts to be ambiguous, incoherent, and open to interpretation.

In Little Rock, for example, we found in 2010 no district-wide literacy program per se and little clarity in how teachers should intervene with students who were falling behind. We saw the same lack of direction and cohesion when we looked at the reading and math programs in Columbus in 2005, Milwaukee in 2006, Buffalo in 2000, and Cleveland in 2005. Districts would sometimes try and compensate with scripted programming for teachers or test preparation, but those strategies rarely built the instructional capacity that teachers or the districts needed to improve or sustain achievement.

WEAK OR UNCERTAIN TEACHER QUALITY

In Jackson, we saw a district with unusually high rates of teacher and staff turnover. The churn was due to the system's weak support of teachers, which is typically the reason they leave. Moreover, while most of the improving districts were intentional in their efforts to recruit and hire high-quality teachers and leaders, Jackson lacked any sort of teacher or leader pipeline, and the human resources department had delegated its primary function—identifying and screening qualified teachers—to principals. On top of that, the district's human resources department, which reported to the chief financial officer, was poorly staffed, unevenly organized, and transactional.

At the time of our review, Jackson operated with 217 long-term substitute teachers, and it had no mechanism for identifying effective teachers. It also had no strategy for retaining the most effective teachers, even if the district knew who they were. Moreover, the new-teacher induction program was focused mostly on procedural issues rather than on content. In fact, only ninety minutes of the professional development new teachers received was devoted to lesson planning, and that occurred after the school year began. There was no mention in the induction program as well about how new teachers should use the district's curriculum.

Philadelphia faced different teacher issues than Jackson, but they were equally debilitating. In Philadelphia's case, the problems emerged from the district's finances and language in the teachers' contract. The situation left the city school system with more students per teacher than other major urban school systems (18.2 versus 15.9). And it left the district with fewer teachers of color (103 African American male students for every 1 African American male teacher and 244 Hispanic male students for every one Hispanic male teacher). The problem went back at least to the tenure of superintendent Arlene Ackerman, who in 2011 faced a $629 million shortfall, resulting in the layoff of 3,024 staff members, including 1,500 teachers. Unfortunately, the cuts continued during the superintendency of Bill Hite, who had to lay off an additional 3,783 staff members in 2013 at the direction of the SRC.

One of the results of the budget cutting in Philadelphia was that more newly hired teachers of color were the first to go, undermining the district's efforts to create a more diverse teaching cadre. And it resulted in significant "bumping" of teachers by seniority into classes, subjects, and grades they may not have taught for some time. We have seen this before in places like Cleveland and Detroit, where the layoff of personnel based on seniority resulted in lower student achievement that took years to reverse.

The turnover of teachers in the nation's urban school systems is a perennial problem—like the turnover of superintendents and school board members. The Council's key performance indicators tell us that the median Great City School system is able to retain only 78 percent of its newly hired teachers after one year; 67 percent after two years; 63 percent after three years; 56 percent after four years; and about 50 percent after five years.[5] The school district of Philadelphia generally reflected those broader trends. On the other hand, Boston, which was producing stronger academic effects as we described in chapter 4, was able to retain 61 percent of their teachers after five years, Miami retained 60 percent, and the District of Columbia retained 74 percent after five years.[6]

Urban public school systems do not function well with a teaching force that is constantly turning over or is absent from work or with classrooms that are staffed with individuals without the requisite training. Teaching and learning require continuity and cohesion, something that is interrupted by constant classroom churn.

FRACTURED PROFESSIONAL DEVELOPMENT AND THE LACK OF CAPACITY BUILDING

The most conspicuous difference between the counterfactual districts and the districts that were making progress was in capacity building. Whereas other districts invested time, energy, and focus on human capital strategies aimed at enhancing the quality of teachers and leaders, Jackson made several decisions that diluted the quality of its people, creating inconsistencies in the district's instructional expectations and limiting its support of schools. Several years before we reviewed the district, its leadership decided to dismantle the school system's curriculum department in favor of outsourcing key instructional functions, like the development of curriculum materials, guidance, and some local testing activities.

This not only left the district beholden to outside vendors who charged an annual subscription fee for access to the district's own instructional materials but also deprived staff of the critical learning and capacity-building process of developing curriculum and providing instructional support and guidance to their own schools. The issue here, of course, was not whether a school system had its own curriculum department but whether it had a way to develop and support good teaching at the school level. In this case, it did not.

Jackson was working to reestablish its curriculum office when the Council reviewed the system, but the impact of this past decision was still evident. In our work with districts, we saw that the strength of district staff and instructional leadership was critical to a school system's ability to move the system forward academically. So, while none of the districts we reviewed were immune to leadership or staff turnover, Jackson was less equipped than others to weather the various academic upheavals it was facing.

All the districts we reviewed over the years worked with outside vendors, but leadership and staff in the improving districts explicitly cited a move away from "buying stuff to fix our problems," focusing their efforts and scarce funding instead on building internal capacity, investing in people, and moving the broader levers of the system.

Finally, the professional development that Jackson offered was essentially a menu of course offerings that were not aligned to district priorities, state standards, or the academic needs of students. This practice of providing professional development for teachers through a catalog of unaligned courses was something we also saw in other reviews.

In Nashville, too, professional development was menu driven when we reviewed it several years ago. Course offerings were not aligned with the district's academic priorities, instructional needs, or student weaknesses. Teachers and others were able to choose their own professional development from course catalogs. The professional development was voluntary and not tracked or evaluated. In addition, it was not differentiated by teacher expertise, experience, or previous professional development, and there was no mechanism to steer teachers toward the professional development they needed most or what students required.

This practice involves teachers going to a listing of course offerings they can take to meet various state continuing accreditation requirements that the district would pay local colleges to provide or would develop in house. Teachers could use these courses to move up the salary scale with no discernible benefit to the district or the students.

Teachers in Philadelphia, on the other hand, had seven days of professional development in their contract, more than most urban school districts have. The district, however, controlled only two of those days at the beginning of the school year, and they were focused mostly on compliance issues. One professional development day was on the last day of the school year.

In a survey of what Philadelphia teachers thought of the professional development they received from the district, most gave it modestly positive marks, but they agreed that they did not receive as much as they needed and there was not much follow-up. Most teachers told us that professional development they received had little district training on the system's curriculum.

Often professional development in urban districts is provided by textbook vendors and is concentrated on how to use the purchased textbook without linking it to the district's curricular expectations, discussing how to bridge between a prior adoption and a new one, or paying much attention to the data on what the district's students needed.

The professional development in Philadelphia, like in many districts, was rarely evaluated for its effectiveness. In addition, Philadelphia had many instructional coaches, but they were not strategically deployed, and their professional learning communities lacked the strength, longevity, or focus seen in faster-improving districts like San Diego.

Neither of these districts—Jackson nor Philadelphia—were particularly unusual, because professional development and other capacity-building measures are challenges faced by many urban school districts. The number of professional development days is usually prescribed in collective bargaining agreements, since most teacher organizations much prefer to design and deliver their own rather than participate in district-provided training. In addition, a good deal of the training controlled by districts is meant to provide information on various procedures and rules. Surprisingly little is devoted to either subject-matter content or instructional strategies.

We ran across this situation frequently as we advised urban school systems on how they could improve. Newark was a good example; superintendent Marion Bolden asked us to look at her instructional program in 2007. She had done an excellent job over the years improving a system that was not functioning well. But at the time we looked at Newark's voluntary program, it was clear that attendance rates in the district-provided professional development offerings were often low.

In addition, participation in professional development in many districts is tracked so that individual teachers could receive credit for it, but the systems make little use of the tracking to help determine who has what capacity and who might need additional training. It was also clear that, because the professional development was not evaluated for how well the lessons were implemented or whether they were effective with students, the district could not determine whether the money they were spending made any difference.

There was another interesting capacity-building situation in Newark. At the time, district leadership under Marion Bolden had done an admirable job of reforming many of the central office functions that could be used to bolster student achievement, but they were almost invisible at the school and classroom levels. In other words, people at one level of the system did not know what people at another level of the system knew. The effort to improve urban schools had to go not only wide but deep.

The inability of many urban public school systems to build their capacity to improve typically stemmed from the fact that much of the professional development on offer was voluntary, was not tracked, was not aligned with system-wide instructional priorities or student academic needs, was not assessed for how well it was implemented, was not differentiated by teacher experience or previous training, or evaluated for its impact on student achievement. Teacher organizations typically give low marks to the professional development they receive from their districts, and it is generally clear why. Much of it fails to build teacher capacity in content knowledge or pedagogical skill. Consequently, because a substantial number of teachers leave after their first five years on the job, a considerable number of them are young and new to the profession, meaning that the potential of professional development to lift the effectiveness of teacher talent is substantial but unrealized.

What was unusual were the practices of the improving districts and the mechanisms they had in place to provide higher-quality professional development and support, build staff who were accountable for student achievement, create a culture of shared responsibility, and enhance system capacity.

INATTENTION TO SCALE

We also saw that the faster-improving urban school districts developed improvement strategies and then applied them at scale across their school systems. Sometimes they phased them in by grade or subject, but they acted in a way that sought to boost the performance of the entire school system. Our counterfactual districts did not do this as well. They were much more likely to allow their schools or regions to act independently on standards, curriculum, materials, professional development, and assessments. Some urban districts have made a school-by-school strategy work, but overall it is not a formula for improving a large, low-performing urban school system.

It was clear that the Jackson public schools did not have a system-wide strategy for improvement. The district did little at scale. Almost everything was defined at the school level. It did not have a universal strategy for the recruitment of talent. It did not have the curriculum needed to drive overall improvement, nor did it have the talent necessary to design and develop an effective curriculum. It did have some content, big ideas, essential questions, links to instructional strategies, performance tasks, and unit resources. But its guidance on how to use it was often vague and lacked clarity on how to introduce concepts or sequence lessons to build students' understanding. Finally, the system's reading and math blocks were not consistently implemented across the system.

Philadelphia also had difficulty applying its improvement strategies at scale. Most of the instructional program was defined at the regional level. And the central curriculum was not aligned consistently with national or state standards, and the curriculum was fractured according to the commercial textbooks being used. In addition, the school district operated many magnet schools and other competitive schools that operated independently. These were often particularly good schools, but other schools in the district often handled instructional direction very much on their own.

In general, over the years we saw a considerable number of districts that piloted programs or materials in small numbers of schools to see what worked, but these districts often did not evaluate these programs sufficiently to draw broader lessons about whether they could boost achievement. Districts that improved were often those that did a lot of research up front and then carefully planned for a broad and aggressive rollout of programming that they had confidence in. That did not mean that improving districts did not pilot test some programs, but they typically evaluated them carefully before proceeding.

FEEBLE ACCOUNTABILITY

The fifth area of contrast between the counterfactual districts and districts that were making progress involved accountability. Staff in the improving districts often spoke at length about a cultural shift in their systems toward shared accountability—that is, a shift away from the kinds of mechanistic accountability measures that were often ascribed to NCLB-type quantitative measures toward broader cultural changes, in which staff members felt like they owned some portion of student progress. Both can work, to differing degrees, but accountability for results is what we saw in districts making progress.

When the Council visited Jackson, the district lacked any mechanism—either qualitative or cultural—for holding personnel responsible for improving student academic outcomes. The personnel evaluation instrument that the district used was the Educator and Administrator Professional Growth System, which was the instrument endorsed at the time by the Mississippi Department of Education as the framework for teacher and administrator evaluations. Principals were evaluated on five domains and nineteen total elements. Each of these domains and elements included examples of evidence that could be used to demonstrate where principals were on a four-point scale, but none of the examples included student outcomes.

The district's teacher evaluation systems also did not include concrete measures of student outcomes or progress. And the district's procedures for evaluating central office administrative staff graded performance across a series of domains and elements—none of which involved student outcomes or their improvement.

This lack of accountability for student progress marked the district's relationships with its partners and vendors. Vendor accountability for results in Jackson was nonexistent. In contrast, we saw in places like Miami-Dade County, where the district had developed a return-on-investment metric for all supplemental materials purchased and implemented by the district. Moreover, Miami developed "Essential Questions" that it sent to all vendors, who were required to show usage data and data on how they met the promises and objectives they set out to accomplish. If they did not meet these criteria, the district did not always renew their annual contracts.

Philadelphia also lacked any universal system of accountability by which staff—individually or in groups—were held responsible for student outcomes. It did not have a mechanism for holding staff responsible for how they implemented programs the district initiated or the services it provided. When we asked whether the district had any mechanism for central office staff evaluations or some way to hold central office staff accountable for student outcomes or program services, we received the following reply by email, "Unfortunately, at this time, the School District of Philadelphia does not have a standardized central office evaluation process. This is a priority for the coming year, but nothing can be included at this time."

At the same time, network or area superintendents in Philadelphia were responsible for setting annual goals in seven areas: activities meant to improve principals' growth as instructional leaders; one-on-one work with principals to help them grow as instructional leaders; principal learning communities to help principals grow as instructional leaders; use of multiple forms of evidence of principals' capacity as instructional leaders; help for principals to create the conditions to be successful as instructional leaders; a formal evaluation process that helps principals improve; and participation in other activities to help principals grow as instructional leaders. Discussions of these goals were held with principals in September, November, February, and June of each year, but no one was evaluated on the extent to which students learned more.

Principals, for their part, were evaluated on a state-developed protocol that included four dimensions: strategic and cultural leadership (organizational vision, mission and goals, use of data, collaboration, continuous improvement, celebration of accomplishments and failures); systems leadership (leverages human and financial resources, ensures high-quality staff, complies with mandates, sets expectations, communicates effectively, manages conflict, and ensures school safety); leadership for learning (leads school improvement efforts, aligns curriculum and instruction, implements high-quality instruction, sets high expectations, maximizes instructional time); and professional and community leadership (maximizes parent and community engagement, shows professionalism, and supports professional growth). Still, the framework did not have a component for progress on student outcomes.

The teacher evaluation handbook, on the other hand, was based on the Danielson framework and was used to evaluate teachers and nonteaching professional staff. (The Danielson framework is a tool that articulates teacher responsibilities in raising student achievement.) The 104-page handbook spelled out a very precise process for teacher evaluations that involved observations (of planning and preparation, classroom environment, instruction, and professional responsibility); student learning objectives (SLOs) for students with attendance at or above 85 percent; a value-added measure; a school performance measure; and a combination of other metrics. The procedure came the closest to anything the district was doing that could be termed an outcomes-based personnel evaluation system.

From top to bottom, however, the system simply had little in place by which to hold staff accountable or expect much shared responsibility for what and how much students learned.

CRISES THAT ARE JUST CRISES

We did not consistently see the counterfactual districts using the various crises they were encountering to leverage improvements in student outcomes like we saw in several of the improving systems. Both counterfactual districts had crises to be sure. Jackson faced the prospect of being taken over by the state, which—to its credit—did spur the system to accelerate its reforms and hire a new superintendent—Errick Greene—who is bringing reform and improvement to the district. The system also used the prospects of a takeover to bring in the Council of the Great City Schools and John Kim's District Management Council to review the system's programs and make recommendations for improvement. What the district did not do, however, was to see the takeover as an opportunity to do something different until their backs were against the wall—and that was how they were different from the improving districts.

Philadelphia, on the other hand, was subjected to one crisis after another, but none of them prompted a focus on better student achievement. The crises that the district faced were related to finances and facilities. Superintendent Bill Hite did a superb job at stabilizing the financial outlook of the district, although the state never did pony up substantial new resources during that period in amounts that would solve the district's structural problems. But the SRC never focused on improving student achievement and staff did not always serve the superintendent academically as well as they might have.

I should note parenthetically the scant evidence of state takeovers of major urban school systems like Jackson and Philadelphia resulting in better student achievement. In fact, a study by Beth Schueler and Joshua Bleiberg concluded, "We find no evidence that state takeover benefits student academic achievement and some evidence that it can be disruptive to student reading performance."[7] Research by Kenneth Wong and Francis Shen found similar results.[8]

The point here is not that a district needs a crisis or should invite one. However, it was clear to us that urban school districts that had had one knew how to take advantage and galvanize instructional reforms that would improve student outcomes. Districts that were less adroit at taking advantage of such crises sometimes were also not as good at a range of other things that might have helped them improve academically.

STRUGGLING SCHOOLS AND STUDENTS

Districts that saw substantial improvement often had several ways to address schools and students who were struggling academically. Districts that did not see much headway in their instructional program, on the other hand, did not have as many discernible strategies for schools and students who were behind—or they sometimes overused remedial instruction rather than high-quality Tier I classroom instruction.

Jackson was a paradigm of how remedial tactics can sometimes be overused or misused in a way that works to the detriment of student performance system wide. I mentioned earlier that the district overly focused on students in the bottom quartile as a way of gaining points on the state's accountability system. The strategy worked for the district up to a point, but it left most students behind. In addition, the interventions that the district was using were poorly defined and not well linked to the broader instructional program, such as it was. It was also clear that the interventions were not applied from school to school in any uniform fashion or in a way that the district could tell how the differences in application were working.

Jackson at the time also lacked adequate professional development for teachers on the use of the interventions and did not monitor the interventions in a way that would give schools or the system any usable data on what worked and what did not. There was also no regular evaluation of interventions at the school or student level. Any evaluation or monitoring of results consisted entirely of whether the district gained any points on the statewide accountability system. In that way, the district's strategy to support chronically low-performing schools or students was really about the adults in the system rather than the students.

Finally, the district's attempts to address school-level or student academic failures were mostly handled by pulling students out of their regular classes, including reading and math, and putting them into separate remedial classes—another way that the district was overusing remedial work and underutilizing high-quality basic classroom instruction. Ironically, the district used a pullout strategy even in its gifted and talented program and then ended it after the sixth grade.

Schools nationally that receive federal Title I funding must prepare school improvement plans on what they are doing to turn themselves around, but we found the plans in Jackson lacked any coherence or strategy and were not carefully reviewed by the district. Instead, they were compliance documents, and that did not drive improvement. The plans were weak and failed to articulate any strategy for how the schools would catch up. The combination of poorly defined interventions, the overuse of interventions, weak professional development, the lack of any evaluations or strategic use of the interventions, the overuse of pullouts, and the inadequate planning at the district or school levels guaranteed that student performance would remain low.

Philadelphia had similar problems trying to support the needs of low-performing schools or students, but to its credit the district did have a more robust way of handling its lowest-performing schools. The district had an Acceleration Network, serving thirty-six chronically failing schools, mostly with grades K–8. These schools were provided with extra funding, leadership support, goal setting, regular monitoring of progress, data reviews, adaptive technology, enhanced professional development, behavioral support, social workers, and additional community support. The district also had forty Comprehensive School Improvement schools under the federal ESSA system, and an internal district system that divided schools into four categories of performance. To its credit, the school system saw the number of its "model" schools increase between 2014 and 2015 and again between 2017 and 2018, while the number of "intervene" schools declined significantly.

Still, the improvements were mostly related to gains in overall "climate" measures and not student achievement. A close examination of the district's writeup of how it was improving its low-performing networks was often vague on how it was addressing its lowest-performing student groups.

Not all the improving school systems had strong mechanisms for addressing chronically low-performing schools and students either, as was the case in the District of Columbia. D.C., however, had implemented other strong system-wide instructional reforms and interventions that positively affected overall results. Districts that were not improving often lacked both a system-wide strategy and a strategy for targeting the lowest-performing schools or students. This was the case for Pittsburgh in 2016, Nashville in 2016, Kansas City (MO) in 2016, and Fresno in 2012.

By itself, supporting or targeting low-performing schools or students is typically not the strategy that improves a district's overall performance. However, it is a good tactic for supplementing broader system-wide improvement efforts because reforms applied across a district are likely to leave gaps with some schools and students who are otherwise immune to system-wide reforms. Generally, it is a promising idea to have a three-pronged improvement strategy that consists of system-wide strategies, strategies that are targeted on specific low-performing schools, and strategies that are aimed at struggling students.

Chronically low-performing schools have been a constant challenge for many urban school systems for years. Strategies for improvement often involve school improvement plans, but the quality in these plans varied significantly from district to district. In fact, some of them were written so vaguely that it was hard to tell what the strategy for improvement was.

An example was Nashville, when we participated in superintendent Sean Joseph's transition team in 2016.[9] Some school improvement plans were quite good and extremely specific. Other plans did not have any description of what the school was planning to do to further improve academic achievement, although many had descriptions of what they had done. Few plans had any description of the school's pedagogy, instructional approach, strategy for reducing achievement gaps, tutoring, or tiered instruction. Several mentioned preparing for the Tennessee state tests. The plans were signed by the district's Title I office, which reviewed them for compliance, but the district's academic department had little say about their approval.

And in Detroit, which in 2008 was under Title I district improvement status, the system had a district-wide plan for improvement, but it lacked sufficient detail to guide the instructional work of the district, much less its individual schools. Identified targets and procedures were not visible in the action section of the plan. Instead of quantifiable targets, the action plan set forth nonnumeric goals for improvement. In addition, the district did not have a coordinated strategy or plan for how it was using its federal Title I school improvement dollars to reform or improve its lowest-performing schools. There was also no coordinated strategy for how the district used its supplemental educational services or other extended-time programs to improve student achievement. These programs at the time appeared to be wholly disconnected from any broader district-wide efforts.

We did find instances in which districts thought they were doing the right things instructionally with their lowest-performing students, but the results were sometimes anything but positive. At its most fundamental, it did not work when districts' plans resulted in lowering the standards or expectations of what struggling learners could do. Doing so resulted in denying students access to high-quality instruction.

Districts often denied access in a variety of ways that dampened performance. Such methods included the use of tracking—where low-performing students were placed with each other in classes that lacked instructional rigor; the use of leveled texts—where students were given texts and lessons that matched their instructional performance but did not stretch them or bring them to grade-level content expectations; or the use of pullouts—where low-performing students were taken out of core courses and provided remedial instruction unaligned to the work their classmates were doing. Other methods included teaching students with remedial strategies rather than core content or subjecting students to excess amounts of test prep to make it look like they were performing when they were not.

The truth is that districts can do lots of things that mimic the language of reform and that call for quality instruction without actually improving it. Districts can adopt standards but not implement them. They can put into place universal curriculum without ever specifying what they expect students to be doing. They can hire more tutors but not train them appropriately. They can provide additional professional development but devote most of it to compliance issues, and they can implement interim assessments but purchase ones that do not align with their standards or curriculum.

We found many instances where one or more of these practices were in use. When we looked at Buffalo in 2000 at the request of superintendent Marion Canedo, we encountered low expectations for student performance and a tendency to fault students for their own low achievement. The result was large numbers of students from low-income families referred to special education and sparse numbers with access to Advanced Placement or honors courses.

In Newark, when the Council reviewed its instructional program in 2007, we saw few classrooms where teachers were challenging students or calling on them to discuss concepts and ideas. Instead, we saw extensive use of worksheets and almost no differentiated instruction. In Dayton, when we went there[10] in 2008—for the third time—we found a curriculum but nothing that told teachers what level of depth they needed to teach various concepts and ideas. Pacing guides did not include all the state standards, such as they were at the time, few high schools offered Advanced Placement courses, and the quality of classroom instruction was low.

Besides not having explicit strategies or having poorly implemented strategies for addressing the needs of struggling students, we often found instructional gaps in the teaching of English language learners and students with disabilities. Urban schools, in general, have higher numbers of these students than other types of schools nationwide, as we saw in chapter 2. The issue that we encountered most often was one of access, that is, English language learners and students with disabilities not having full access to the rich instructional offerings that other students had. This lack of access was often rationalized around these students' welfare, but the effect was often not academically beneficial to them.

The public schools in Des Moines exemplified the risks of poorly implemented strategies for English language learners.[11] In 2016 Des Moines' well-regarded superintendent Tom Ahart asked us to look at their efforts to improve instruction for the district's ELLs. Of the approximately thirty-two thousand students enrolled, about 21 percent were learning English as an additional or new language. The district had done substantial work to develop its school board and bolster the work of its principal supervisors to support instruction, but it struggled to address the English acquisition needs of a very unusual mix of immigrant and other English learners, who spoke Spanish, Karen, Somali, Arabic, Vietnamese, and Nepali—seventy-five languages in all.

English language learners in Des Moines were not included explicitly in the district's strategic plan. School improvement plans did not include English learners, and comprehensive achievement data on ELLs were not regularly presented to the school board. ELL department procedures were mostly focused on federal compliance issues rather than on improving English language acquisition and content knowledge. Curriculum and pacing guides contained little information for teachers on working with English learners. Data on ELL performance were hard to obtain. ELL instruction was at a low level, and ELL materials were often not aligned with general instructional guidance. Language development instruction was inadequate. ELLs in middle and high school grades were disproportionately placed in special education, had little access to the core curriculum, and very few English learners were being educated in gifted and talented programs, Advanced Placement or International Baccalaureate classes, or other high-level math and science classes.

The Providence public schools had many of the same access issues when we reviewed its English learner programs in 2012 and 2019.[12] The district had an enrollment of about twenty-four thousand students in 2019, 29 percent of whom were English language learners—over half of all English learners in Rhode Island. In general, our ELL team found that there was little sense of shared responsibility for the academic welfare of its English learners. No one in the district—administrators or teachers—were held explicitly accountable for the academic well-being of English learners. Little attention was paid by the school board to the status or progress of English learners. School improvement plans did not include components for English learners. The system used a "seat-based" ELL resource allocation procedure that essentially capped services to students. The district had limited access to various school choice options. There was an uneven trajectory of English acquisition programming across grades and schools and inadequate numbers of language-certified staff to place or teach the district's English learners. Curriculum guides were inconsistent from grade to grade and provided little direction for teachers in instructing English learners and implementation of district ELL instructional models was irregular. As in Des Moines, very few English learners in Providence participated in the district's most rigorous courses.

We saw some of the same access issues when we reviewed the bilingual programming of the Seattle Public Schools in 2008. Maria Goodloe-Johnson was the superintendent at the time and had asked for the review. What we found was an instructional program for the district's English language learners that was highly fragmented, weakly defined, and poorly monitored, which was producing unsatisfactory academic results.[13]

There was no broad theory of action about teaching English language learners in Seattle at the time, and individual schools were left to their own devices to define and implement their own programs without any technical assistance from the district. The system did not have a clear set of goals for improving the outcomes of ELLs, provided little professional development to their bilingual teachers, relied on a cadre of instructional assistants who had far-reaching responsibilities beyond their bilingual support duties, and made use of a pullout model that curtailed basic instruction for English learners.

Access issues also existed with students with disabilities. Again, the issue was restricted availability of high-quality instruction. Disproportionate identification of students of color, out-of-school suspensions, and isolation of students with disabilities in classrooms without access to the district's Tier I instruction was often the main problem. The school district of Stockton was an example when we reviewed it in 2019 at the request of superintendent John Deasy.[14]

Stockton identified African American and Native American students as having a disability at twice the rate that one would expect, given their percentage of the student body. English language learners were also disproportionately identified. In addition, the district had fewer students with disabilities in general education classes more than 80 percent of the day than state or national averages. It also had more students than average being educated in general education settings less than 40 percent of the time. And more students with disabilities were placed in separate schools than was expected by state targets or national averages. To complicate matters, the district's collective bargaining agreement limited the extent to which the district could create inclusive environments, a situation we found in other places as well.

Stockton was not the only district with such patterns. When we looked at Buffalo in 2014, we saw many of the same issues.[15] The district identified about 16.5 percent of its students as having a disability; African American students were more likely to be identified with either an emotional disability or an intellectual disability; more English language learners were identified as having a disability than one would expect from their share of total enrollment; and about 11 percent of students with disabilities were educated in separate schools, compared to the national average of 3 percent.

Austin was similar when we went there in 2010 at the invitation of superintendent Meria Carstarphen to assess their special education program.[16] The percent of the district's enrollment that was identified for an individualized education plan was about 10 percent—lower than national averages, but the percentage of African American students labeled as having an emotional disability or intellectual disability was two to almost four times what one would expect from their portions of the district's student body. Only about 58 percent of students with disabilities at the time were educated in a general classroom at least 80 percent of the time, while about 12 percent of students with disabilities were in such classes for 40 percent or less time.

In general, what we found from these reviews simply did not work with struggling students. These students were often subjected to the overuse of interventions to address seeming deficits or segregated through either pull-out efforts or placement in classes where less rigorous instruction was provided.

LACK OF INVESTMENT OR SCATTERSHOT COMMUNITY ENGAGEMENT

Finally, neither of the counterfactual districts had unusually strong or coherent community involvement compared with the districts that showed substantial improvements. Each of them had a considerable number of community partners and supporters that the school districts could count on. But what we did not see in either district—like we saw in the improving districts—was community partnerships that were aligned in a way that could help the districts strategically improve student outcomes.

We saw this in other major city school systems as well. There were lots of players in their respective communities, but their expertise was not always marshaled in ways that would help their school systems attain strategic goals. In some cases, in fact, the numbers of community actors could be so overwhelming as to bog down a school district that was not thinking strategically about what outside resources and expertise it needed on behalf of students like we saw in the District of Columbia public schools.

We should note here that the community "ecosystems" in these two urban districts, Jackson and Philadelphia, were similar to those in the faster-improving systems. The racial composition of the two counterfactual districts was like that of the improving systems. The teachers union in Philadelphia was no less aggressive than the one in Chicago, and there was no collective bargaining for teachers in Jackson. Both systems had modest community support. Still, there were differences.

In both cases, Philadelphia in particular, the state played an outsized role in what the local school system was doing. Pennsylvania seized the school district of Philadelphia, altered its governance system, and shifted its priorities. Instead of focusing on improving student outcomes, the state's intervention shifted the district's priorities to budget, finance, and charter school management. The School Reform Commission in Philadelphia spent nearly all its time on these issues, and it hired as superintendent Bill Hite, who was skilled in these challenges. What it did not do was insist the system improve student achievement like other districts did.

We should also remember that both systems operated in a broader context of abject poverty and a legacy of racial discrimination. We found from our analyses that traditional urban school systems with NAEP scores in reading and mathematics below what we expected often had unusually high rates of abject poverty. (See the appendix.) This negative overall district effect appears to apply to systems where 10 percent of the population or more had annual income levels at or below $15,000 *and* at least 50 percent of the population with annual incomes below $50,000 in 2019. All low-performing districts, except Albuquerque and Los Angeles, had these characteristics.(See the appendix.) Albuquerque and Los Angeles, however, had unusually high rates of English language learners, which might produce similar effects. Nonetheless, one TUDA district with high abject poverty showed better-than-expected results in 2019 in three grade-subject combinations (fourth-grade reading and eighth-grade reading and mathematics): Cleveland.

In addition to abject poverty, the legacy of discrimination and urban disinvestment also informs student performance in these and other districts. Several cities in the TUDA sample have a history where Black communities were subject to sustained legal isolation, oppression, and a lack of investment that left them without the social and economic capital they needed to support educational progress. This historical pattern, to be sure, is seen in Baltimore, Cleveland, Detroit, Jackson, Milwaukee, Philadelphia, and other cities.

The segregation or "redlining" of many Black communities and their institutions in these cities over considerable time made it difficult for individuals of color to buy homes, borrow against the value of their homes, or start businesses and improve their properties.[17] The result was that owner occupancy was reduced, property values were lowered, housing quality slipped, and racial segregation increased. Many of these communities also saw the exit of grocery stores, gas stations, movie theaters, and banks, which further isolated the communities, lowered the quality of life, and left these communities without the wherewithal to compete with other, better-endowed school systems.[18] The reduction in property values alone reduced the financial investment in schools, which is often reliant on this critical revenue source.

Our analysis also indicated that concentrated numbers and percentages of English language learners may have similarly outsized effects on district performance, as may be the case in Los Angeles and Albuquerque. Both city school districts had student ELL rates above 15 percent. Still, districts like Boston (29.2 percent), Chicago (18.2 percent), Dallas (40.7 percent), and Denver (27.4 percent) have higher rates of ELLs but have shown significant positive district effects and improvements. In each case, these districts pursued reforms over an extended period. Other factors, of course, may be at work in these school districts, but it is important to remember the context in which they have operated over many decades.

The Council of the Great City Schools made a series of proposals to our two counterfactual systems, Jackson and Philadelphia, encouraging them to refocus their work on improving student achievement.[19] We made 41 separate recommendations to Jackson that ranged from revamping and realigning their organizational structure to strengthening accountability for results; developing an aligned curriculum and professional development system; improving instructional monitoring; and creating an in-house teacher and principal pipeline program.

In Philadelphia, we made 99 proposals, starting with an overhaul of how the board of education does its work and including detailed recommendations on shifting the district's priorities, aligning its curriculum, retooling its reading and math programs, strengthening its ELL and special education programs, overhauling its professional development and staff capacity-building efforts, boosting its instructional interventions, and revisiting its assessment system.

By 2023 the results from a new study by Sean Reardon and Tom Kane showing state test score change since 2022 showed that both Jackson under superintendent Errick Greene and Philadelphia under new superintendent Tony Watlington Sr. were among the most academically improved school districts in the nation.[20] It can be done.

In general, urban school districts that do not show much improvement are often plagued by practices that hamper their achievement. They lack a focus on student outcomes. They often do not improve student achievement because it is not a priority for the system or what they do does not have any discernible effect on the quality of classroom instruction district wide. In many cases, the problems start at the top of the system with school boards that pay inadequate attention to how well students are doing academically.

Instead, their focus is on adult issues like contracts and hiring, vendor agreements and procurement, budget modifications, and operations. These are all critical issues, to be sure, but we often see them displace attention on student welfare in places that do not show much improvement.

We also saw in the slower-improving districts less attention to the standards and to overall curricular issues. These districts often had no curriculum or curriculum that was fractured, incoherent, unaligned, or of mediocre quality. And these districts often lacked the internal staff capacity to correct the situation. We saw situations in which curriculum existed, but individual schools and teachers were free to ignore it. Anchoring one's instructional program in college and career readiness standards and a curriculum that flows from it makes it clear to teachers what the expectation is for what students should know and be able to do. These expectations were not always as clear as they needed to be in districts that had shown less improvement. In other words, these districts did not show as much improvement because they had little way to systemically enhance the quality of their classroom instruction.

In addition, districts that did not experience as much academic gain often had less capacity to develop their staff or their systems to instruct children better. This often meant inadequate professional development, but it could also involve a district's inability to provide aligned and high-quality support or coaching to their teachers and staff. And we frequently saw districts that were plagued by inequities in struggling students' access to high-quality instruction.

Finally, one of the abiding features of these districts that set them apart from their improving colleagues involved their lack of attention to continuous academic improvement. They did other things well, but they paid a price for their lack of focus on achievement and its enhancement. Sometimes, like in Philadelphia, they had data and research operations that were every bit as good as the improving systems, but the district did not use the data to regularly monitor or improve their instructional operations like the faster-improving districts did.

Not all slower-improving districts were characterized by all the features described in this chapter, and not all the faster-improving districts had solved all the issues described here. The differences between the two sets of districts were not always black or white. The improving districts, however, often recognized where improvement was needed and why. As I said at the outset, most districts thought they were doing what works, but it often took someone from the outside to figure out how it differed from places that were getting better results.

The themes that I describe in this chapter and chapter 4 go a long way, I hope, in explaining whether an urban school district was likely to improve—or not. Table 5.1 below summarizes many of the differences between the two sets of districts, but the reader should keep in mind that not all circumstances apply to each district.

The good news is that a considerable number of issues identified in this chapter have since been addressed in these systems over the years. Not all of them, but many have. Other problems cropped up, but the cities remained at each other's disposal in figuring out what was not working and what they needed to do about it. And it was these efforts to identify why systems were not working the way they should that helped urban schools improve.

In chapter 6, we will look at what was going on behind the scenes during the pandemic and how it shifted the work of urban school systems across the country from improvement to crisis management.

Table 5.1 Summary of key differences between faster-improving districts and districts that did not show as much progress on NAEP

Characteristic	Improving/higher performing	Less improvement
Leadership	Strong and consistent focus on improving teaching and learning	Greater focus on financial, operational, and other issues than on instruction
	Longer or more stable leadership tenures focused on instruction	Shorter tenures or less instructional focus during longer tenures
Standards and instruction	Attention to high-quality college and career-readiness standards and their implications for the curriculum and instruction	Less attention to standards or weak alignment of instructional program with standards
	Clear academic goal setting and academic expectations with regular monitoring of goals	Vaguer academic goals and/or little monitoring of goals
	Strong, system-wide implementation of standards to boost the quality of instruction	Implementation of standards that was misaligned or weak
	Coherent, clear system-wide instructional expectations, curriculum, and program	Less coherent or poorly articulated instructional expectations and program
Teacher and leader quality	Ability to distinguish effective from less effective staff	Less ability to determine which staff were effective
	Focus on improving the quality of area and school leadership	Less emphasis on enhancing the skills of instructional leaders
Capacity building	Focused and coherent efforts to continually enhance the instructional knowledge and skills of teachers and staff	Professional development and other capacity-building efforts were weak, less focused on instruction, and less coherent
	Districts had good data systems that were used to monitor academic progress and modify strategy	Less use of sometimes good data systems to drive academic improvement
Acting at scale	Once researched and designed, reform efforts were rolled out systemically, monitored, and adjusted	Reform efforts were more piecemeal, regional, school-by-school, or defined by individual teachers
	Implementation efforts were aligned across the system	Less attention paid to program or reform alignment

(continued)

Table 5.1 (*Continued*)

Characteristic	Improving/higher performing	Less improvement
Challenges	Agility to turn problems, challenges, or new situations into opportunities to spur results	Challenges were handled but not exploited
Struggling schools/ students	Districts had cohesive improvement efforts not only at systems level but at school or student-group levels Emphasis on improving core class instruction rather than disconnected remedial efforts	Improvement efforts were regionally defined or were disconnected to system-wide reforms More emphasis on remedial efforts or poorly defined instructional interventions rather than boosting core instruction
Community engagement	Broad community support that was aligned to system goals	Community support that was either weaker or less aligned to district priorities

6

Behind the Scenes
During the Pandemic

In March 2020, when the pandemic started to shut down operations across the country, Eric Gordon was the chief executive officer (CEO) of the Cleveland Metropolitan School District and chair of the Council of the Great City Schools. He was in Washington, D.C., with me to discuss the upcoming legislative conference of the organization when Cleveland Mayor Frank Jackson called him about returning to town to participate in a press conference with the city's three main hospitals. The pandemic had started. And it was only the beginning of a journey that neither of us wanted to make.

As we walked down the hall of the Council's D.C. headquarters on Pennsylvania Avenue, I asked Gordon if he thought it made sense to arrange an emergency conference call later that week with the group's superintendents, CEOs, and chancellors to talk through the emerging crisis. He thought it made sense but wondered if we could gather everyone so rapidly.

Our uncertainty about whether our colleagues would respond quickly proved unfounded: everyone showed up. We invited Seattle superintendent Denise Juneau, whose schools were among the first in the nation to close, to update the group on what she was learning. It quickly became clear to everyone that we were facing something unprecedented. The existential threat that the pandemic posed to urban public education was unmistakable.

What did not happen, as we will see, was chaos, confusion, mismanagement, and incompetence that some in the press and in various advocacy organizations and think-tanks depicted. The leaders of these systems were not always able to respond jointly or convincingly to every issue that came up, to be sure, but the information sharing, discussion, and coordination over the two years helped these systems weather the challenges the pandemic was creating better than anything else we might have done.

At the same time, the reader will see crisis management in real time. You will get to listen in on a series of weekly calls that I facilitated with the nation's urban school leaders. Crises, by definition, are typically low-probability and unpredictable events that can cause severe damage to an enterprise. The causes and consequences of these kinds of events may be unclear or unknown, but leaders must see the threats posed by the crisis and act quickly to mitigate them. Big-city school leaders all have crisis management plans for events like hurricanes, earthquakes, strikes, transportation snafus, snowstorms, and school shootings, but this was different.

Two Harvard researchers and business experts, Leonard and Howitt, differentiate "routine emergencies" from "true crises" as events that cannot be dealt with using predetermined plans and capabilities.[1] Leonard and Kaplan[2] indicate that in true crisis situations that no one has ever seen before and where there are no ready answers, the process leaders use to respond can make all the difference. They suggest that leaders attend to the structures, people, and problem-solving approaches that will allow them to understand the elements of the situation, generate options, predict outcomes of various courses of action, decide on the best courses of action based on an organization's values and priorities, execute action, and learn from the results.

In this chapter you will see how the superintendents, school boards, and line officers took these steps. At the same time, you will see how urban school leaders struggled with the elements that made this crisis so unique. There was no end in sight, and it affected everyone. The crisis appeared to be accelerating; it created high levels of uncertainty because there were no known solutions. No one knew how many dimensions the crisis would have. Multiple actors inside and outside the institution were responding differently. No one was sure who was leading the response at the national level or what the exit strategy was. School officials were getting ever-changing and contradictory guidance. Disparate interests were able to blur communications, and the crisis was sufficiently all encompassing to distract school leaders from their core mission.

When everything was said and done, urban school leaders were much better at managing this unprecedented crisis than they thought they would be, but it pulled them off their efforts to continuously improve, and considerable learning time was lost.

DEFINING A STRATEGY

One thing was established on that first call that set the tone and tenor of our collaboration throughout the difficult months to come: we had agreed to initiate weekly Zoom sessions for the superintendents, CEOs, and chancellors of the Great City Schools to share the steps that everyone was taking to address the challenges facing our urban schools and communities. Within weeks, these meetings evolved into regular role-alike calls with school board members, general counsels, chief academic officers, chief financial officers (CFOs), chief operating officers (COOs), bilingual directors, communications directors, and many others.

In any one week, fifteen groups of urban school leaders met virtually. Within the first several months, we made over a thousand group calls as leaders worked to stay ahead of the obstacles that the pandemic was creating. The gatherings proved to be a critical way to provide direction, cohesion, and support when schools were getting little consistent guidance from the federal government or the states about what to do. It did not mean that all school leaders did the same things, but they were able to talk through their strategies with trusted colleagues on a regular basis.

It took no time on these calls for big-city school superintendents to agree on the scope of the crisis and its potential threat to public education, but there was considerable back and forth among urban school leaders on the first several calls about how to respond. Those early calls were devoted to how the school districts in the group could collaborate with one another, how we could bolster each other's resolution to do everything we could on behalf of our students, and how we could remain realistic about what we could do. We also talked about urgent matters, such as how to get lessons to students, how attendance was being calculated, how grading would be handled, how staff was being paid, how students and district personnel were being tested for the disease, how meals were delivered, and how graduations were going to be held.

In an early call, Miami-Dade County superintendent Alberto Carvahlo and Dallas superintendent Michael Hinojosa argued that we had little choice but to meet the challenge in front of us with whatever means we had, however inadequate.

Gordon and others, however, were worried about whether schools should be treated like everyone else who was being shut down. He was concerned that the tools we had at our disposal were insufficient to keep our students on track and deliver all the other services that the public expected us to deliver. We might be trying to do too much, and we knew that remote learning simply could not take the place of in-person instruction. He fretted that we were setting ourselves up for failure.

At the end of the first several meetings, however, everyone concurred that the situation was one that would test the very viability of urban public education and that we had little choice but to throw everything we had at the challenges in front of us. The strategy going forward would be to provide as much instructional time remotely as we could arrange, meal services to as many students and families as we could reach, and we would keep everyone as healthy as possible. In pursuing this strategy, we would aim to uphold the values of excellence and high standards, stakeholder involvement, safety and health, equity, consistency and stability, collaboration, and attention to trauma and family difficulty. We knew that it would be hard to keep our students at grade level, given the limitations of distance learning, but we vowed to do everything we could to provide for our students and families.

The downside for some of our poorest districts was that they and their families would have inadequate technology to provide students the access to online instruction that everyone else had. But the urban school superintendents shared the same values, goals, and sense of determination, and they agreed to go forward together. It was a risk because we knew we would encounter criticism no matter what we did. But we agreed that it was a risk worth taking and we were going to have to figure this out on our own—and this was the group to do it.

The superintendents generally assumed in the early spring of 2020 that the pandemic would be over soon enough to reopen the buildings by the end of that school year, an assumption that faded as the pandemic raged on, and it became clear that this was a longer-term situation.

At the same time, school leaders were faced with what seemed to be an endless stream of questions and concerns.

Sonja Santelises, Baltimore City's school CEO, for instance, asked about how districts were distributing instructional lessons to students, particularly those without internet connection. Jason Kamras, superintendent of the Richmond (VA) public schools, wondered how his colleagues were paying staff, like bus drivers, who were not being used and how districts were hiring teachers for next school year, since this was the time of year that hiring was typically done.

Brenda Cassellius, the Boston superintendent, wondered how her colleagues were planning for summer school, since grading had been upended. Jesus Jara, superintendent of the Clark County (Las Vegas) schools, asked about whether the US Department of Education would provide some flexibility in various IDEA (Individuals with Disabilities Education Act) requirements. The Philadelphia superintendent, Bill Hite, looked for guidance from his colleagues on whether they would hold traditional or alternative graduation ceremonies. The calls were collaboration at their finest because what they were doing was creating, on the fly, the game plan for managing a novel global pandemic that did not otherwise exist.

SECURING RESOURCES

Amid all the information sharing in the early weeks of the pandemic, there was a nagging concern that public schools would not receive the kind of deep support and financial aid that would be required for our recovery.

There was even some concern that the efforts we were making would signal that we had everything we needed. The superintendents were profoundly worried about being compensated for the resources they were laying out but had not budgeted for.

Gordon, the Cleveland CEO, was convinced that we would need to devote our political wherewithal to convincing Congress that financial aid was going to be necessary and that we could not sustain our efforts without support.

By the end of March that year, President Trump and Congress had approved the first tranche of funding for elementary and secondary schools, $13 billion. The money was meant to stem the COVID-19 virus, support school district efforts to protect the public, and reopen an economy that had shut down. Funds would start arriving that summer.

It was obvious to everyone, however, that the initial $13 billion would not be enough, and Council staff began working with other national education organizations to advocate for some $200 billion in aid to help with recovery. The superintendents each signed a joint letter to Congress calling for massive assistance beyond what was initially provided. The Council became increasingly focused over the months not only on ensuring that Congress appropriated the aid but on making sure that it was distributed according to the poverty-based Title I formula.

PROBLEM SOLVING

As the weeks ticked by that spring, the superintendent calls became focused less on sharing information and more on collaborative problem solving. On April 16, 2020, I was on a call with about forty-five superintendents, including Bob Nelson of Fresno, Deborah Gist of Tulsa, Sonja Santelises of Baltimore, Michael Hinojosa of Dallas, and Jesus Jara of Las Vegas to discuss issues of assessment and how we were measuring the learning that was likely being lost because of the reduced instructional time that came with students being out of school.

Bob Nelson indicated that his district was using his interim assessments, in this case iReady, as a diagnostic tool to identify learning gaps. Deborah

Gist said that they were using MAP in similar ways, while Sonja Santelises described her district's use of iReady and their curriculum-imbedded assessments and Michael Hinojosa was using MAP in their transition grades only. Jesus Jara described their efforts to do online assessments before giving up. The leaders batted back and forth the benefits and liabilities of using these tools in this way.

The conference calls continued throughout the early days of the pandemic and facilitated a collaborative and problem-solving spirit. In April 2020 I was on another call devoted to the COVID-19 testing of staff and other school personnel. The Boston superintendent was concerned that getting parents to send their children back to schools might depend on our ability to guarantee that personnel had been screened for the disease.

The superintendents formed a smaller, off-line working group with Deena Bishop from Anchorage, Aleesia Johnson from Indianapolis, Bob Runcie from Broward County, Deborah Gist from Tulsa, Sharon Contreras from Guilford County, and Brenda Cassellius from Boston to talk through what they were doing short term and how their work on this front would need to improve if the pandemic stretched well into the future. The working group would report back to the full group on subsequent calls with a series of options on screening staff and students. These small working groups designed to think through options became standard practice from then on. They also resulted in a series of reports and guidelines that we used throughout the pandemic. (See the appendix for a list.)

Other early calls devoted to one problem or another addressed internet connectivity, the delivery of school meals to students and community members, the retention of school bus drivers and other staff, support for students with disabilities, the identification and assessment of English language learners (ELLs), the use of community hotlines, hybrid instructional models, and many other topics.

The Council also used the calls to encourage the superintendents to brainstorm out-of-the-box ideas to get us through the pandemic and rethink our traditional practices. Eric Gordon from Cleveland proposed making greater use of evening learning sessions to create more extended learning time; developing an "essential learning" curriculum for the next year or so to address lost instructional time; getting rid of the summer vacation; creating shared instructional platforms with local colleges; incorporating social/emotional lessons into the ongoing instructional program; designing hot spot technology that could be imbedded into student backpacks; developing more blended classrooms and co-teaching strategies across grade levels; getting rid of seat time and moving toward a purely mastery model of learning; and using a "Blue Apron" strategy, where some master teachers created content kits for other teachers. Others came forward with ideas as well.

Most of these ideas and many others were meant for after the pandemic, but I wanted to encourage as much creativity as possible to help us weather the storm.

By mid-April 2020, it was becoming increasingly clear that schools were likely to remain closed for the balance of the school year. The prospects tested everyone's resolve, because it was clear we were in this situation for the long haul. At one point, Gordon quipped, "This is not what I signed up for." Everyone agreed but the consensus was to move forward.

ADDRESSING ISSUES OF ACCESS

Attention in the weekly discussions among the Great City School superintendents as time marched on became more focused on internet access, technology device availability, supply-chain bottlenecks, meals for students and community members, and learning loss. Albuquerque superintendent Scott Elder reported that his district had provided approximately 300,000 meals in just 15 days. The El Paso superintendent indicated that they were preparing and distributing some 150,000 meals a week. By the end of May, the Council of the Great City Schools estimated that its member urban school systems would have distributed some 150 million meals.

Broward County superintendent Bob Runcie recounted how they had already distributed 90,000 devices and hot spots to students. Kyla Johnson-Trammel, the Oakland superintendent, reported that they had given out 17,000 devices within one month of the pandemic's start. New

York City chancellor Richard Carranza informed the group that they had distributed 175,000 devices and were prepared to send another 247,000 pieces to students in the coming days. And Cleveland, Baltimore, and Birmingham began realizing that their lack of devices was likely to cost them dearly in lost learning.

Deborah Gist from Tulsa and Marty Pollio from Louisville called their colleagues' attention to the fact summer school was likely to be all-virtual and that everyone was simply going to have to get better at remote instruction. And everyone had reconciled themselves to starting school earlier in August for the fall semester.

In addition, that spring, Boston began reporting the first spikes in shootings and other acts of violence among young people in the city.

THE WORK OF BIG-CITY SCHOOL BOARDS

In these early months of the pandemic, the school boards began to meet as well at the suggestion of Michael O'Neill, who was vice president of the Boston School Committee and chair-elect of the Council of the Great City Schools. He would come to dub the stressed-out but genial group his "Friday Friends" since the calls were held at 1:00 p.m. each Friday. The name stuck, and urban school board members across the country would regularly refer to each other for years afterward in this way.

These early school board meetings were often dedicated to receiving legislative updates from the Council's legislative team of Jeff Simering and Manish Naik and to briefing each other on the state of play in their respective districts. Of special interest were updates on the status of possible federal relief and the latest guidance from the Centers for Disease Control and Prevention (CDC). Everyone was worried about revenue shortfalls and overspending due to unforeseen expenses from the pandemic. At that point, the districts were bankrolling pandemic mitigation efforts and technology enhancements out of their own overstretched budgets. David Lee Evans from the San Diego school board reported at the April 10, 2020, meeting that his district had already spent $19 million of its own dollars on mitigation efforts.

School boards also shared strategies on how they were remotely holding their regular school board meetings, how they were receiving public input, and whether the structure of their meeting agendas had changed. There was considerable back-and-forth about what technology platforms the boards were using, what their features were, and how school board sessions could be improved. Most people had never heard of Zoom before then. And everyone noted that public attendance had spiked markedly.

The issue of public input was the subject of considerable discussion from the very first meetings. Everyone agreed that their virtual platforms allowed for greater public input and debate than their regular in-person sessions. No one knew how proficient they would become on these platforms as time marched on.

Many of these early school board sessions struggled with how to represent their communities and provide feedback to their superintendents and administrative staff without overwhelming them. In calls with both superintendents and board members, I noticed a striking consensus about the nature of the problems they were having. To their credit, most of the boards saw the issues mostly as managerial and operational, not governance, and deferred to the administration on an unusual array of problems. Some school boards, like in Providence, Newark, and Los Angeles, granted their superintendents special emergency powers to expedite operations.

As the weeks ticked by, school board attention during these calls increasingly turned to graduations and how the districts were going to handle the ceremonies remotely. Miami school board member and former chair of the Council, Larry Feldman, was particularly good at this point in keeping spirits high and the group focused on what we were trying to achieve.

One of the serious issues that the boards struggled with, however, during the early days of the pandemic involved data and metrics by which they could monitor how students were doing. The superintendents and staff were dealing with the same things because it was becoming increasingly difficult to gather data from staff and students when they were not in school. Instead, there were considerable discussions about both how data could be collected remotely and how it could be aggregated and reported.

In addition, the boards were getting increasing pressure from their bargaining units to create revisions to the contracts to manage new hours and workloads. Amy Kohnstamm from the Portland school board reported that pressure was building on their district for new contract language. Oakland reported the same.

THE INVOLVEMENT OF OTHER DISTRICT LEADERS AND STAFF

The value of these early calls and the need to resolve some issues at a more granular level compelled us to begin parallel calls with district line officers, whom we had worked with regularly over many years. We began with group calls to big-city school chief financial officers, chief operating officers, chief human resource directors, general counsels, chief academic officers, research directors, communications directors, and chief information and technology officers.

Quickly, the calls with the chief academic officers evolved into separate meetings of the bilingual education directors and directors of special education. The meetings with the chief operating officers evolved into separate sessions with the directors of transportation, food services, facilities, and security. And meetings of the human resource directors eventually included collective bargaining staff, risk managers, and others.

Each of the line groups dug into the details of the work in front of them in ways that augmented the broader strategic conversations that the superintendents and school boards were having. The chief academic officers spent considerable time in the early weeks sharing information on such things as how to launch their digital instruction; how they were addressing technology and device shortages; what platforms they were using for remote instruction; how they were getting information from parents and guardians about home access to technology; and how student logins were being tracked. They also shared how they were training staff and parents on the use of instructional technology and how to conduct hybrid instruction where some teaching was done in classrooms and some remotely. And they spent considerable time discussing how to create and encourage networks of teachers who could share their strategies and approaches.

After the first week of being shut down, for instance, the Long Beach schools had created their Google classrooms for dissemination to students and parents; trained teachers on the rudimentary use of the platform; launched their remote instructional program; set up technical assistance for staff and parents to resolve glitches; set up call centers; created crowd-sourcing procedures so that teachers could share online lessons; began distributing meals to the community; and distributed paper lessons to students without immediate access to technology. The Los Angeles schools were already enlisting their parent academies to assist and had arranged for their PBS stations to provide instruction. Guilford County, Orlando, Albuquerque, and others picked up on the Los Angeles example and began partnerships with their PBS stations.

By the second week of being closed, the chief academic officers had already turned their attention to the prospect of unfinished learning and began sharing information on the content materials they were using and the gaps that were created by the lack of instructional time. Dallas began partnering with Univision to provide instruction in multiple languages. Tulsa was using its central office academic team and the district's CANVAS platform to push out classroom lessons to augment teacher-created ones. Baltimore city was using videos from Eureka Math on their website. Broward County was already incorporating social-emotional supports into their instruction. And Denver was moderating their scope and sequence documents to focus on power standards.

Issues about grading and graduation credits, attendance, professional development, actual instructional time, and upcoming summer school plans absorbed the group. It was becoming increasingly clear that the amount of instructional time using remote platforms had fallen off substantially from the learning time students had in their classrooms.

In the meantime, the CFOs were spending their time tracking what districts were spending and figuring out how to pay for everything. The CFOs from Fresno and Palm Beach County developed templates to track their spending and distributed the models to their colleagues on the calls.

Districts like Des Moines and Columbus were reporting to the group on how they were making their spending and revenue projections for the balance of the school year and next.

San Diego reported that it expected losses in the tens of millions. Long Beach reported a loss of $4.8 million. Los Angles projected a $200 million shortfall, and Norfolk expected losses of about $13 million. Clark County indicated that Nevada had already announced cuts of 4 percent across the board, while Buffalo said that New York state was talking about a 20 percent cut to schools.

Everyone was concerned about how they were paying their staff, when it was not clear whether schools would even be open by the end of the school year. And the uncertainty about how districts were going to pay for all the meals they were providing was widespread. At the same time, the CFOs were sharing strategies on pay freezes, reserve dollars, maintenance of effort, and carryover funds along with methods on how to best prioritize limited dollars. Congress could have used this group to negotiate the debt limit.

The chief operating officers focused on the myriad details that running and maintaining the schools in the middle of a global pandemic entailed. They oversaw safety procedures involving masks, social distancing, hand washing, air quality, building and equipment disinfecting and sanitizing, classroom and building setup, cleaning, signage, water management, shipping and deliveries, and the like.

On top of that, they had responsibility for student transportation, security, and meals. The security directors realized quickly that there were spikes in school break-ins to steal equipment and food. Security staff were also being called on to protect district workers who were distributing meals and devices in sometimes dangerous areas of their cities.

The facilities directors, for their part, devoted their energies to building access, the continuation of capital projects, custodial and maintenance services, groundskeeping, and management of the staggered use of school buildings.

Transportation directors worked on strategies to retain drivers and contract language with transportation providers. Districts shared information on how they were disinfecting and cleaning buses and deploying their bus fleets and drivers to deliver meals and instructional packets and how they were providing transportation for private and independent charter schools. Of particular interest was how the transportation directors were reconciling the differing standards that the CDC and the Occupational Safety and Health Administration (OSHA) used for cleaning buses.

Food service directors worked out strategies for providing what became hundreds of millions of meals to urban residents across their communities. And the technology directors shared strategies for obtaining instructional devices that were increasingly in short supply because of supply chain issues; programming them; distributing, safeguarding, repairing and replacing equipment; creating and distributing hot spots; training people on their use; and ensuring internet security.

Everyone was focused, in those early months, on giving students and families the tools and resources everyone thought they needed as the world was being turned upside down. As each of the groups met on a weekly basis, we also formed working groups to develop guidance for the membership at large—and anyone else who was interested—on what we were learning about best practices to meet the challenges we were facing. (See the appendix for links to the guidance that the teams developed in the early months of the pandemic.)

SUPPORTING SCHOOLS, SUPERINTENDENTS SUPPORTING EACH OTHER

It became clear over the weeks and months that the calls we were holding had benefits beyond sharing best practices, developing solutions, and trying to stay realistic about what we could do. Much of the press attention at the time was devoted to the exhaustion that teachers were feeling in trying to juggle their instructional responsibilities. But the exhaustion was felt by the leaders and line officers of these systems as well.

Every so often we devoted at least part of our calls to surveying everyone's mental health and what they were doing to manage the stress they were under. Superintendents reported that they were gaining weight, losing weight, losing sleep, and losing hair. Some people started reading poetry. Others found a new love for classical music. Others renewed their religious faith. Some turned to their families. Some bought pets. And others cried or found that they were drinking more.

Sharing became more than a way of collaborating on common issues each week; it became group therapy. Sonja Santelises once remarked, "I so value these calls because they remind me that I am not crazy. All this is really happening."

By the end of the school year, the school districts had provided an extraordinary amount of support to their communities, but everyone hoped that they could open early in the fall and bring back some sense of normalcy. Graduations that spring went off remarkably smoothly with the recent technology that districts were getting used to operating, even though families clearly missed having in-person ceremonies.

But on May 25, George Floyd was killed in Minneapolis, and the nation was rocked with protests and upheaval.

I do not know of any formal polling that was done nationally that spring about what the public thought of its schools. Many school leaders at the end of that first school year thought we had done about everything we could have done. It may not have been enough, but it was all we could do. In a matter of months, our urban public school systems, like many others, had pivoted to remote instruction, acquired and distributed millions of devices and hot spots to connect students with their teachers, provided tens of millions of meals across our urban communities, worked to keep students and staff as healthy as possible, and spoke out for racial justice as ramifications of the George Floyd killing became clear.

Still, the more difficult period was yet to come.

THE CRISIS MARCHES ON

What all the school closings meant to students in terms of lost learning was sinking in with the superintendents on their weekly calls. Most districts planned for extensive summer school programming, and most thought they would be able to start early in the fall to make up for lost time. Places like Miami-Dade County had already arranged for many of their best teachers to staff their summer schools. Cleveland was thinking increasingly of designing its summer schools around activities that would address the social-emotional problems they were beginning to see. Boston was thinking about using the summer for independent study and credit while doing small group academic intervention services in person. And San Antonio considered starting the fall semester in mid-July.

Michael Hinojosa from Dallas reported that they were already experimenting with a hybrid model with students in school two days a week and remote for three. El Paso was doing something similar. Most everyone, however, was required to conduct their summer schools remotely and were unable to test hybrid models until later.

Discussions over the summer turned to the potential for greater privatization of education and how a new normal might involve a hybrid of brick-and-mortal schooling alongside online instruction, all decoupled from traditional notions of seat time.

Alberto Carvahlo from Miami was particularly vocal about pointing out to his colleagues that there was no going back to whatever we thought was normal. We could design effective summer schools and we could start the fall term early, but parents now had an open seat to what schooling looked like for their children and their demands were rising. Brenda Cassellius from Boston argued vigorously that urban school leaders needed to take the reins in our own reinvention.

The possibility that remote instruction might be required in the fall or might be part of the ongoing services of the districts was getting increasing attention from the superintendents. The spring semester revealed gaping holes in who had access to technology and who did not. Eric Gordon from Cleveland estimated that at least one-third of all students in the city did not have internet access. Ed Graff from Minneapolis was reporting that families were having increasing difficulty paying for internet service as people were being laid off work.

At the same time, Michael Hinojosa was launching "Operation Connectivity" to create universal internet access nationwide, arguing that access to the internet had now become a civil rights issue. Superintendent Meria

Carstarphen of Atlanta reported that Comcast was starting to use their school system to bolster internet access throughout their community. Aleesia Johnson from Indianapolis shared her community's efforts, and Eric Gordon described their work to provide and co-brand internet services citywide.

Reports of child abuse and mental health problems were also emerging. Jesus Jara in Las Vegas was reporting an extraordinary spike in student suicides. Deborah Gist from Tulsa was particularly vocal about the steps that schools needed to be taking to address the issues or students would never be able to concentrate on their schoolwork. The district was already making home visits and partnering with local social service agencies and organizations.

Superintendents during this period were also noticing that many students were simply disappearing from school. They did not sign in when they had remote access, and many had moved or could not be found. Philadelphia reported that between seven and eight thousand students could not be located, although an aggressive door-to-door campaign in conjunction with the mayor eventually located about half of them. Boston reported that nine thousand children were missing initially, but most were found in shelters across the city. Providence was initially missing four thousand students, but the district whittled the number down to about fifty. And Chicago was initially missing some thirty-seven thousand students, but partnerships with community organizations eventually found all but about three thousand.

On their calls, the superintendents shared their strategies, like their door-knocking campaigns, phone calls, public housing visits, community partnerships, and interviews, to ensure they were thinking of everything. Neighborhood interviews, for instance, revealed that some families had simply returned to their home countries to wait out the pandemic. As a result of their information sharing, superintendents encouraged staff to contact parents in their native countries and tell them that their children would be welcomed back.

The issue of missing children would plague the districts for years as enrollment dropped.

It was also becoming obvious by mid-summer that some states were off-setting the $13 billion in federal spending with cuts from their own education spending. Nonetheless, the superintendents moved forward with their food services, technology purchases, and other spending out of their own district coffers.

REOPENING SCHOOLS

In the middle of all these challenges, the districts continued planning to reopen schools in the fall. Districts like Dallas, Tulsa, Chicago, Baltimore, and Kansas City (MO) had initial draft reopening plans for the fall that they shared with their colleagues on the calls and with their communities for input.

Options for how to reopen were tossed out among superintendents that summer as the pandemic continued to kill thousands of Americans. Barbara Jenkins from Orlando reported that parents in her community were divided on the reopening. A survey from Broward County, Florida, which had some 72,000 responses, found that 26 percent of parents wanted to continue remote instruction in the fall; 37 percent wanted a hybrid model where some time was spent in person and some time was spent online, and 27 percent of parents wanted campuses fully open. Other superintendents reported that their surveys were showing the same three-way split in community opinions.

Still, the districts had no option but to continue planning to reopen. Everyone knew that students needed to be back in school. Fresno was thinking about a staggered schedule and requiring masks. Cleveland was considering a staggered schedule by grade band with the youngest and the most in-need coming back first. Atlanta was considering weekly cohorts. Des Moines was surveying parents; Oakland and Denver were talking with their unions; and Philadelphia was holding virtual town-hall meetings. Everyone was flummoxed by the transportation challenges and scheduling complications. But all the superintendents listened intently to each other describe their options and offered reactions to them.

Everyone faced the same problem: if the districts reopened the schools, they could not staff them fully because too many teachers and administrators were likely to call in sick, or the quarantine periods would force random school closures when there were not enough personnel. As it was, superintendents were emptying the central offices to cover classes—and teach classes themselves.

It was difficult for the districts to act in unison when it came to reopening schools. The public was divided. Each state had different rules and varying responses to the pandemic. Guidance from the CDC was inconsistent. The unions were resistant, and the ground rules seemed to constantly change. The result was often divergent decisions from one city to another, because the pressure points in each locale varied. It was the source of ongoing frustration by the superintendents that they could act together in some circumstances but not all. The reopening of schools was one of those cases. Nonetheless, they were constantly leaning on one another.

By early summer 2020, the US House of Representatives had passed a second tranche of federal funding for schools, but there was no action in the Senate.

Around the same time, the US Department of Education under Secretary Betsy DeVos approved guidance that would shift funds under the first tranche of support toward less-poor private schools in defiance of the Congressionally approved Title I formula. The Council's executive committee authorized the organization to file suit against the Department, the first time that the group had ever done so, an effort that would eventually prove successful. Here was a circumstance where the cities could act jointly.

That summer, the US Supreme Court also ruled in *Espinoza v. Montana Department of Revenue* that state-based scholarship or voucher programs that were funded with public money to allow students to attend private schools could not discriminate against religious schools. The decision underscored for superintendents how vulnerable their institutions were and how critical it was to do everything they could to meet the needs of their communities. At the same time, national protests over the killing of George Floyd spilled into the schools as many urban districts were under pressure to end their school resource officer (SRO) programs. It was one more pressure point on the districts as they were working to reopen in the fall.

Ultimately, only a handful of big-city school districts ended their SRO programs; most stayed with them because the threat of school shootings was still real. Everyone listened intently to Bob Runcie, whose experiences in Broward County with the Parkland High School shooting sent chills down everyone's spines.

SUMMER 2020

While the struggle raged over how to reopen schools that fall, most big-city school leaders used the summer of 2020 to provide professional development to teachers on instructional technology, update union agreements, and find missing students. Agreements that were wrapped up first, like in San Diego, were passed around among all the superintendents.

The superintendents also used the calls that summer to talk through what worked and did not work during the spring. What had they learned from the spring about remote instruction? It was starting to look like everyone would operate virtually again in the fall. Leadership was frustrated with their inability to reach students with specialized needs. Instructional leaders were exasperated with the small amount of instructional time students were experiencing. And everyone was upset about the mixed messaging they were getting from above and below. Janice Jackson from Chicago was particularly forthcoming in describing her difficulties in creating quality learning experiences remotely for her city's children.

In the meantime, COVID-19 cases were rising all over the country, and there was still no vaccine.

Still, the superintendents continued to work on their shared problems together. Jesus Jara from Las Vegas, for instance, raised an employee pay issue his district was having. The Clark County team had produced a draft reopening plan to have cohorts of students return to school in the fall in person for two days per week while participating in distance learning three days a week. Their legal counsel indicated that they believed that employees would be eligible to take paid leave on the days their children were participating in remote instruction if they did not have other childcare options, according to the Families First Coronavirus Response Act. Depending on how many employees needed and used this option, the district could face significant staffing shortages.

This was also a problem that the human resource officers were dealing with in their weekly meetings. Both groups talked the problem through and developed a series of workarounds that had teachers working at home for part of the day and taking leave for the other part, while staggering student schedules. It was a good example of the many complicated issues that everyone was dealing with and how they solved them.

In Tulsa, superintendent Deborah Gist was being pressed by a school board member for a metric the district could use to decide on reopening. The Wichita assistant superintendent of student support services, Vince Evans, wanted the same thing, as did Rochester superintendent, Lesli Myers-Small. Denver shared the statistical model that a neighboring district had developed, but Michael Hinojosa from Dallas cautioned that no number or statistical model would override the political calculations that leaders were having to make. Still, the search for an acceptable metric districts could use and the public could understand remained a need throughout the pandemic. Despite our requests, the CDC never came up with one.

ENCOUNTERING PUSHBACK

Toward the middle and end of July 2020, districts were starting to release their draft reopening plans for the fall, knowing full well that politicians, the press, and the public would have lots to say about them. Most of the initial plans involved having schools return in hybrid form or return remotely for an interim period before transitioning to a hybrid or staggered schedule. In other cases, like Florida, the governor announced in July that he wanted schools open five days a week to all children.

The draft reopening plans brought out the unions as well. In Minneapolis and St. Paul, for instance, the teacher unions organized a march between J. J. Hill Montessori Magnet School and the governor's house on July 24, 2020, to call for a delay in returning to in-person instruction that fall. They were trying to get a jump on Governor Tim Walz's expected plans.[3] The American Academy of Pediatrics had endorsed a return to in-person instruction in the previous month, but infection rates nationwide were increasing. An unscientific Minnesota statewide survey found that 36 percent of parents were uncomfortable sending their children back to class. Some 64 percent of parents, however, said they were comfortable sending their children to in-person classes.[4]

Carrying signs that read "I can't teach from a grave" and "Exactly how many dead kids are acceptable," the union argued that the risk of reopening schools to in-person learning was too great. When St. Paul superintendent Joe Gothard released his draft plan to start the school year with remote instruction, he was met with more protests from the teacher group, arguing not only against returning to school but also against mandated screen time. Instead, the teacher organizations wanted asynchronous instruction, where teachers and students could teach and learn on their own schedules.

As the fall drew closer, St. Paul was not the only big-city district that experienced protests, sickouts, walkouts, and lawsuits from the unions as their criteria for reopening was a moving target. The District of Columbia public schools were met with protests and on-again, off-again negotiations over months and could not reopen until February 2021. Teachers in New York City marched through the streets of Manhattan in August 2020 to protest the mayor's plan to reopen the schools that fall. It was the same struggle over reopening and under what conditions in Chicago, Los Angeles, Cincinnati, Milwaukee, Philadelphia, Boston, Detroit, Broward County, and San Francisco and other cities. The American Federation of Teachers called for "safety strikes" if teachers did not think schools were safe.[5]

MOVING AHEAD THAT FALL

When schools began to reopen in August and September that year, most provided instruction virtually, although some districts allowed their teachers to teach remotely from their classrooms rather than from home. By that time, most of the districts had worked out their distance learning protocols and reported mostly smooth openings.

Still, there were problems to solve. In the first several hours of school that fall, the state IT system in North Carolina went down, knocking students offline. The Reno schools had phased in their return but had to close again when smoke from the California wildfires polluted the air. Portland was seeing violent clashes in the wake of the George Floyd killing that some teachers and students were participating in. And the Clark County schools experienced a ransomware attack as they went online.

Debates also broke out across the country about allowing students to participate in athletics when their schools were closed. Many of the big-city school superintendents who participated in the weekly calls decided to allow some sports where there was little personal contact, like tennis, but to ban sports where students were in direct contact, like wrestling. Even that common-sense decision had critics.

Districts were also seeing a shortfall in students despite their efforts to get everyone back, although Broward County saw 260,000 students return within the first few days of reopening that fall. Districts also struggled with how to deal with the opening of some schools and the closing of others when the pandemic was unevenly experienced across their communities. And everyone was having difficulty in providing remote services to students with disabilities.

In the meantime, negotiations between Capitol Hill and the White House had broken down over a second tranche of funding for schools.

Nonetheless, early that fall, technology devices had been distributed, although there were shortages. Union agreements had been resolved, although not to everyone's satisfaction. And professional development had been provided, although more was needed.

The Council's lawsuit against the US Department of Education over the distribution of pandemic aid and one by the NAACP were well received in the federal courts in northern California, Seattle, and the District of Columbia. And Gabriela Uro from the Council's staff had worked out an agreement with the Department of Education about how to provisionally count English language learners remotely.

ASSESSING THE FALLOUT

The calm opening of schools that fall allowed districts a momentary breather for school leaders to reflect on what they had been through and share lessons learned, but no one thought we were out of the woods.

The early enrollment numbers that fall showed that districts had lost students, particularly in the youngest grades, but attendance was stronger than expected. Denver reported attendance at 88.6 percent, Rochester was at 83 percent, Baltimore City at 85 percent, Kansas City (MO) at 84 percent, Oakland at 91 percent. The Council estimated that most of the big-city school systems had daily attendance between about 85 and 90 percent early that fall. We also estimated that total urban public school enrollment was off about 4 percent, although some superintendents reported higher down-turns. El Paso's enrollment was down almost 10 percent, Dallas was down about 7 percent, Kansas City was down about 8.5 percent, and Anchorage was down about 9 percent.

In addition, several districts decided to administer their interim assess-ments at the beginning of the school year to get an early fix on how far behind students were. Districts like Dallas, Atlanta, Des Moines, and Cleveland re-ported significant academic learning loss, particularly in mathematics.

The public, for its part, was of mixed minds about what they were see-ing from their schools. Decisions about whether to open or close schools, require masks, and mandate social distancing in addition to screen time and COVID-19 testing all created debate, controversy, and passion. Most districts reported that parent engagement was at an all-time high but that parent anxiety had waned at least briefly as clarity was emerging about their children, and people settled into new routines.

Political and partisan differences, however, soon began feeding the pub-lic's temperature, as the nation headed into the 2020 November elections. And schools were seeing some of the first signs of cultural issues spilling into their territory. Library books, gender identity, mandatory masks, critical race theory, and parental rights were all emerging as hot-button political issues, and school board meetings were becoming intolerably hostile.

Adding to the frustration among the superintendents, school board members, and staff was the mixed signals they were getting from the federal government and the states about when to open or close schools. There was no protocol or toolkits coming from the White House, Department of Education, CDC, or anyone else that laid out clearly the criteria for keeping children and adults safe in school despite the emerging data suggesting that schools were not hot spots. Eventually, the superintendents developed their own protocol and distributed it to each other.[6]

Most big-city school superintendents believed as they were starting school virtually that fall that the public was largely with them, despite the clamor and fall off in enrollments. Of special interest at this time was the differing responses to closures that the districts were seeing by race. African Americans, Hispanics, and Whites were often in different places when it came to reopening. African American parents, for instance, appeared more reticent to send their children back into the buildings.

Pedro Martinez, who was then superintendent of the San Antonio schools, was quick to remind his colleagues to "do the right thing for students, do what will allow you to sleep at night, tell everyone who will listen about it, and get up tomorrow and do it again."

FALL AND WINTER 2020

Despite the closures and online instruction during the fall of 2020, districts found ways to partially open some schools in less-infected areas, set up instructional pods and hubs for fragile students, and provide some remedial instruction for students who needed tutoring. Many districts, however, found that they had to reclose some of the reopened schools midway through the semester as infections in some parts of the cities rose and resistance to reopening by some continued.

By the time the fall semester ended, the districts had discussed and worked through thousands of problems large and small—from air quality and ventilation to teacher shortages and grading practices—but it was still clear that the upheaval from the pandemic had taken a toll on district staff and teachers, students, parents, and the public. At the same time, districts were experiencing a sense of renewal and hope as the national elections foretold new political leadership in the White House and Congress, a new aid package of approximately $54 billion was on the cusp of approval, and a COVID-19 vaccine was about to be launched. President-elect Biden's desire to get the schools open was the first real signal to district leaders that their long struggle to reopen the buildings had an ally in high places. And Council staff began assembling their recommendations to the new Biden education transition team.[7]

Most superintendents and outside researchers continued to report that schools did not drive community infection rates, but everyone wanted teachers and school staff to be among the first in line for the new vaccines. The Council and its member districts stated publicly that they were in favor of having teachers go first whenever a vaccine became available, which it did in December 2020.

On one of the last calls of 2020, Orlando school board member Teresa Jacobs remarked that "we only get stronger through adversity, and I am grateful for life, for the patience and generosity that everyone has shown on these calls, and for our communities." There was an audible "amen" from the group, for everyone was ready for a holiday break.

The calendar turned uneventfully on January 1, 2021, but the calm was broken less than a week later when allies of the outgoing president stormed the US Capitol in Washington. To educators in the major cities and elsewhere across the country, the incident told youth that the country was not stable and that the chaos they were seeing at some of their school board meetings was becoming a new normal. It did not take students long to draw parallels with their own experiences, because both superintendents and school board members reported that January that they were seeing rising rates of gun violence and mental health breakdowns in their communities. And students could see the lack of public civility everywhere.

Public trust in our institutions, including schools, seemed to be at a low ebb.

Still, the nation's urban public schools were eager to throw their resources and expertise into the struggle to bolster democracy, support civility, fight the global pandemic, teach the children, and keep everyone healthy and safe as best we could.

THE VACCINATION CAMPAIGN

On January 22, 2021, the Council of the Great City Schools wrote to President Biden volunteering our twelve thousand schools to the nation as vaccination centers, arguing that our schools were in every corner of our urban communities and could help address potential inequities in vaccine distribution. The White House never formally took us up on the offer, but the proposal made it clear that the nation's major urban public schools could be a significant player in vaccinating the American people, ending the pandemic more quickly, and getting our schools open faster.

Even without formal support from the White House, the nation's urban schools took the initiative in the vaccination effort. The Albuquerque schools began vaccinating city residents in conjunction with their healthcare agencies when the vaccine first became available at the local level. Anchorage was one of the first school districts in the nation to provide vaccine sites for its community. The Cleveland school district provided round-trip transportation from fifteen of its high schools to the city's Wolstein Center for students, families, and community members that were interested in receiving the COVID-19 vaccine. The Dayton schools partnered with the Dayton Children's Hospital in Ohio to have in-school vaccination clinics for both students and their family members.

In concert with community health partners at the Detroit Health Department, Henry Ford Health System, Ascension Health, and the NAACP Youth Council, the Detroit school district launched its Teens for Vaccines campaign. The initiative provided vaccine education and accessibility to COVID-19 vaccines for district teachers, staff, families, and eligible students. In East Baton Rouge, the school district worked with the mayor's office and LDH and OLOL Hospital to provide individuals twelve and older with vaccines at ten high schools.

The Houston Independent School District (HISD) partnered with the City of Houston Health Department, Texas Medical Center Partners, and elected officials to host in-school COVID-19 vaccination clinics for both students and families. All HISD nurses were trained to administer the vaccination at district schools. The Newark Public Schools in New Jersey hosted testing and vaccination locations for community residents and all district, private, parochial, and charter school employees.

The stories were similar in Birmingham and Oklahoma City and Orlando and Pittsburgh and St. Louis and Seattle and every major city school system across the country. There is no way to know exactly how many people were vaccinated because the schools stepped up, but the numbers reached into the millions.

The Council's superintendents and board members continued to coordinate their work on the weekly calls through the first half of 2021 and kept White House staff and the COVID Collaborative, led by John "Bridge" Bridgeland, informed of their efforts. No major daily newspaper anywhere in the nation ever covered what urban schools across the country were doing to vaccinate the public, although *Education Week*, to its credit, ran a story about Anchorage.[8]

By the first week in March 2021, districts were reporting that between 50 and 75 percent of their teachers had been vaccinated.

THE BLESSING AND CHALLENGE OF FEDERAL AID

Later that same month, Congress approved and President Biden signed the third tranche of funding for schools. The aid package, the American Rescue Plan, included $122 billion for schools, 20 percent of which had to be spent on learning loss. The Council estimated that its members would receive somewhere around $50 billion from the three tranches of funding.

House Education and Labor Committee chair Bobby Scott came remotely to the Council's legislative conference that March and said bluntly to the assembled urban school leaders of the new largess, "Don't screw it up."

The aid was unprecedented, but it came with new challenges. Districts were required to spend these exceptional amounts by September 2024, do it in a way that was sustainable, coordinate it with aid to states, counties, and local governments whose aid expired on a different date, and do so quickly without making it look like you were spending indiscriminately.

Consequently, the Council immediately assembled a national task force to formulate a model plan for how urban schools could use the new dollars most effectively and efficiently. The task force included working groups of school board members, superintendents, chief academic officers, chief financial officers, chief information officers, communications directors, and others. The Council released its final guidance, *Investing American Rescue Plan Funds Strategically and Effectively: Guidance for School Districts*, in June that year and circulated it widely.

Discussions among urban school leaders that spring turned to postponing end-of-year state testing, procedures to involve the public on ways to spend the new federal dollars; efforts to vaccinate staff, students, and the citizenry; uses of the first two packages of federal aid; mental health challenges; and policies for promoting and graduating students.

Meanwhile, the Council partnered with Walmart Pharmacies to provide supplemental assistance to districts that needed aid in vaccinating teachers and others, and the group successfully argued to the National Assessment Governing Board for a one-year delay in administering NAEP. And one of the group's own, who had participated in the weekly superintendent calls—Cindy Marten, superintendent of the San Diego schools—was named Deputy Secretary of Education.

SPRING 2021

Many of the districts had reopened at least some of their schools in late winter and early spring of 2021, although the public was conflicted about it, and resistance from the teacher organizations continued. Minneapolis found in a survey that 65 percent of families wanted the elementary schools to open, but the teacher group filed a temporary restraining order, arguing that reopening would constitute an unfair labor practice.

The issue of unfinished learning was a major issue as schools began to reopen that spring, especially at the elementary grade levels. The Council issued a report on unfinished learning and how to address it while keeping students at grade level. But the districts were also working on tutoring strategies, extended-time instruction, enrichment and acceleration efforts, digital support, and intercessions as ways to regain what students had lost.

Barbara Jenkins from Orlando, Jill Baker from Long Beach, Janice Jackson from Chicago, Deborah Gist from Tulsa, and others were particularly good on the weekly calls at helping their colleagues think through the academic strategies to use. Leaders were becoming increasingly excited about the new resources heading their way and what they could do with them to stem unfinished learning, address social-emotional needs, fix facilities, and stabilize their technology systems.

Planning turned to virtual graduations, summer school, hiring for the 2021–2022 school year, and the possibility of permanent blended schooling. High school graduations went well that spring, but the decline in enrollment was on everyone's minds for next year.

A NEW SCHOOL YEAR

Most of the nation's urban school systems opened in person in the fall of 2021, although hybrid instruction was an option for students and families in many places. Some districts, like Cleveland, set up their own virtual high schools to compete with online charters that were emerging. Enrollment continued to be lower compared to prepandemic levels, but there was a sense of normalcy as the school year began and the pandemic was on the wane.

The sense of routine was soon broken, however, as the Delta and Omicron variants of COVID-19 swept the nation later that summer and fall, and school closures began again. This time, the infection rates across the country were worse than ever, with numbers peaking in January and February of 2022. By May, one million Americans were dead from the pandemic.

TURNING THE PAGE: 2020 IN THE REARVIEW MIRROR

The COVID-19 years had taken a harsh toll on urban school systems. Of the seventy-eight big-city school superintendents in the Council alliance, many did not make it through the entire pandemic. In fact, most of them reported that the 2021–2022 school year was the hardest and most difficult of their professional careers. Untold numbers of urban school board members decided not to run for reelection. And over a quarter million students lost a parent or guardian to the disease.

People were exhausted from the experience, but leaders also found that the big-city school districts held fast, although badly bruised, under their stewardship. They had set up the processes they needed to think through their options and mull over the consequences when ready answers to the crisis were not at hand. Michael O'Neill, the Boston School Committee member who chaired the Council during the 2020–2021 school year, said, "This may be the most important year that we have ever had as urban educators." He was right. The challenges were unlike anything we had ever experienced before.

The discussions among the nation's urban school leaders about what to do in response to the global pandemic started in March 2020 with a stark set of choices about whether to do anything. We could have cast ourselves as victims of the disease as so many others did. We could have decided to do the minimum and just sat out the pandemic.

Instead, one can see that the leaders of these often-cash-poor districts decided to do the opposite and devote everything they had and more to support their students, staff, and communities. One can see the trajectory of their deliberations around every detail of how these large organizations functioned. And one can see that leaders understood that the ground was shifting under them. At the same time, one can see that for the better part of three years, urban school leaders were sidetracked from their central priority of improving classroom instruction to managing a crisis that no one knew how to handle.

In a matter of a few years, the institution had been rocked in ways both profound and trivial. The nation's urban school leaders grasped the implications and did everything in their power to put their schools into a position to thrive in a new world after the pandemic subsided. In my opinion, the nation should be grateful for the determination and courage of so many local leaders. They were not flawless, to be sure, but it is hard to imagine what any other group of leaders might have done in their shoes.

The nation faces the question why a disaster of this magnitude fell so disproportionately on school officials and others at the local level. The ineptitude and confusion of the federal government over much of this time and the muddled leadership of many of the states left local leaders flying blind as to how to respond. It need not have been this way in a country with such talent and expertise.[9] Urban school leaders did not handle everything expertly, but the fact that they banded together at the outset of the crisis and stuck together throughout helped them and their communities weather the storm like nothing else could have. The fact that they worked together not only held the institution together, however damaged, but allowed our schools the capacity to build back more effectively for the future.

When Dutch Leonard and Arnold Howitt, the Harvard business school experts, talked at the beginning of the pandemic about the need to set up processes during crises for which there were no procedures, this is what they meant. Urban school leaders set up those processes to collaborate on challenges that no one saw coming and no one had a playbook for. And they did it as well as anyone could have.

In chapter 7 we look at the effects of the pandemic on our students. After that, we look to the future.

7

Effects of the Pandemic and District Responses

By the Numbers

When the nation's big-city school superintendents met in March 2020 to discuss how to respond to the pandemic, many predicted that the next year or so would be among the toughest periods that any of them had ever faced. They were right.

The three years between 2020 and 2023 brought unprecedented challenges to America's system of public education. An editorial by the *New York Times* asserted that the "pandemic may prove to be the most damaging disruption in the history of American education."[1] There is little in this chapter that will contradict that assessment.

As it turned out, big-city school leaders were better than they thought at managing a crisis of this magnitude. They set up processes that allowed them to think through their options, figure out what they were up against, and see what was working among their colleagues. Still, their efforts to improve classroom instruction, a priority that had defined their work for years, took a backseat to steering their institutions through a crisis of unparalleled dimensions.

At the same time, it is worth remembering that they had learned a thing or two over the decades about how improvement was attained in urban education. They saw that they could address what the pandemic threw at them in ways that few other public institutions could have done.

These districts put the best remote instructional systems into place that they could. They served hundreds of millions of meals to their students, families, and others, no questions asked. They purchased and distributed millions of devices for those who had none. They created internet access for countless families. They devised innovative mental health interventions. They put masking policies into effect to keep students and adults disease free. They stepped up to vaccinate not only their own staff but citizens across their regions. They took in and welcomed refugee children from across the globe who had nowhere else to turn. And they worked to ensure an accurate census count. It was an impressive body of work.

Nonetheless, the pandemic took a significant toll on public schools. The broader public narrative suggested that the nation's urban schools bore the brunt of the pandemic. This was true in some cases but not others. Sometimes the damage was worse in our urban schools than elsewhere; sometimes urban public schools came out better or recovered faster than many others. The experience told us a lot about our strengths and weaknesses.

In this chapter, I summarize the impact the pandemic had on the nation's urban school systems and their students. I look at school district enrollment, attendance, student achievement, and other indicators between 2019 and 2023. I examine how the districts began to respond with the federal funds they received from the American Rescue Plan. And I look at preliminary evidence of an academic rebound in 2023.

WHAT HAPPENED TO STUDENT ENROLLMENT?

Much has been made of the enrollment losses in public education, particularly urban public education, over the pandemic years. Indeed, there were significant declines in the traditional big-city school systems. The Council of the Great City Schools has complete enrollment data for the 2019–2020

Figure 7.1 Enrollment change in preK to 12 grade levels in the Great City Schools between 2019–2020 and 2022–2023

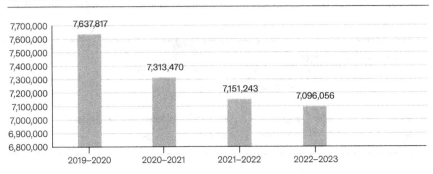

to the 2022–2023 period on its seventy-eight-member urban school systems.[2]

Between 2019–2020 and 2022–2023, pre-K–12 enrollment in these systems dropped by 541,761 students or 7.1 percent (figure 7.1). Most of this decline occurred in the first year of the pandemic, when enrollment fell by 324,347 students or 4.2 percent. The slide during the second year was an additional 162,227 students or 2.2 percent. Data on 2022–2023, however, suggest that the enrollment decline slowed to −0.8 percent, while twenty-seven districts posted gains between 2021–2022 and 2022–2023

The loss of students, however, was uneven from grade to grade. During the first year of the pandemic, the number of kindergarten pupils fell by 12.3 percent.[3] Likewise, the number of kindergarten students ticked up by 2.8 percent in the second year of the pandemic but fell again by 1.6 percent in 2022–2023, leaving kindergarten enrollment some 11.3 percent lower than before the pandemic (figure 7.2).

In other grades, changes between 2019–2020 and 2022–2023 ranged from a decline of 11.0 percent in grade 2 to an increase of 1.3 percent in grade 10. Enrollments were down most in grades preK to 7 but less so in grades 8 to 12. Grade 10 was the only grade higher in 2022–2023 than before the pandemic (figure 7.2).

Figure 7.2 Enrollment changes in the Great City Schools by grade between 2019–2020 and 2022–2023

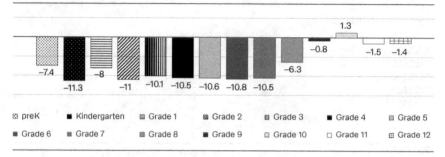

Table 7.1 Percentages of Great City School students by race/ethnicity, 2019–2020 to 2022–2023

	% Black	% Hispanic	% White	% Asian
Great City Schools				
2019–2020	25.8	43.5	18.5	7.0
2020–2021	25.8	43.7	18.2	7.0
2021–2022	25.5	44.0	18.0	6.9
2022–2023	25.2	44.4	17.8	6.8

Source: Council of the Great City Schools, https://www.cgcs.org/enrollmentdashboard.

We also have data by race and free or reduced price lunch (FRPL) status on urban school enrollment through 2022–2023, but data on English language learners (ELLs) and students with disabilities only through 2021–2022. Intriguingly, the demographic composition of the Great City Schools remained about the same over the pandemic years, but there were exceptions. For instance, there were slight declines in the percentages of Black, White, and Asian American students in these urban school systems, but there was a slight increase in the percentage of Hispanic students in these districts (tables 7.1 and 7.2).

The percentages of ELLs, students with disabilities or those with individualized education plans (IEPs), and students from low-income families or FRPL-eligible students increased only slightly over the same period.

Finally, changes in enrollments were uneven from city to city between 2019–2020 and 2022–2023. The enrollments in East Baton Rouge,

Table 7.2 Percentages of Great City School students by language status andindividualized education plan (IEP) status, 2019–2020 to 2021–2022, and FRPL status, 2019–2020 to 2022–2023

	% ELL	% IEP	% FRPL
Great City Schools			
2019–2020	15.9	16.6	71.7
2020–2021	15.7	16.9	NA
2021–2022	16.8	17.0	71.0
2022–2023	NA	NA	72.7

Source: Council of the Great City Schools, https://www.cgcs.org/enrollmentdashboard.

Phoenix Union, Newark, Hillsborough County, and New Orleans, for instance, increased slightly between 2019–2020 and 2022–2023. All other districts fell by differing degrees. The declines ranged from a loss of –0.6 percent in Orange County (Orlando) to –16.9 percent in Jackson, MS (table 7.3).

Where did the students go? More research is needed to answer this question, but the preliminary evidence suggests that they were homeschooled, went to charter or private schools, or left the cities. The National Alliance for Public Charter Schools reported that between 2019–2020 and 2020–2021 charter school enrollment increased by 240,000 students, or 7 percent, and it held steady in 2021–2022.[4] The *Washington Post* reported that, in the thirty-two states that kept comparable data, there had been a 51-percent increase in the numbers of students being homeschooled between 2017–2018 and 2022–2023, with the biggest spike in participation in 2020–2021.[5] The same article refers to a 7-percent increase over the period in private school enrollment. And the Brookings Institution reported in 2022 that there were outsized population losses across the 88 US cities with populations of 250,000 or more people in 2020–2021.[6]

It is not clear whether this pattern is temporary or it signals a permanent shift in the enrollments of big-city public schools. Of course, the population of cities and their public schools have waxed and waned over the years due to changes in the economy, the housing market, domestic migration, birth rates, and immigration. I expect these factors and the effects

Table 7.3 Percent enrollment changes by city between 2019–2020 and 2022–2023

Districts that increased enrollment	Districts that decreased enrollment 0.0% to 5.0%	Districts that decreased enrollment 5.1% to 10%	Districts that decreased enrollment 10.1% or more
East Baton Rouge (+4.8)	Orange County (−0.6)	Wichita (−5.1)	St. Paul (−10.2)
Phoenix Union (+1.1)	Charleston (−0.7%)	Tulsa (−5.1)	Los Angeles (−11.5)
Newark (+0.8%)	Cincinnati (−1.2)	Jefferson County (−5.1)	New York (−11.5)
Hillsborough County (+0.6)	Duval County (−1.2)	Anchorage (−5.2)	Pittsburgh (−11.6)
New Orleans (+0.1)	Fresno (−2.1)	Guilford County (−5.2)	Fort Worth (−12.2)
	DC (−2.5)	Broward Cty (−5.4)	Santa Ana (−12.4)
	Memphis (−3.0)	Oakland (−5.5)	Providence (−13.1)
	Dayton (−3.0)	Arlington (−5.7)	St. Louis (−13.8)
	Palm Beach County (−3.0)	Nashville (−5.8)	Indianapolis (−13.9)
	Omaha (−3.2)	Clark County (−5.9)	Puerto Rico (−14.0)
	Winston-Salem (−3.4)	Hawaii (−6.0)	Rochester (−15.2)
	Charlotte (−3.7)	Pinellas County (−6.1)	Minneapolis (−15.6)
	Miami-Dade County (−3.8)	San Antonio (−6.8)	Richmond (−16.2)
	Bridgeport (−3.8)	Columbus, OH (−7.0)	Jackson, MS (−16.9)
	Baltimore (−4.0)	Birmingham (−7.0)	
	Atlanta (−4.0)	Chicago (−7.4)	
	Detroit (−4.2)	Oklahoma City (−7.4)	
	Washoe County (−4.2)	San Francisco (−7.6)	
	Fayette County (−4.4)	Little Rock (−7.7)	
	Denver (−4.6)	Portland, OR (−7.9)	
	Toledo (−4.7)	Des Moines (−8.0)	
	Kansas City (−4.8)	Sacramento (−8.1)	

Table 7.3 (*Continued*)

Districts that increased enrollment	Districts that decreased enrollment 0.0% to 5.0%	Districts that decreased enrollment 5.1% to 10%	Districts that decreased enrollment 10.1% or more
	Aurora (−4.9)	San Diego (−8.2)	
		Dallas (−8.3)	
		Boston (−8.3)	
		Norfolk (−8.5)	
		Seattle (−8.5)	
		Cleveland (−8.5)	
		Long Beach (−8.6)	
		Austin (−9.3)	
		Philadelphia (−9.4)	
		Buffalo (−9.5)	
		El Paso (−9.5)	
		Albuquerque (−9.6)	
		Milwaukee (−9.6)	
		Houston (−9.6)	

Source: Council of the Great City Schools, https://www.cgcs.org/enrollmentdashboard.

of an emerging alternative sector to continue affecting public school enrollments in the future.

WHAT WERE THE EFFECTS ON ATTENDANCE?

The effects of the pandemic were not limited to enrollment. Student attendance in the nation's major cities—and nationwide—was significantly altered. Here we look at data collected by the Council of the Great City Schools between 2019 and 2022.

The Council collected absenteeism data or Key Performance Indicators (KPIs) on grades 3, 6, 8, and 9 on students who were absent five to nine days, ten to nineteen days, or twenty or more days cumulatively over the course of the school year.[7] The following table summarizes the number of responding districts where absenteeism of twenty or more days fell into specified ranges (table 7.4).

Table 7.4 Number of districts whose students were absent twenty or more days, by grade and year

	Grade 3		Grade 6		Grade 8		Grade 9	
	2019	2022	2019	2022	2019	2022	2019	2022
70 and over	0	0	0	0	0	0	0	0
60%–69%	0	1	0	1	0	1	0	3
50%–59%	0	0	0	1	0	1	2	0
40%–49%	0	2	0	1	0	1	1	6
30%–39%	2	5	2	5	3	14	2	20
20%–29%	4	22	3	25	4	23	15	19
10%–19%	16	18	13	15	26	9	21	2
Less 10%	20	1	21	1	9	0	1	0
Total districts	42	49	39	49	42	49	42	50

One can read the table this way: of the forty-nine major urban school systems on which we have data on third grade, twenty-two of them had average absenteeism rates of twenty or more days that was between 20 and 29 percent in 2022, compared with only four districts in 2019.

Absenteeism rates at this level ranged across districts from 12.8 percent to 68.2 percent among third-grade students in 2022. In 2019 the range was 4 percent to 35 percent. The median rate in 2022 was 25.8 percent, up from 9 percent in 2019.

In grade 6, this high level of absenteeism ranged from 9.6 percent to 66.2 percent, with a median rate of 25.9 percent in 2022. This was an increase from 2019 when the range was 4 percent to 35 percent, with a median of 10 percent.

In grade 8, absenteeism at this level ranged from 14.7 percent in 2022 to 66.0 percent, with a median rate of 23 percent. In 2019 the range was 7 percent to 38 percent, with a median of 12 percent.

And in grade 9, this absenteeism ranged from 12.0 percent to 66.1 percent, with a median of 28.4—up from a range of 6 percent to 52 percent in 2019 and a median of 12 percent. In other words, high absenteeism across these urban school systems more than doubled during the pandemic, a situation that is bound to affect student achievement.

Unfortunately, absenteeism rates were higher still among student groups of special concern. For instance, while the overall chronic absenteeism rate among third graders in 2022 was 25.8 percent, the median chronic absenteeism rate among urban African American male students in the third grade was 31.0 percent. In other words, almost one-third of African American third-grade males were absent for more than 20 days in the 2022 school year. The median rate among third-grade ELLs was 25.5 percent, and the rate among third-grade students with disabilities was 26.3 percent.

Absenteeism is not a problem solely in the nation's big city schools, it is a national phenomenon. But the situation appears to be more severe in the nation's urban schools.

HOW EXTENSIVE WAS TEACHER TURNOVER?

Nationwide teacher shortages have garnered a lot of attention since the pandemic. Researchers disagree on the existence and degree of the problem. Unfortunately, there is not a database on the big-city public schools that would settle the debate once and for all, but there is a long-standing database on teacher retention in the big-city schools after one, two, three, four, and five years of hiring.[8]

The data from the most recent report indicate that, between 2018–2019 and 2021–2022, the percentage of newly hired teachers who were retained by their urban school districts fell after one year from 78 percent to 73 percent. Even districts in the highest-performing quartile[9] on this key performance indicator reported a fall-off in their teachers retained, from 87 percent to 80 percent. Districts in the lowest-performing quartile on this indicator reported falling from 72 percent after one year to 64 percent.

Interestingly, the data do not suggest a decline in retention rates among teachers who were hired two, three, four, and five years ago. The median two-year teacher retention rate in the big-city public schools increased slightly between 2018–2019 and 2021–2022, although there were dips among the highest and lowest quartiles between 2020–2021 and 2021–2022. Teacher retention rates after three years remained steady at about 60 percent.

After four years, the median rates held at about 55 percent, and after five years, the rates remained around 50 percent.

These numbers do not suggest that there were no shortages, however. They indicate that districts had a harder time holding onto their most recently hired teachers. And the data on individual cities indicate that some cities had more difficulty than others. Any shortages would have been on top of the ongoing problems urban districts have in recruiting math, science, bilingual, and special education teachers.

In addition, the database indicates that the districts struggled to place substitute teachers when regular teachers were absent during the pandemic. The data show that the percentage of student attendance days where a substitute teacher was successfully placed in a classroom fell from 77 percent in 2018–2019 to 59 percent in 2021–2022. On top of that, the percentage of substitutes with an undergraduate degree fell from 88 percent in 2018–2019 to 73 percent in 2021–2022.

WAS THERE CHURN AMONG SUPERINTENDENTS?

There has been considerable speculation about the turnover of urban school superintendents during the pandemic as well. Turnover in the superintendency in big-city schools is normally high compared with other kinds of public school systems. What we saw during the pandemic was something different, though. In March 2020 the Council of the Great City Schools had seventy-six members, each one with a superintendent, CEO, or chancellor. At the time this book was written, only thirteen of those remained in the same jobs, in the same districts.[10]

In other words, only fifteen of the seventy-six (22.4 percent) Great City School superintendents who were leading one of these big-city school districts in March 2020 were still in office when this book was written. It was a time of unprecedented turnover of urban school leaders. In the almost thirty years that I headed the organization, I never saw more than twenty districts experience superintendent turn over at any one time. In this case, over sixty districts did.

Despite the extraordinary turnover in superintendents in the nation's major cities, the demographic composition of the group remained about the same. By the fall of 2023, forty-eight of the seventy-eight superintendents (61.5 percent) were male and thirty (38.5 percent) were female. In addition, thirty-seven (47.4 percent) of the superintendents were African American, twenty-three (29.5 percent) were White, seventeen (35.4 percent) were Hispanic, and one was Hawaiian Native.

Obviously, some of the leaders who left their districts were at the end of their tenures. Some were worn out from the pandemic; some were the victims of the culture wars; and some simply retired. Whatever the reason, a considerable amount of talent and experience was lost. It was one of the reasons why I decided to write this book. We were at risk of losing too many lessons at exactly the time urban education is trying to recover.

HOW DID THE PANDEMIC EFFECT MENTAL HEALTH, SAFETY, AND SECURITY?

Staff, teachers, and students routinely report that their mental health and social-emotional well-being were affected by the pandemic. At a town hall meeting held at the annual conference of the Council of the Great City Schools in the fall of 2023, big-city school students from across the country passionately voiced their concerns about how the pandemic, the isolation, and the overall global upheaval were affecting them and how their anxieties were accelerated by the ubiquitous nature of technology and social media.

Unfortunately, there are not good quantifiable indicators on student mental health in the big-city public schools, but sometimes mental health and social/emotional problems will show up in a school district's safety and security data.

The same Council member KPI performance management database that has information on teacher retention rates also has data on safety and security incidents in schools and suspensions.[11] The data on assault and battery incidents per one thousand students in the big-city public schools indicate that rates fell from 7.0 incidents in 2018–2019 to 0.9 incidents in 2020–2021 but they spiked in 2021–2022 to 4.4 incidents per 1,000 students when more children were back in school.

Over the same period, the overall number of "people-related" security incidents fell from a median of 34.2 incidents per 1,000 students in 2018–2019 to 14.0 in 2020–2021 before rising again in 2021–2022 to 15.5. And the total number of bullying or harassment incidents dropped from a median of 2.4 incidents per 1,000 students in 2018–2019 to 0.5 incidents in 2020–2021, when most students were not in school—before increasing again to a median of 1.9 incidents in 2021–2022.

Suspensions also declined in 2020–2021, but there were significant spikes in 2021–2022, and in some cases suspension rates were higher than before the pandemic.

Overall, the number of reportable incidents in the schools over the pandemic was low, probably because schools were often closed, and students were typically at home or on the streets. And most incident rates have not returned to what they were before the pandemic. Still, these are only indirect measures of mental health and do not specifically address the emotional and psychological effects that many students are facing. It is this toll that schools will be dealing with for years to come.

HOW MUCH LEARNING WAS LOST?

As we saw in chapter 2, reading and math scores on the NAEP went up significantly in the Large City Schools and many individual urban school districts between 2003 and 2019. In fact, the improvements were substantial enough to narrow the gap between these schools and the rest of the country by almost half. The data also showed that the Large City Schools and many individual urban school districts were producing an educational effect that was larger than other schools once one considered the differences in the demographics of students served by these school systems.[12]

The 2022 results on the NAEP, however, showed significant declines both nationally and in the Large City Schools. What most coverage missed

Table 7.5 Differences in NAEP scale scores by subject and grade between the national public and Large City School samples, 2019–2022

	National public sample		Large City Schools		Difference: national public and Large City Schools	
	2019	2022	2019	2022	2019	2022
Reading						
Grade 4	219.4	216.1	211.7	208.9	7.8	7.2
Grade 8	262.0	259.1	254.7	254.9	7.3	4.2
Mathematics						
Grade 4	240.0	234.9	234.8	226.6	5.2	8.3
Grade 8	281.0	273.1	274.2	266.5	6.8	6.7

was that the gap between the nation and the Large City Schools did not widen for the most part. Table 7.5 shows NAEP scores in reading and mathematics in grades 4 and 8 in 2019 and 2022 for both the national public sample and the Large City public schools and the differences between the two groups over time.[13]

The results show the national sample of fourth graders declined about three scale score points in reading and approximately five scale score points in mathematics between 2019 and 2022. The drop among eighth graders nationally was about three and eight points, respectively. These declines were large enough to have wiped out the modest gains that the nation had made over about the last twenty years.

The Large City Schools also saw declines, although the pattern was different. The large city fourth graders declined by 2.8 scale score points in reading and 8.2 points in math. Large city eighth graders did not see any significant change in their reading performance over the pandemic, unlike the nation's average public school performance, but it saw a 7.7-point decline in mathematics, about the same decline as the nation at large. The losses in mathematics among the large cities were large enough to take their scale scores back to approximately 2005, while the losses in reading took the scores back to 2007 in grade 4.

Another way to look at the differing effects of the pandemic on the nation and the Large City Schools is to look at the differences between the two before the pandemic and afterward. One can see from the two far right-hand columns in table 7.5 that the large cities were 7.8 scale score points behind the national sample in fourth-grade reading and 7.3 points behind in eighth grade reading in 2019. By 2022, the Large City Schools were 7.2 points behind the national average in fourth-grade reading and only 4.2 points behind in eighth-grade reading. In math, Large City School fourth graders were 5.2 points behind the nation in 2019 but 8.3 points behind in 2022, losing ground. And Large City School eighth graders were 6.8 points behind in 2019 and 6.7 points behind in 2022.

In other words, the Large City Schools either made up ground nominally on the national average or held steady in three grade-subject combinations and lost ground in one. The large city school losses mirrored those of the nation in some respects, but they also showed some strength that was not apparent in the national discourse about the results.

As with the enrollment, the changes in NAEP results over the pandemic varied from city to city. Table 7.6 shows changes among Trial Urban District Assessment (TUDA) districts on NAEP scale score points between 2019 and 2022, ranked in the left-hand column by their changes in fourth-grade reading.

In fourth-grade reading between 2019 and 2022, fourteen of the twenty-six participating large city school systems either nominally gained NAEP scale score points or lost no more points than did the nation, while twelve large city school systems lost more scale score points at least nominally than the nation at large.[14] In eighth-grade reading, twenty large city school systems either nominally gained scale score points or lost no more than the nation at large, while only six districts lost more scale score points than the nation.

In math, the Large City Schools lost ground on the nation in the fourth grade, and only four cities lost less nominally than the national average. At the eighth-grade level in math, thirteen cities lost less ground than the nation at large, while thirteen cities lost more.

All in all, the changes between 2019 and 2022 were better than or the same as the national average in all four grade/subject combinations in three

Table 7.6 changes among TUDA cities on NAEP scale scores by city, grade, and subject, 2019–2022

City	Scale score point change in grade 4 reading	Scale score point change in grade 8 reading	Scale score point change in grade 4 math	Scale score point change in grade 8 math
Austin	+3.7	−2.9	−4.1	−9.3*
Hillsborough County	+2.5	−1.9	−1.3	−7.1*
Los Angeles	+2.2	+9.4*	−3.7*	+1.7
Dallas	−0.1	−0.4	−3.4	−4.1*
Miami-Dade County	−0.3	+0.4	−5.3*	−1.9
DC	−1.0	−1.7	−11.2*	−11.7*
San Diego	−1.0	−2.0	−8.2*	−8.3*
New York City	−1.1	+0.7	−8.9*	−4.0
Houston	−1.6	−2.0	−9.4*	−9.4*
Philadelphia	−2.0	−1.1	−8.1*	−4.1
Milwaukee	−2.1	−0.8	−9.2*	−6.0*
Albuquerque	−2.5	−0.8	−6.5*	−6.8*
Large City Schools	−2.7*	+0.2	−8.3*	−7.8*
Boston	−3.3	−2.1	−7.0*	−8.9*
Chicago	−3.3	−1.4	−10.3*	−12.2*
National public	−3.3*	−2.9*	−5.1*	−7.9*
Jefferson County	−3.4	−4.3*	−8.3*	−10.7*
Fort Worth	−3.6	−0.6	−7.1*	−6.0*
Denver	−4.7	−1.8	−7.7*	−10.7*
Detroit	−6.1*	−4.6	−11.7*	−6.3*
Guilford County	−7.1*	−6.1*	−7.2*	−10.1*
Duval County	−7.3*	+0.2	−7.3*	−4.9*
Shelby County	−7.8*	−6.4*	−11.8*	−14.4*
Baltimore	−7.9*	−0.4	−15.4*	−8.8*
Clark County	−8.0*	+0.3	−9.2*	−4.8*
Atlanta	−8.1*	−1.4	−7.1*	−5.5*
Charlotte	−9.6*	−3.8	−12.7*	−10.5*
Cleveland	−16.5*	−7.1*	−14.9*	−8.4*

* Change is significant at $p < .05$.

urban districts (Hillsborough County, Los Angeles, Dallas), while five districts lost more ground than the nation in all four grades and subjects (Charlotte-Mecklenburg, Cleveland, Guilford County, Jefferson County, and Shelby County).

The 2022 results also showed substantial variations in how the pandemic years affected large city school results by race. The modest increases that both the Large City Schools and the national public sample saw in reading scores of African American fourth graders between 2003 and 2019 had largely evaporated in 2022. On the other hand, most of the gains among Hispanic students between 2003 and 2019 were retained in the Large City Schools, while Asian American students moved forward in both the Large City Schools and the national public sample (table 7.7).

The following tables summarize the net scale score changes by subject and grade of students in Large City Schools and the national public sample by race.

Table 7.7 Net NAEP scale score changes in fourth-grade reading in Large City Schools and the national public sample by race between 2003–2019 and 2019–2022

4th-grade reading	Scale score point change 2003–2019	Scale score point change 2019–2022	Net point change 2003–2022
African American			
Large City Schools	+6.5*	−5.9*	+0.6
National public	+5.7*	−4.8*	+0.9
Hispanic			
Large City Schools	+7.9*	−2.7	+5.2*
National public	+8.8*	−3.9*	+4.9*
Asian American			
Large City Schools	+6.0	+1.1	+7.2*
National public	+12.7*	+1.3	+13.9*
White			
Large City Schools	+5.2*	+1.7	+6.9*
National public	+2.2*	−3.3*	−1.1

* Change is significant at $p < .05$.

Table 7.8 Net NAEP scale score changes in eighth-grade reading in Large City Schools and the national public sample by race between 2003–2019 and 2019–2022

8th-grade reading	Scale score point change 2003–2019	Scale score point change 2019–2022	Net point change 2003–2022
African American			
Large City Schools	+0.5	+0.9	+1.4
National public	+0.2	−1.1	−0.8
Hispanic			
Large City Schools	+8.3*	+0.3	+8.7*
National public	+7.3*	−1.3	+6.0*
Asian American			
Large City Schools	+14.9*	+0.7	+15.6*
National public	+12.9*	−0.2	+12.7*
White			
Large City Schools	+6.2*	−2.5	+3.7*
National public	+0.8	−4.1*	−3.3*

* Change is significant at $p < .05$.

- In the eighth grade, the fall-off in NAEP reading scores between 2019 and 2022 was not as great by race as that in the fourth-grade except for White students. By and large, none of the racial groups in the Large City Schools declined between 2019 and 2022 as much as the same groups did in the national public school sample (table 7.8).
- In fourth-grade math, there were substantial declines in every racial group in 2022, but the declines were more severe in the Large City Schools than they were in the national public school sample. These were students that would have been in second grade when the pandemic started (table 7.9).
- Finally, in eighth-grade math, the decline in NAEP scores was greater between 2019 and 2022 in the Large City Schools among African American, Asian American, and White students than was the case in the national sample. The large city schools lost less ground nominally among Hispanic students than the nation (table 7.10).

Table 7.9 Net NAEP scale score changes in fourth-grade math in Large City Schools and the national public sample by race between 2003–2019 and 2019–2022

4th-grade math	Scale score point change 2003–2019	Scale score point change 2019–2022	Net point change 2003–2022
African American			
Large City Schools	+9.3*	−9.1*	+0.2
National public	+8.0*	−7.4*	+0.7
Hispanic			
Large City Schools	+10.6*	−8.6*	+2.0
National public	+9.2*	−7.0*	+2.2*
Asian American			
Large City Schools	+12.4*	−12.5*	−0.1
National public	+14.9*	−3.9*	+11.0*
White			
Large City Schools	+9.0*	−4.7*	+4.3*
National public	+5.8*	−3.7*	+2.1*

* Change is significant at $p < .05$.

Overall, African American students in the large city schools fared worse than any other group during the pandemic, except in eighth-grade reading, and Asian American students in the large cities lost the most ground in math.

There were substantial differences among cities in the performance of various income and language groups. Table 7.11 shows gains and losses among students from low-income families in each major city participating in TUDA between 2019 and 2022. The results indicate that students from low-income families in the Large City Schools, on average, held up better nominally than students from low-income families in the national public school sample in fourth- and eighth-grade reading and eighth-grade math, but Large City School fourth-graders from low-income families suffered disproportionately large losses in fourth-grade math compared with the national sample.

Table 7.10 Net NAEP scale score changes in eighth-grade math in Large City Schools and the national public sample by race between 2003–2019 and 2019–2022

8th-grade math	Scale score point change 2003–2019	Scale score point change 2019–2022	Net point change 2003–2022
African American			
Large City Schools	+11.1*	−9.0*	+2.1
National public	+7.5*	−7.1*	+0.3
Hispanic			
Large City Schools	+10.9*	−6.6*	+4.2*
National public	+9.8*	−7.2*	+2.7*
Asian American			
Large City Schools	+26.3*	−12.0*	+14.4*
National public	+20.0*	−5.5*	+14.5*
White			
Large City Schools	+10.8*	−8.1*	+2.7
National public	+4.9*	−7.9*	−2.9*

* Change is significant at $p < .05$.

The story among English language learners was somewhat different (table 7.12). Here, English learners in the major cities mirrored national trends in reading but did somewhat worse than national averages in math among fourth and eighth graders.

In the fourth grade, eleven TUDA cities showed at least a nominal gain in reading performance among ELLs, while thirteen showed declines—only one of which was statistically significant, Charlotte-Mecklenburg. In eighth grade, English learners in twelve cities showed at least nominal gains, while eight showed either nominal or significant declines.

Math losses among urban English learners were larger than the nation in grade 4. Only two urban school districts (Jefferson County and Hillsborough County) showed even nominal increases in their fourth-grade math scores among English learners. All other cities showed either nominal or significant declines. In eighth grade, only six cities showed at least

Table 7.11 Changes in scale scores of students from low-income families by subject, grade, and city, 2019–2022

City	Scale score point change in grade 4 reading	Scale score point change in grade 8 reading	Scale score point change in grade 4 math	Scale score point change in grade 8 math
Miami-Dade County	+0.8	+1.0	−5.3*	−0.9
Austin	+0.6	−2.1	−7.1*	−6.0*
Hillsborough County	+0.4	0.0	−3.9	−4.3
Dallas	+0.1	−1.6	−5.4*	−3.4
New York City	−1.4	−1.4	−9.6*	−3.6
San Diego	−1.5	−2.1	−11.3*	−8.5*
DC	−1.5	+2.5	−12.4*	−9.1*
Milwaukee	−1.8	−2.1	−7.9*	−6.2*
Jefferson County	−2.0	−0.6	−7.6*	−10.7*
Los Angeles	−2.3	+7.7*	−7.7*	+0.6
Houston	−2.8	−2.2	−10.4*	−9.4*
Philadelphia	−2.8	+2.1	−8.5*	−3.2
Boston	−2.8	−3.3	−7.3*	−10.5*
Clark County	−3.0	+8.2*	−4.6*	+2.7
Large City Schools	−3.2*	+1.4	−8.7*	−6.1*
Baltimore	−3.6	+1.9	−13.5*	−7.5*
National public	−4.2*	−1.5*	−6.4*	−6.6*
Albuquerque	−4.7	−1.2	−5.5*	−5.4*
Fort Worth	−4.9	−1.5	−8.5*	−6.4*
Detroit	−5.6	−4.9	−12.2*	−7.7*
Chicago	−6.0*	−1.8	−13.9*	−12.5*
Denver	−6.2*	−0.2	−6.8*	−9.0*
Duval County	−6.9*	−0.2	−8.9*	−5.6*
Shelby County	−8.7*	−6.3*	−12.5*	−12.5*
Guilford County	−9.3*	−6.9*	−9.9*	−7.9*
Atlanta	−11.6*	−3.0	−13.1*	−4.2
Charlotte	−13.0*	−6.1	−16.8*	−8.5*
Cleveland	−16.4*	−5.9*	−14.7*	−6.6*

* Change is significant at $p < .05$.

Table 7.12 Changes in scale scores of English language learners by subject, grade, and city, 2019–2022

City	Scale score point change in grade 4 reading	Scale score point change in grade 8 reading	Scale score point change in grade 4 math	Scale score point change in grade 8 math
Jefferson County	+14.6*	+5.5	+0.4	—
New York City	+9.1*	−1.1	−4.2	−2.2
Hillsborough County	+6.8	—	+0.7	—
Austin	+3.7	+3.1	−8.6*	−5.3
Dallas	+3.6	+4.0	−4.1	−1.2
Milwaukee	+3.3	+14.0	−8.4*	+12.9*
Miami-Dade County	+2.6	−3.3	−3.6	−7.7
Chicago	+2.4	+16.9*	−5.4	+1.5
Los Angeles	+2.4	+7.2	−3.1	+2.7
Houston	+2.2	+4.6	−5.9*	−6.1*
Shelby County	+1.8	—	−5.2	—
National public	−1.2	+4.3*	−4.1*	−1.9
Large City Schools	−1.4	+4.7	−7.2*	−2.1
Denver	−1.9	−3.0	−5.7	−12.6*
DC	−2.0	+0.3	−8.0*	−10.4
Philadelphia	−2.8	−6.2	−3.7	+9.9
Albuquerque	−3.3	+11.2*	−5.6	−1.7
San Diego	−3.9	+6.0	−11.5*	−6.5
Fort Worth	−5.6	+12.2*	−8.6*	+5.0
Clark County	−6.0	−4.0	−9.1*	−7.2*
Boston	−7.2	−4.6	−11.5*	−11.7*
Detroit	−7.7	−3.1	−11.5*	−4.6
Guilford County	−9.0	—	−3.1	—
Cleveland	−13.3	−25.4*	−19.5*	−7.9
Baltimore	−15.7	—	−12.3*	—
Charlotte	−16.3*	+6.1	−14.8*	+5.3
Duval County	—	—	−10.8	—
Atlanta	—	—	—	—

* Change is significant at $p < .05$.

nominal gains in math, but overall losses were somewhat larger than the national average.

In general, these patterns held up if one looked at students from low-income families and African American, low-income and ELL, or low-income and disabled. That is, the scores of the students in each one of these groups in the Large City Schools tended to fall less in reading than their counterparts in the national public sample. At the same time, African American students and ELL students from low-income families in the Large City Schools fell further in math in both grades than did students elsewhere across the country, but students with disabilities from low-income families fell less in the Large Cities than in the national sample.

As I demonstrated at the outset of this discussion, the Large City Schools did not lose any overall ground on the national public school sample, but everyone in both categories dropped significantly. Data from the Education Recovery Scorecard project also demonstrated that test scores in math declined more in districts where schools closed for 90 percent or more of the time than in districts where schools were closed for 10 percent or less of the time.[15] Analysis conducted by the National Center for Education Statistics, however, of NAEP data at the state level and Program for International Student Assessment (PISA) data at the international level found that the correlation between closings and learning loss was weak.[16] I suspect that the more local analysis of schools depicts the more accurate situation.

It is also interesting to note that large city charter schools lost more ground between 2019 and 2022 than did the traditional large city public schools. This may sound unlikely given that so many advocates made such a big deal about the historic achievement decline in the nation's traditional public schools, but the numbers do not lie. (See the appendix.)

For instance, between 2019 and 2022, the math scale scores of fourth graders in independent charter schools in the large cities fell from 238.2 to 228.6, a decline of 9.6 points, while the traditional large city schools fell from 235.0 to 226.9 percent, a drop of 8.1 points. Eighth-grade math scale scores in the independent charters fell from 278.0 to 262.9, a drop of

15.1 points, while traditional large city schools fell from 274.4 to 267.0, a decline of 7.3 points.

Reading scores among fourth graders in large city independent charter schools fell from 217.2 scale score points in 2019 to 214.2 in 2022, or 3.0 points, while the traditional large city schools declined from 211.8 to 209.1, or 2.7 points. And reading scores among eighth graders in independent large city charter schools fell nominally from 256.9 to 256.3, an insignificant 0.6 points, while eighth graders in traditional large city public schools went from 254.9 to 255.0, a nominal increase of 0.1 points.

Finally, there was also a fall-off in other indicators of academic performance in the traditional big-city schools along with the decline in NAEP scores. For instance, between 2018–2019 and 2021–2022, there was a small drop in the percentage of ninth graders with a B or better in all core courses and a small decline in the percentage of students who took one or more Advanced Placement courses.[17] At the same time, there were slight improvements in the percentage of ninth graders who failed one or more core courses; the percentage of ninth graders who had completed Algebra I by the end of ninth grade; the percentage of all AP exam scores that were three or higher; and the four-year cohort graduation rate.

HOW DID URBAN SCHOOL DISTRICTS RESPOND?

In 2020 and 2021 Congress approved some $190 billion in funding for schools across the country to help them make it through the global pandemic. Funding was targeted on school systems with the largest numbers and percentages of students in poverty and was flexible in how local school districts could spend it.

In the spring of 2021, the Council of the Great City Schools formed a national task force to recommend ways to spend the dollars effectively and efficiently.[18] And in 2023, the organization conducted an extensive survey of how the nation's big city public schools used the dollars. Early results show how several cities were spending their federal Elementary and Secondary School Emergency Relief (ESSER) dollars. I describe three examples of districts that had their detailed plans released to the public before many others did. They were particularly good in their comprehensiveness and clarity.

Clark County School District

The pandemic interrupted the five-year strategic plan of the Clark County (Las Vegas) school district after year one. Schools in the district were in remote instruction for a full year in what would have been year two of the strategic plan, while year three was devoted to fully opening schools, meaning that the district was three years behind on its initial plan before it could recoup any sense of normality.

Recovery in the district meant reinstituting the initial goals that the strategic plan had set and adding new priorities around proficiency and proficiency gaps, teacher shortages, safety, community engagement and financial accountability, and mental health.

The school district saw some $771 million in ESSER funding from the three tranches of federal recovery aid. District leaders set up two community organizations, involving some fifteen hundred people, to advise the school system on expenditures, along with multiple community surveys.

Most of the district's American Rescue Plan (ARP) funds were devoted to student success in one form or another; $616.5 million was devoted to Tier I instructional materials in English language arts and science, instructional technology, materials to bolster social/emotional supports, summer learning programming, mental health services, community learning partnerships, direct allocations to elementary schools per state law, online curriculum and instructional resources, ELL endorsements for teachers, and crisis response teams. An additional $96.9 million was devoted to teacher recruitment and retention bonuses, professional development, educator pipeline, and teacher leadership activities. Some $57.8 million was devoted to COVID-19 mitigation efforts and responses, including funding for charter schools, health services, and operations. Some $6.9 million was allotted for parent and community engagement activities and data and transparency activities to keep the community informed. And $339,000 was directed to project coordination, strategic planning, and governance.

The district set up a formal project management system and publishes quarterly updates of every investment, along with monthly status reports of planned versus actual spending levels. Each initiative has implementation milestones and interim measures—all pointing toward the district's five main goals: student success, retaining and recruiting teachers, partnering with parents and the community, sustaining efforts for the future, and mitigating COVID-19's impact.

All information is presented on the district's website, at regular school board meetings, at press events, and to the state in scheduled reports. The district expects to spend its total federal allocation within the required time limit.

Saint Paul

The Saint Paul school system in Minnesota received some $334 million in federal funds across all three tranches of federal funds, with plans to spend all by September 30, 2024. The district is using funding to meet four main goals: safely reopen schools, address pre- and postpandemic unfinished learning, build lasting and equitable systems for teaching and learning, and support for student and staff social-emotional needs.

Specifically, the district formulated seven focus areas, in which it is spending ESSER dollars: effective and culturally responsive instruction, college and career readiness, family and community engagement, school safety, positive school and district culture, systemic equity, and program evaluation.

Approximately 44 percent of the district's COVID-19 aid is devoted to improving instruction. Included in these expenditures are investments in preK and early learning; special education; curriculum and professional development for teachers; classroom supports for students; culturally responsive instruction; reforms to high school schedules, credit recovery, and grading; multilingual learning supports; and technology supports and improvement. Within each category of spending, the public can find what activities are being supported with federal funds, along with a logic-model showing expected short-term and long-term outcomes.

The district uses its interim assessment system to regularly track and report on its goal to improve student achievement. It has created an "innovation team" to steward the work and make regular course corrections as its data system determines what works.

The district's efforts are regularly updated at scheduled school board meetings, and the public can view a regularly updated online dashboard of the district's expenditures by goal, initiative, and year. And the district's superintendent, Joe Gothard, indicates that the work is fundamentally changing how the district is organized and how it operates.

Baltimore City

The Baltimore City Public Schools expect to receive some $689.7 million from its three federal ESSER grants. A total of $800 million in federal and state grants along with philanthropic aid is being put at the district's disposal. The district's Recovery Plan—Reconnect, Restore, and Reimagine—is based on two preconditions for success: health and safety, and connectivity and technology support.

The plan employs five main strategies: wellness, school culture, and climate; personalized learning; acceleration; reimagined time for students; and expanded enrichment and academic opportunities for students. About 35 percent of the funds are centrally coordinated and managed, and about 65 percent go directly to schools for supplemental resources and services.

Specifically, ESSER dollars are being devoted to facilities and air-conditioning upgrades ($130.1 million); accelerated instruction to address learning loss ($118.2 million); summer programming and extended time opportunities ($109.1 million); technology devices, infrastructure, and support ($77.2 million); curriculum materials and personalized learning ($36.3 million); support for students with disabilities ($28.9 million); virtual learning ($24.8 million); health, safety, and COVID-19 mitigation ($19.1 million); COVID-19 testing and contact tracing ($19.0 million); high-dosage tutoring ($16.5 million); expanded enrichment and academic opportunities, including expanded athletics, fine arts, and extramural activities ($14.0 million); professional development $13.4 million); in-person learning supports and staff redeployment ($9.7 million); student transportation ($9.6 million); wellness and school culture and climate activities ($8.1 million); and student re-engagement initiatives ($3.6 million).

The district expects to spend out all ESSER funds by the federal deadline in 2024.

These three districts are particularly good examples of the use of federal funds, because they lay out clear goals and priorities, emphasize how resources are being spent on unfinished learning, gauge progress, and demonstrate transparency.

A survey by the Council of the Great City Schools of its member districts in late 2023 yielded thirty-six responses as of this writing to an open-ended question about investments being made with ESSER and ARP funds to address academic recovery. Some 94 percent of the districts had publicly available websites or dashboards by which they kept the public, parents, teachers, and staff up to date on how they were spending funds. Districts reported that they were using funds to boost academic performance in the following ways:

- Some 75 percent of districts (twenty-seven districts) indicated that they were using funds for teacher professional development
- Some 69 percent of the districts (twenty-five districts) reported that they were making major investments in high dosage tutoring or similar strategies
- 64 percent of the districts (twenty-three districts) used funds for additional instructional staff
- 56 percent of the responding districts (twenty districts) reported that they were using their funds for summer school programming
- About 56 percent (twenty districts) said that they were using their funding for curriculum enhancements or for the purchase of higher-quality materials
- Approximately 53 percent (nineteen districts) indicated that they were investing in various reading and math interventions, personalized learning, or expansions to their multi-tiered systems of support

- 47 percent (seventeen districts) indicated that they were using ARP dollars for various extended learning-time opportunities like before or after school or Saturday classes
- 33 percent (twelve districts) used funds for various technology based instructional efforts or to enhance the technology capacity of the district
- 28 percent (ten districts) used their funding for instructional coaching in reading and mathematics
- 25 percent (nine districts) used their funds to bolster their English language learner and special education programming
- About 14 percent (five districts) were focusing ARP dollars on improvements to their core instructional program
- 14 percent (five districts) used funds for teacher and staff retention incentives
- 8 percent (three districts) used funds for credit recovery programming
- 6 percent (two districts) used funding for college access programming
- 3 percent (one district) used funding for student mentoring initiatives
- 3 percent (one district) used funding for Advanced Placement or dual enrollment programming

These findings are largely positive and suggest that sizable investments of ARP dollars are going into unfinished learning. Still, there are signs in these data that recovery may be slow, and the pattern of expenditures may have been influenced by pressure from the unions, parent groups, vendors, states, the press, and other interests. For instance, 69 percent of the districts used funds for high-dosage tutoring, but only 14 percent used funds to improve their core instructional program. Tutoring can, if done well, boost achievement quickly, but it may not leave the districts with any longer-term capacity to improve instruction like strengthening their Tier 1 instructional efforts would.

On the other hand, if the 75 percent of districts that used funds for professional development and the 56 percent that used their ARP dollars to improve the quality of their materials did so in a way that bolstered the basic instructional program, then improvements might be at hand. In addition, some 64 percent of districts used funds for additional staff, which may leave some districts with the prospect of laying off people when funds run out, something the Council warned its members about in the spring of 2021 when funding was approved.[19]

ARE THERE SIGNS OF RECOVERY?

Finally, there were preliminary signs that student achievement on state tests was starting to tick upward in the spring of 2023. The gains were modest in many places, suggesting that it will take schools in both the large cities and the nation several years before they would regain all that was lost during the pandemic. Here is a sample of spring 2023 results on state exams:

- In 2023 **Baltimore** City Public Schools (City Schools) students reached achievement levels in English Language Arts (ELA or literacy) on the Maryland Comprehensive Assessment Program (MCAP) that exceeded prepandemic outcomes while demonstrating growth in math and science. The district's growth in ELA aligns with similar gains at the state level. The district's grade 3–8 increase of 4.5 percentage points was the fifth highest in Maryland compared to the 2021–2022 school year. The district's growth in math and science mirrored the performance of Maryland students overall.
- The 2022–2023 Illinois Assessment of Readiness (IAR) results showed that the **Chicago** Public Schools saw growth of nearly 6 (5.9) percentage points in students meeting or exceeding expectations on the ELA IAR exam, returning to prepandemic levels, and a nearly 3-percentage-point gain (2.6) on the math IAR. Overall, 428 out of 491 elementary schools (87 percent) administering this assessment increased the percentage of students meeting or exceeding expectations in ELA, while 359 out of 491 schools (73 percent) increased the percentage of students meeting or exceeding expectations in math.[20]

- The **Cleveland** Metropolitan School District (CMSD) made significant growth on the state test in several areas and exceeded expectations in others, placing CMSD in the top 10 percent of Ohio districts in growth. Of note was CMSD's number-one ranking among the Ohio 8, urban districts. Tied with Toledo in its four-star rating, the report card shows CMSD outpaced all seven of its urban peers in its two-year growth.

- In reading, **Dallas** students either showed gains or held steady in eleven of the eighteen categories on the TEA STAAR exam compared to last year. In addition, Dallas ISD students had a higher growth rate than the state in sixteen of the eighteen assessment categories. Strong math gains continue to be noteworthy, with students in grades 3 through 8 improving their performance at two performance levels. Of note, fourth-grade students saw their strongest growth with a 9-percentage-point increase.

- The **District of Columbia** public schools saw modest gains in reading and math on their spring 2023 Partnership for Assessment of Readiness for College and Careers tests. Students reading at or above grade level increased from 31 percent in 2022 to 34 percent in 2023, and students performing at or above grade level in math improved from 19 percent to 22 percent over the same period. Reading gains were largest at the middle school level, and math gains were largest in the elementary schools.

- Every demographic group in the Jefferson County (**Louisville**) Public Schools (JCPS) improved their proficiency rates in reading, and all demographic groups either improved or maintained proficiency rates in math according to results on the 2022–2023 Kentucky Summative Assessment. The assessment showed almost 70 percent of JCPS schools increased or significantly increased their reading and math scores. Elementary schools showed improved proficiency rates in every content area among all student groups, with 81 percent of elementary schools increasing or significantly increasing their reading and math scores. The number of middle and high school students who increased their scores in reading and math outnumbered students whose scores decreased. While overall test scores for middle and high schools declined in some content areas, their overall rating remained the same as last year.

- **Los Angeles** Unified School District students in grades 3, 4, and 11 had higher percentages meeting or exceeding reading standards compared to last year on the California Assessment of Student Performance and Progress, with grades 5, 6, 7, and 8 all decreasing. In math, the percentage of students meeting or exceeding standards increased to 30.5 percent, up from 28.5 percent in 2021–2022. All grades saw improvements in student achievement levels, with elementary grades showing slightly greater gains than later grades.

- The School District of **Philadelphia** saw improved student test scores in thirteen out of seventeen areas for students in grades 3 through 12 on the Pennsylvania System of School Assessment, including increases in Proficiency and reductions in Below Basic attainment categories. The percentage of grades 3 through 8 students who scored Proficient or Advanced in math increased by 4.2 percentage points from 16.5 percent in 2021–2022 to 20.7 percent in 2022–2023. The percentage of students who scored Proficient or Advanced in grades 3 through 8 in ELA remained stable, at around 34 percent.[21]

Finally, an analysis of 2023 spring state test scores by Tom Kane and Sean Reardon using the Stanford Educational Data Archive, found a "surprising" rebound in student achievement, particularly among students attending large city school districts.[22] Of the forty-one Great City School districts on which they had reading data, twenty-five (61 percent) showed gains in grade 3 through 8 that exceeded the average gain nationally. And of the forty-four Great City School districts on which they had math data, forty-two (95 percent) showed gains in grades 3 through 8 that exceeded the average gains nationally. In addition, 60 percent of the districts posted math gains above their respective state gains, and 49 percent posted reading gains that exceeded their state gains. And ten urban school districts posted the largest math gains in their respective

Figure 7.3   Change in math scores in grade equivalents, 2021–2022 to 2022–2023

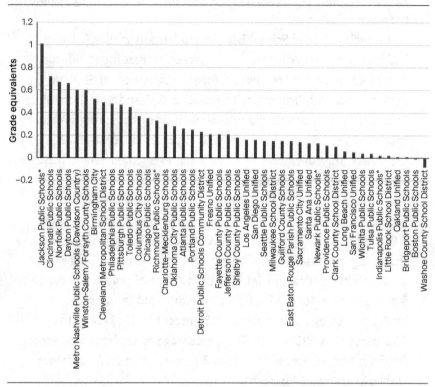

states, while seven posted their state's largest gains in reading (figures 7.3 and 7.4).

***

It is undeniable that real damage occurred both in the Large City Schools and nationally, and in schools across the globe because of the pandemic. I take little comfort in the fact that students in the nation's urban school districts sometimes fell less than other students. Everyone was harmed academically.

A recent analysis by the United Nations Educational, Scientific and Cultural Organization (UNESCO) of public education worldwide found that the pandemic contributed to lost learning, poor nutrition, family

Figure 7.4 Change in reading scores in grade equivalents, 2021–2022 to 2022–2023

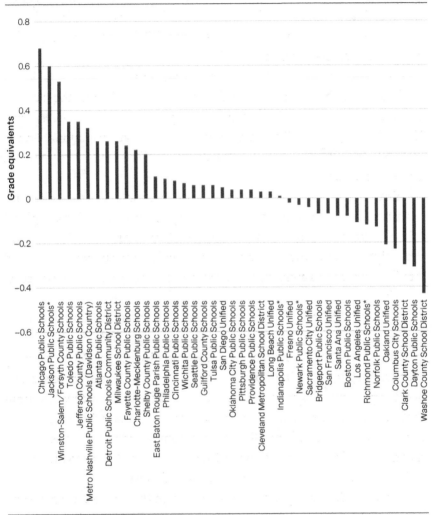

dysfunction, stress and social-emotional trauma, child-care gaps, strain on health-care systems, increased dropout rates, social isolation, child abuse, and other problems in countries all over the world.[23]

A second study by noted economist Eric Hanushek for the Organization for Economic Cooperation and Development (OECD) showed educational effects from the pandemic that were like the UNESCO analysis.[24] Other studies done by the Annenberg Institute,[25] the University of Chicago,[26] and the Wharton School at the University of Pennsylvania[27] reached similar conclusions. The results of the most recent PISA exam showed too that math results across the globe tumbled.

A subsequent study by Hanushek and Strauus indicated that total learning loss in the United Stated over the pandemic could lower the national Gross Domestic Product by 3 percent through the balance of the century.[28] If this does not sound like much, then consider that this amount equals some $31 trillion in lost economic activity over the next 80 years in the United States alone.

What is clear was that we saw a national, even international, phenomenon; it was not a unilateral failure of big-city public schools. It was a global crisis that urban school systems were better at managing than they thought they might be. Still, the pandemic resulted in lost instructional time, and it pulled our schools away from their improvement agenda in ways that set them back.

What is encouraging, if one can use that term, at least among the big city public schools in the US, is that there were substantial improvements in achievement among students in the nation's Large City Schools during the period up to 2019. The fact that we fell somewhat less in some subjects over the pandemic suggests that we had some "instructional muscles" from that period, some educational torque, if you will, that will serve us well coming out of the pandemic. Recent data from Reardon and Kane suggest that this muscle might be flexing in 2023.[29] The data also say to the nation, "We did it before and we can do it again—and more."

In chapter 8, I pull together the themes from the previous chapters and discuss where urban public education goes from here. I summarize some of the major lessons learned about what it took to improve; offer recommendations for how urban schools regain and accelerate the momentum they had before the pandemic; briefly discuss some of the pitfalls that present themselves from our national culture wars; and articulate a better future for our urban public schools and their contributions to the nation.

8

Where Do We Go From Here?

The pandemic took a toll on public education and its students by almost any measure. The country's major urban school systems were not immune to those effects, as we saw in chapter 7. In some cases, they held up better than public schools elsewhere; in other cases, they took the brunt of the damage. Without question, enrollment and attendance in traditional urban public schools dropped and student achievement declined. Nonetheless, the nation's urban public schools showed signs of a rebound in 2022–2023 and have a track record of improvement over the last twenty years or so. Urban educators can learn from that legacy of improvement as we regain our momentum.

LESSONS LEARNED

There are two major questions that confront us now: What did we learn from the pandemic? What did we learn from those two decades or so of improvement?

It may be too early to answer the first question. We may need more time and distance from the pandemic to know whether we learned the right lessons. Still, the question is worth asking even if we end up rethinking the answers later. To help with some preliminary thoughts on lessons from the pandemic, I posed the question to some of the best thinkers and practitioners in urban education today. They included Michael Hinojosa, former superintendent of the Dallas schools; Kaya Henderson, former chancellor of the District of Columbia public schools; A. J. Crabill, former chair of the Kansas City board of education; Jesus Jara, former superintendent of the Clark County (Las Vegas) public schools; Janice Jackson, former CEO of the Chicago public schools; Barbara Jenkins, former superintendent of the Orange County (Orlando) public schools; and Eric Gordon, former CEO of the Cleveland public schools. What follows is my synopsis of their responses.

- Every time we get distracted or compromise on instructional time, the futures of our students are diminished. As discussed in chapter 6, the leaders of the nation's major urban school systems found themselves in an impossible position and made a judgment call to do everything they could to address the immediate needs of their students, staff, and communities. While these districts did all they could to focus on student achievement, we were, in fact, pulled away from our main priority of improvement to manage the crises in front of us. Our students lost considerable instructional time that summer school and tutoring can only partially make up for. What we learned was the difference between what was urgent and what was important. We learned that it was critical to know what to protect and what to let go. And we learned that students suffer when their needs are secondary to those of adults. The lesson here is that while the unprecedented nature of the pandemic forced us to focus on the immediate crisis in front of us, that is not what we should focus on moving forward.
- We should never overestimate technology and what it can do to improve achievement. Urban school leaders made a choice at the beginning of the pandemic to use technology to provide as much learning as possible in lieu of doing nothing. It was the right call, but nobody should ever think that instruction with technology is an adequate substitute for a live teacher working directly with their students. Still, we did not need the pandemic to learn this lesson. Every time a new technology comes along, educators are often lured into thinking that it will replace, enhance, or augment the quality

of instruction that students receive. Technology needs to be better infused into instruction, to be sure, but we should not think that it can solve all problems or serve all students. The lesson here is that we are almost always wrong about technology. (We are looking at you, AI.)

- We have considerable impact, but we are not always in control of our own fates or the fates of our school districts. To be sure, the pandemic underscored that our schools were often at the mercy of inconsistent medical advice, self-serving political direction from above that sometimes prevailed over common sense, and ever-changing pressure from below. Superintendents and school boards were often left hanging out to dry, which did not feel fair. Still, it may be useful to remember that we were often the clearest voices for common sense. If we keep the welfare of our students in mind, work relentlessly to improve their outcomes, and never give up hope, then we will more successfully navigate the distractions that others put in front of us. The lesson here is to remain centered on the work when others attempt to pull us away.
- When we refer to student outcomes, we often mean student achievement. But the pandemic reminded us—again—that children are more than their academic records. We provide more than instruction, and our families often require us to provide more than families in other settings do. Our efforts to provide meals and mental health support were critical alongside all the other things we were doing. The lesson here is that our students are multidimensional and need our support both during the pandemic and now that it is over.
- Public support for its schools is fragile. This has been the case for some time, despite the high rating that parents often give to their neighborhood schools. Confidence in public schools, like confidence in institutions public and private of all kinds, has been declining for several years. There are all kinds of explanations for this, but we have learned that the public's trust is frailer than we might have guessed. The public wants both good education and safety for their children. Our job is to give the public what it wants. The lesson we relearned: never take the support of parents and the public for granted.

These lessons are likely to change over time as more people talk about the big takeaways from the pandemic. Nonetheless, it is worth pondering what came out of the pandemic that we can use to improve public education. And while we may need more time to ruminate, we have had plenty of time to think about what we learned over the last twenty years or so, before the pandemic, when we saw significant improvements in urban school performance. Before we present proposals for how urban education proceeds from here, I thought it would be useful to summarize some of the lessons learned about our improvement before the pandemic disrupted our progress.

TWENTY YEARS OF PREPANDEMIC IMPROVEMENT

First, it was clear that the improvement of urban public education is possible. The data in chapter 2 demonstrated that Large City Schools had, in fact, made substantial headway in reading and math achievement between 2003 and 2019. It was also clear that the Large City Schools produced a greater academic effect than All Other Schools. The data indicated that gains occurred across all student groups, although gaps among the groups did not narrow appreciably. And we demonstrated that urban schools added value for their students, and they produced a return on investment that was no different from public education generally. In other words, the nation's big-city schools are worth the nation's time, attention, and investment.

Second, the impetus for reform and improvement can begin for any number of reasons, with any number of people, inside or outside the school districts. It was clear that major improvements are sometimes prompted simply because people inside the district see that the institution can do better. This was the case in our six case study districts. Sometimes these leaders were prompted by a compelling vision of what could be; in other cases, they were simply angry that the schools were failing students. In every case, the desire and passion to make improvements were matched by the expertise to make it happen.

Three, the reform and improvement of urban public education do not need to start at any one place. We saw school leaders leveraging differing parts of the institution to get the ball rolling. Alberto Carvahlo used a huge budget cut to start reforms. Michelle Rhee and Kaya Henderson started overhauling the school district's human capital. Chicago was outraged by being called the worst school district in America, and it leveraged its school leadership and the standards to pull itself up from the bottom. In each situation, district leaders took their opportunities for improvement where they found them. They sized up the culture, strengths, and weak spots in their districts to identify which levers to pull first. It was not always the same levers in each district. In contrast, districts that tried to improve everything at once often found it impossible.

Four, leadership was a key ingredient in whether a big-city school system improved or not. And by leadership, I do not mean solely the superintendent of the school district. I am referring to the school board, the superintendent, and the district's senior staff working together to create a culture of improvement. The ability of these people to be on the same page, work on the same goals, and define those goals around better outcomes for students over an extended period was the secret sauce in most of these urban school improvements. It was also clear that the frequency of superintendent turnovers could be mitigated by the district's ability to maintain an agenda of improvement across leaders. This is easier said than done, but it was achieved in Chicago; Charlotte-Mecklenburg during the tenures of John Murphy, Eric Smith, James Pughsley, Peter Gorman, and Ann Clark; and Dallas under Michael Hinojosa (1.0), Mike Miles, Michael Hinojosa (2.0), and Stephanie Elizalde. Otherwise, districts are prone to lose momentum by changing up their agendas every time they switch superintendents. Momentum is critical.

Five, every big-city school district that improved marshalled strategic and systemic levers to boost the quality of instruction in their classrooms. That is why they got better. Often the Common Core State Standards were the fulcrum around which the districts could better define instructional quality, coherence, and alignment than anything they were doing before. But it was not solely the standards. It was how the districts accompanied the standards with parallel reforms to their curriculum, professional development, organizational structures, mid-management capacity, accountability, and data systems that made the standards as powerful as they were. The standards also allowed these districts to make managed instruction work, because they provided more universal expectations about the quality of teaching and student work than was the case if they allowed each school to do what they wanted. Finally, in each one of these cases, the districts pursued their reforms at scale.

RECOMMENDATIONS

At this point, we have learned more than enough lessons to get out of the hole we are in. In my opinion, our main challenge over the next few years is to address the unfinished learning that occurred during the pandemic, raise student achievement to higher levels than what we saw before the outbreak, and return to a clear focus on student outcomes. Our second critical challenge is to build public and parental trust. The dozen recommendations in this chapter are formed around getting those things done.

Reorient the Work of School Boards

School boards in the nation's major cities continue to be devoted to the needs of adults and obsessed with district inputs rather than student outcomes. It would not require much time watching any random school board meeting to conclude that their main purposes were to approve contracts, hire staff, move money around, and argue with one another. Discussions of student well-being happen too rarely. The Council of the Great City Schools, however, has devoted considerable effort over the last several years to improving how school boards in our major city school districts do their work.

Most of this work has been led by A. J. Crabill, the Council's director of governance, who has developed a framework for student outcomes–focused governance that turns the orientation of school board work on its head. In short, it entails having school boards and their superintendents develop a concise list of academic goals that it wants to achieve and then devoting a substantial portion—typically 50 percent or more—of each school board meeting receiving and discussing status reports on the progress students are making on those goals. Along with each goal is a series of indicators that the boards use to determine whether the progress is real.

This reorientation means focusing school board meetings not on adult inputs, but on student outcomes. The change is in keeping with a reform idea that has had currency for over thirty years, that is, flipping school reform from inputs to outputs. Up until recently, however, the work of school boards was out of step with this orientation.

The proposal I am making here assumes that school staff, including the superintendent and his or her direct reports, will spend their time and energies on what they think are the priorities of the board. If staff think that the board's priorities are vendor contracts, then that is what they pump their expertise into. On the other hand, if staff members see that the board's priorities are focused on improving student performance, then the system and its people will be devoted to that. It is not a complicated idea.

The benefit of reorienting staff work around student achievement is that more time and expertise will go toward this priority, but there is also a benefit for the public and parents in seeing their elected or appointed school board members talking about their children and their children's well-being. It is small wonder that an aggressive parents' rights movement has cropped up across the country when parents everywhere see school system leaders arguing mostly about things that only affect them.

I recommend that school boards in the nation's large cities reorient their work around this student outcomes–focused governance. Even if boards do not follow every detail and precept of this approach, I think it would not only boost student achievement, when and where it is needed most, but also prop up public confidence in our schools. Districts might look to the board reforms initiated in Philadelphia under the leadership of Joyce Wilkerson for a good example of the power of this approach and how it can spur academic improvement.

Double Down on College and Career Standards

Many commentators, scholars, and observers were skeptical about whether the Common Core State Standards would improve student outcomes when they were first rolled out. Some skeptics now declare the standards dead and propose doing away with them. I would recommend doing the opposite. Double down on the standards now, more than ever.

As schools emerge from the pandemic, there are numerous issues that are taking staff time and attention. Among the things that many districts are losing sight of is the college and career-ready standards. They are not in the news much; they are not getting much commentary; and they came online over a decade ago. But the research that we have done indicates that the standards were anything but a waste of time. Where they were implemented with any semblance of fidelity, student achievement improved, not because of the standards themselves, but because of the complementary efforts that made them effective. They provided instructional coherence across grades, boosted the quality of instruction, gave purpose to professional development and technical assistance, increased system and staff capacity, guided the purchase of instructional materials, and informed student assessments.

Rather than treating the standards as yesterday's reform, the standards need to anchor the instructional efforts that urban school systems make to recapture the gains they made before the pandemic. This means reviewing your curriculum's alignment to the standards or your state's version of them. It also means ensuring that the materials you purchased align with those standards and replacing materials that do not. Do not take your vendor's word for it; review the materials in detail yourselves to make sure that what is used in the classroom is consistent with the standards. Artificial intelligence (AI) can actually help with that.

It also means grounding your professional development in the standards and how they link to the curriculum, materials, and instructional practices. Over a decade has passed since the standards were launched, yet a sizable portion of your teaching force may not have been trained on them. Training materials on the standards continue to exist and should be used to bolster staff capacity.

Above all, pay no attention to the skeptics who claim that the standards were a waste of time. The research on major urban school systems and how they improved over the years says the opposite. The foundation for getting out of the academic situation that big city schools and others are in rests in the standards and your attention to them. Districts should look for good examples from the District of Columbia and Chicago.

Align Your Curriculum and Instruction

The curriculum is your main guide to what is essential to teach and how deeply to teach it so that every child has access to rigorous academic experiences. A district curriculum is not your textbooks or other materials. It is the district's guide for a coherent instructional experience that systematically builds student readiness for college and/or career within and across grade levels from pre-kindergarten through high school. As such, it should effectively shepherd the work of all instructional staff.

The lack of a clear and coherent curriculum leaves teachers and administrators to individually determine what the district wants or expects, and it leads to a variety of interpretations that may not align with district expectations. This is especially detrimental in urban settings, where high staff turnover requires structures to define and maintain a continuity of expectations.

Moreover, high student mobility in urban centers means that students may miss key concepts by transferring from one school to another, when they are all doing something different. Student achievement should not depend on which school students attend.

Many urban school districts have not revisited their curriculum for some time, but now is the right moment to make sure that all instructional tools are aimed in the direction of improving student outcomes and are aligned with each other.

We recommend that districts look at their curriculum to ensure that it achieves the following:[1]

- reflects college and career-readiness standards and the district's values and philosophy about how students learn and what learning is essential at each grade level
- provides coherent instructional experiences that increase complexity over time within and across grade levels from pre-kindergarten through high school and systematically builds student academic and social emotional readiness for college and careers
- addresses the trends in district data in which large numbers of students are likely to have unfinished learning and provides teachers

guidance for addressing those gaps, while leveraging student assets, in the context of grade-level instruction

- provides clarity on required and optional resources for all instructional staff, including those who support and supervise teaching
- provides teacher guidance on how to incorporate texts, tasks, and resources that respect and celebrate the cultural, ethnic, and linguistic diversity of students
- provides guidance on the multiple roles of technology to enhance grade-level teaching and learning across multiple learning environments
- articulates a continuum of learning that delineates the content knowledge, academic language, and skills that should be taught, and at what point during a school year, so that students who transfer between schools have a coherent learning experience
- creates a floor, not a ceiling, for learning at every grade level and in every course. In this way, the curriculum should support and challenge the full range of learners, from struggling students to gifted and talented students
- illustrates exciting learning opportunities within and outside school to keep students engaged as they learn challenging content, skills, and concepts in every setting
- allows for as much individualization as possible to meet the diverse learning needs of students while maintaining an elevated level of rigor and accessibility for all
- addresses the importance of social-emotional learning opportunities that will increase student preparedness for rigorous learning experiences and collaborative tasks
- communicates why, when, and how to use assessments, including formative assessments, to determine how well students are progressing on individual standards or sets of standards
- employs a two-way communication process to respond to feedback and meet evolving student and educator needs

A good example of a district that has done excellent work aligning their curriculum with their standards is Long Beach, California, under the leadership of Jill Baker and her predecessors, Chris Steinhauser and Carl Cohn.

Do Not Rely Solely on Tutoring

Almost every time one reads a newspaper article on the subject or a new set of recommendations for how schools should make up the unfinished learning that students experienced over the pandemic, one will see an emphasis on "high-dosage tutoring" and summer school. This is, in fact, a good short-term strategy for boosting student results, particularly if it is done well.

Summer school, as well, has proven to be most effective when it is aligned to the curriculum, when it is taught by teachers who know the curriculum, when it is differentiated by student needs, when it lasts at least five weeks for 60 to 90 minutes per day, and when students are encouraged to participate.

Experience also shows that it is hard to do high-dosage tutoring at scale. Many school systems will employ these strategies by hiring a tutoring company and risk the possibility that their services will not align with either the district's standards or the curriculum. Doing so will also leave school district staff with little added capacity to do the work once American Rescue Plan funds are gone and the district must curtail its tutoring contracts. They are also likely to use this strategy without improving the overall quality of their basic Tier I instruction.

Instead of relying disproportionately on high-dosage tutoring, the Council would propose using six overarching principles for supporting students with unfinished learning during regular class time. "Districts and schools should (1) stick to grade-level content and instructional rigor and (2) focus on the depth of instruction, rather than pace. To provide this grade-level instruction, districts should help teachers (3) prioritize content and learning. And educators should (4) include every learner and (5) identify and address gaps in learning through core instruction, avoiding the misuse of standardized testing to place kids into high- or low-ability groups or provide low levels of instructional rigor to lower-performing students. Finally, districts should consider (6) focusing on the commonalities that students share, not just their differences."[2]

Districts should also avoid the temptation to cover all the "gaps" in learning from the pandemic. The pace required to cover all this content will leave many students discouraged. Moreover, at a time when social-emotional well-being, agency, and engagement are more important than ever, instructional haste may eclipse the patient work of building academic motivation.

As educators, we need to remain focused on the learning that could and should be happening today and not allow ourselves to be distracted by remedial tactics. These distractions shift our attention from "just in time" learning to "just in case" teaching. "Just in case" teaching wastes time teaching content and skills from earlier grades just in case students need it for grade-level work. "Just in time" concentrates time on needs that come up during grade-level work.

In other words, taking the time to provide patient, in-depth instruction allows for issues related to unfinished learning to arise naturally when dealing with new content, allowing for "just in time" instruction and reengaging students in the context of grade-level work.

We recommend that districts rely on "just in time" core instruction supplemented with "high-dosage" tutoring and social-emotional supports—not the reverse. I fully endorse this approach.

Stop Buying Poor-Quality Instructional Materials

The quality of instructional materials available to the nation's schools is vastly better now than it was when the Common Core State Standards were launched in 2010. Considerable resources and attention to the importance of high-quality instructional materials were provided by the Bill and Melinda Gates Foundation and others, and substantial research was done on their effectiveness.

It is still the case that materials—by themselves—are not sufficient to improve student achievement. They need to be accompanied by strong standards, coherent professional development, on-time technical assistance and other capacity-building measures. It remains true now like it was true years ago: you cannot buy reform and improvement off the shelf.

Two developments over the years have significantly improved access to high-quality materials. The first involved the founding of EdReports, which reviews materials for their quality and alignment with the standards. The second is the purchasing consortium developed by the Council of the Great City Schools and its staff members Gabriela Uro and Denise Walston that uses the joint buying power of the big-city school systems to encourage publishers to improve their materials. Both have been powerful levers, but they are not always used to the extent that they could be.

School systems still buy materials that do not address the standards or are of poor instructional quality. In other cases, individual schools and teachers are free to purchase their own materials, which can be high quality but are not necessarily so.

Part of the problem is that school systems do not always attend to the standards when they review materials for purchase. And part of the issue is that districts do not consistently train teachers and staff on the materials they have purchased, even when they are aligned. When the latter happens, teachers often resort to sites like Pinterest and others to find materials they think might be more effective.

I recommend that school districts ensure that they are continuing to use EdReports reviews and the Council's purchasing consortium, along with appropriate training, as part of their game plan to improve academic results.

Sharpen Your Capacity-Building Efforts

Ironically, one of the most poorly used tools in the arsenal of public education is professional development. One would think that this is what schools would be good at doing, but they are not. Most professional development, at least in major city public school systems, and the time devoted to it are tightly constrained through collective bargaining agreements. And a good deal of that time is devoted to procedures and rules that school district staff must abide by. The amount of time devoted to improving instruction is quite small.

A good deal of the blame for this situation rests with district leadership. The teacher unions typically do not want their members sitting through ineffective training or would prefer to offer it themselves. It is hard to blame them. The solution rests in districts offering professional development that adds value to teachers' classroom work. They would show up for that and would want as much of it as they could get.

One of best things that districts could do while they recover from the pandemic is to provide professional development on how to teach on grade level while addressing unfinished learning as it becomes evident during day-to-day instruction. This would help anchor high-dosage tutoring and expanded summer schooling. It would also help teachers after the crisis is over because unfinished learning is not something that occurred solely because of the pandemic. Urban schools and others have dealt with this issue for many years.

Another feature of professional development in many urban school systems involves the use of professional development units, or PDUs. This typically involves requiring teachers to take a specified number of course credits to retain their teaching credentials. The concept is not a bad one, but its implementation involves districts offering courses through their local colleges of teacher education that teachers may select at their discretion to fill the credentialing requirement. Unfortunately, the courses are often chosen from catalogs that have little to do with the instructional priorities, weak spots, or needs of students. Still, millions of dollars go to this practice every year. The groups that benefit include the states, the colleges of education, and the unions. Students garner little from this.

I recommend getting rid of PDUs where they still exist and replacing them with professional development that helps teachers build their instructional craft and better meets the needs of their students.

I also offer two related proposals. The first involves the evaluation of teacher effectiveness. And the second involves teacher seniority rights. I am all in favor of raising teacher salaries. There are several proposals to set floors on what teachers earn and to allow for additional pay for added responsibilities. I think all of these, including hiking salaries across the board, are good for the profession and would help solve the teacher shortage in quick order. At the same time, it is well past time to evaluate teachers not solely on their duty hours, lesson planning, parental engagement, and the like, but on their effectiveness in improving outcomes for students. This applies to other personnel as well.

The second issue involves the ability of senior teachers to bump junior teachers when budget cuts occur. This practice not only harms student achievement, but it also undercuts the ability of school districts, particularly large urban school systems, to retain teachers of color who are typically newer to the systems. I would recommend that district leaders and unions develop new ways of solving these issues once and for all, and that their national organizations encourage them in that pursuit.

Moreover, I would suggest reconsidering the use of differentiated staffing in our schools, particularly at the elementary school level. The truth is that, as good as many of our teachers are, it is hard for them to be good at all things. We should start having teachers who are well trained in math and/or science devote their expertise to teaching those subjects. The research on this is promising, and it would make better use of talent.

Finally, our districts need to seriously consider the use of coaches for school boards, superintendents, principals, and teachers. I have heard numerous objections to boards and superintendents having coaches, because it might suggest that they do not know what they are doing. But I noted that Patrick Mahomes, Super Bowl–winning quarterback, brought not only one coach with him to the big game but lots of coaches. No one claims that Mahomes does not know what he is doing.

Boost Student Attendance

The data in chapter 7 indicate that absenteeism in many of our districts is alarmingly high. There are numerous efforts throughout the country to better understand the reasons for this, but this research is likely to point to multiple factors driving the problem. Unfortunately, this will mean that no one strategy that our school systems put into place is likely to work on its own.

Although the problem persists, our districts are already implementing a variety of tactics to address the issue. Los Angeles staff are going door-to-door to locate missing students; Cleveland was enlisting local sports figures to place robocalls to students; and Oklahoma City initiated its "No Empty Seats" campaign. Wichita works with its local Communities in Schools group to check on students, make sure they are going to class, and connect them with community resources. In Charlotte-Mecklenburg, the school district employed "Street Teams" to make home visits after hours and on weekends, along with mediation teams to problem solve with parents. Other districts assign attendance aids to call families and ask if they need help. So far, we are not sure how successful these efforts have been, but districts like Newark under the leadership of Roger Leon, the District of Columbia under Lewis Ferebee, and St. Paul under Joe Gothard have indicated that enrollment and attendance are starting to bounce back. It is worth learning from these and other districts about the measures they put into place to get students back in class.

In St. Paul, the school district spent some $30,000 on an advertising campaign directed toward families who were looking for schools. The effort included digital and social media marketing, community outreach, open houses, school choice fairs, and special events. They have also placed additional emphasis on programming that is popular with parents and students, like the district's East African Magnet School and its Hmong language offerings. Renovations to schools are also attracting families back into the district.

The initiatives that prove effective will look different from community to community, but our urban school systems need to bear down on this challenge if we are to raise student academic achievement. We recommend that the nation's urban schools collect information through the Council of the Great City Schools on what the districts are doing to address this issue and monitor attendance rates through the organization's KPI system. Which districts are regaining students fastest, and what are they doing?

Rethink Time and Technology

Throughout the pandemic, we heard a great deal about making up for lost time by extending the school year, school day, or even adding a bridge year to the school calendar. Some advocates even proposed retaining everyone in grade until they were all caught up. These proposals are all about extending time to address unfinished learning, generally a good thing to do. But for many schools, this is likely to mean doing the same things stretched over a longer period. The result will be anything but satisfactory, as the research on year-round schools shows.

It is a fact that time is essential in education, just like it is in every other aspect of life. We lost a lot of it during the pandemic. Teachers often say that they do not have time to do everything we ask of them. The same is also true for students. Extending time may be a good thing, to be sure, but we can make better use of the limited time we have by spending more of it on high-quality instruction rather than on many of the disruptions, paperwork, and pointless activities that we often require of staff and students.[3]

Rethinking how we use and optimize time and revisiting the school calendar ought to go together with any discussion of extending time that we may not have the resources to pay for anyway.[4]

In addition, much has been made of the emergence of AI. We knew that instructing students remotely was likely to be a losing proposition, and it was. It does not mean that we should abandon technology or run away from AI. In fact, AI has enormous potential for school districts. I can easily see it being used to align districts' many commercial instruction products, simulate classroom settings for professional development, identify holes in risk management, optimize bus routes, develop budgets, analyze how district staff could be better deployed to maximize student achievement, synthesize the ocean of data that districts possess, and so many other benefits.

The future is going to be shaped by these technologies, and we need to ensure that our urban students are equipped to handle what the future brings. The notion that AI might encourage cheating is not sufficient reason to abandon it.

Bolster Your Auxiliary and Support Systems

It is clear to school people and casual observers alike that the pandemic took a toll on more than academic achievement. It affected adult and student mental health in ways that we are only now beginning to understand. It is also becoming evident that, to recover academically, we will have to pay attention to the mental health needs of our staff, teachers, parents, and children in ways that we have only started doing. Preliminary indicators suggest that our ability to address unfinished learning from the pandemic may be hampered by the many nonacademic worries that our students carry, the staff shortages that everyone is experiencing, the chronic absenteeism we see, the disciplinary issues that we are facing, and some of the demographic shifts that are occurring.

If we do not complement our academic work with parallel efforts to take care of the mental health needs of our young people, then their issues will serve as a drag on our ability to boost their academic success. That means that we cannot return to the kinds of exclusionary disciplinary strategies that too many of our districts employed before the pandemic, since all those do is to teach our children how to be chronically absent. And we cannot solve our staffing issues by lowering the bar on who we hire, as some states are suggesting.

What I propose instead is that we think through the kinds of mental health supports that are likely to work, based on the good research and best practices that have emerged over the years. I would also propose incorporating more extracurricular activities for our students to help them reconnect with each other and offset the mental health costs of social isolation and social media.

The Council and other groups have developed many good tools and compilations of effective strategies that big-city schools are using. Those strategies may also mean bolstering the ranks of our counselors and social workers, along with providing substantial professional development for our teachers on handling the social-emotional needs of our students. Certainly, it will mean collaborating with other organizations, public and private, to build more seamless supports for our students and families.

Expand Public School Choice

It is not always clear that broader choice within a large public school district directly improves achievement among children. Still, there is little doubt that parental satisfaction and student commitment to a school are stronger when families have chosen what school to attend. Public school choice may also improve student attendance because of that satisfaction and commitment.

At a time when public schools, particularly traditional public schools in our major cities, are struggling to regain parental confidence and boost attendance, it only makes sense to give families a greater selection of public schools and courses within a district. Both Miami and Dallas used public school choice effectively to bolster public confidence and strengthen attendance. And they both provided more choice without fracturing the cohesion of their core instructional program. At a recent seminar for aspiring big city school superintendents, Los Angeles school superintendent Alberto Carvahlo argued, "School choice is here to stay; why not use it to your advantage?" And Michael Hinojosa, former superintendent of the Dallas Independent School District asserted, "Public school choice was one tool in my toolbox to build public ownership of our schools and increase attendance."

At the same time, there are students who are compelled to go to a school outside of their neighborhoods not by choice but because the district has not invested enough to make every neighborhood school a good one. It is past time to ensure that every school in every neighborhood is high quality so that you do not have to leave your neighborhood if you do not want to.

Ensure Your Improvement Strategy Is Broad and Deep

We talked in chapter 4 about the theories of action and strategies that school systems used to improve their results. The truth is that most school boards and many superintendents do not think very deeply about what a theory of action means. Considerations are often reduced to a choice between a centrally driven system or a system in which schools are left alone to do what they want. Sometimes, district leaders create incentives for schools to work themselves out of central office guidance—what some people refer to as "earned empowerment." The evidence from chapter 4 suggests that this approach is more effective for large urban school districts when achievement is low than other strategies, but we saw that there are exceptions to the rule. Understanding why the exceptions work is critical because for a theory of action to work, it must bolster the quality of classroom instruction.

Still, school leaders rarely think about the appropriateness of these various theories of action or strategies. District leaders need to gauge their staff and teacher capacity and the academic performance of students when deciding on what approach to take. They also need to think about when and how changes to those approaches are warranted as capacity and achievement improve. And leaders need to think about the need to layer their strategies.

Our experience with big-city school systems over the years suggests that any one strategy to improve the entire system—no matter how effective— is likely to leave some schools and student groups behind. Some schools and students will appear to be immune to the district-wide strategies that leaders put into place. Some would argue that this is why it is not good to have a "one-size-fits all" approach to improvement, and they consequently abandon putting a system-wide effort in place. That is not what the evidence shows.

We would argue that a district-wide strategy is imperative if you want the system to improve at scale but that a system-wide strategy needs to be paired with tactics that take on individual schools that chronically fail despite the broader reforms. This suggests having in place a convincing turnaround strategy for a small number of struggling schools.

In addition, there will be student groups with special needs or who need dedicated support on top of system-wide and school reforms, like English language learners, students with disabilities, or African American males. The data in this volume clearly suggest that our urban schools need to devote more instructional attention to our African American students. Dallas demonstrated the possibilities with more economic integration and accountability. I would also suggest strengthening English language acquisition programming, foundational literacy skills, and content instruction with your English learners.[5] All of this argues for a three-tiered strategy or theory of action that combines system-wide reforms, individual school supports, and assistance to student groups that need extra help.

This three-tiered strategy then needs to be connected one to another to make sure that the overall reforms are coherent. One of the ways to do that is to ensure that academic staff is well coordinated with school supervisory staff and that principal supervisors are trained and deployed to monitor the quality of instruction from a data-informed system, school, and student perspective. It is also critical that a series of feedback loops are built throughout the system so that information can flow easily, and monitoring is facilitated.

Finally, it is important to think about which theory of action your school system is ready for. Sometimes an exceptionally low-achieving school system will install a site-based system when its schools, teachers, and staff simply do not have the capacity to improve on their own. The approach you choose and the reform you emphasize make all the difference in your success.

There is much more I could say on this issue, but the crucial point is that I recommend thinking through your improvement strategy in ways that do not leave gaping holes in your academic achievement by school or student group.

Overhaul Your Assessment System

Several years ago, we did an inventory of tests that students took in the Great City Schools over the course of their elementary and secondary school careers. The results indicated that the average student would take some 112 standardized tests during that period. It was not clear to us whether that was too many tests or not enough, although lots of people took positions on that question, based on our study.

What was particularly disturbing in our inventory was that much of the testing was not aligned with the standards and not very coherent from grade to grade. This was particularly true of interim or formative tests that are given two to four times over the course of the school year to keep track of how students are doing before it is too late.

Some of these formative assessments are high quality and well aligned with college and career readiness standards. Others are not. The problem is that districts sometimes use the results of low-quality exams to hold teachers accountable for results, and sometimes teachers use misaligned results to teach their students the wrong things. Accountability and quality instruction are affected. In addition, these assessments often are used to predict the results of end-of-the-year state exams. However, often they are not well aligned to the state exams and may provide a statistical prediction but not a useful, substantive one.

School districts do not spend a great deal of time conducting tests, despite claims to the contrary. We estimated that they were devoting about 3 percent of classroom time to testing. The amount of time is not really the problem. The main problem is that they often measure the wrong things and contribute to the overall instructional misalignment of the school system. In these cases, no one is served except the test publishers.

We recommend that school systems review their interim testing system, in particular, and replace them if the assessments do not align with college or career readiness standards or do not accurately predict substantive performance on end-of-the-year state assessments. There are several commercial tests that fit the bill, or the district could develop its own. Either way, conducting tests that do not align with what you want your students to know and be able to do is a waste of everyone's time and money.

POLITICS AND OUR FUTURE

Did we learn the right lessons from the pandemic? Have we correctly interpreted why we made as much progress as we did between 2003 and 2019? Time will tell.

At this point, the reader may have noticed that nowhere did we mention anything about the culture wars that the nation is obsessed with waging. We did learn, among our other lessons, that we should stay with our values around excellence, equity, and opportunity. It does not serve our students, our staff, and our communities to get mired in the culture wars. Once we engage, there is no end to it. There are lots of people who would like to see us get involved in what I consider an empty debate. That is all some people do. But there is little benefit for us in engaging. Sometimes the best politics is no politics.

One of the advantages that urban public school districts have is that the culture wars do not always have the same resonance in the more progressive big cities as they do in the suburbs and small towns. It does not mean that we are immune, but we should press our advantage and not take the bait when it is tossed in front of us. If we—as urban school systems—take our eye off the ball to fight the nation's culture wars, then we are likely to fail in our attempts to improve. And if we fail to get better, we will prove our critics right, and many people will conclude that it is not worth investing in us because we are too focused on ideology to get better. It is a circular firing squad.

Now more than ever, it is important for urban public schools to stay focused on improving student achievement—on regaining the momentum we built before the pandemic and exceeding that level of achievement moving forward.

There is room, of course, to rethink what we have done in the past and to try something new. Our strategies for improvement worked well for many children before the pandemic, but we are on the cusp of wasting an excellent opportunity to transform our systems so that they work well for all students. For instance, we should rethink the wisdom of letting our schools do whatever they want with curriculum and instruction. It might work well in districts with uniform, high capacity, but it does not work well in major city school systems whose academic performance needs to improve. We need to reassess the wisdom of our pullout tactics for providing remedial instruction. We should be conducting more research on why some of our students did well during the pandemic using remote instruction and why others did not. And we should use these data to configure our instructional programs going forward.

In addition, we still need to figure out why our efforts to improve are not narrowing the achievement gaps as we made gains overall. We need to better harness both the academic and social/emotional benefits of our multitiered systems of support. We need to treat digital connectivity as a public utility. We need to rethink the cultures and benefits of our workplaces to attract and retain top talent for our students. We should test ways to expand the amount of learning time each day and week. And we need to harness the innovation, resourcefulness, and nimbleness that we exhibited during our time of crisis in service of raising student achievement over the long run.

Observers have called for a complete and bold rethinking of the institution at large. I hear that public education in the US needs a Moon Shot, a Marshall Plan, or a Mars Rover for schools. Most of these calls, however, typically involve structural reforms or additional choice options that are not likely to produce noteworthy progress in student achievement. While there are certainly things that need to be rethought, we also need to be careful not to change things for the sake of change. I would argue that more than rearranging the deck chairs in public education, we need to spend the next few years focusing on what we have learned about what works and does not work in improving student outcomes—and apply those lessons with a sense of urgency.

As we rethink how we do our work, we should also keep in mind that our highly decentralized and multilayered institution is faced with a distinct lack of national consensus about which direction to move in. There are disparate pressures on these systems from above us and below us—and few people agree on anything.

When advocates argue for systemic transformation, we should rightly ask what that means. What makes us think that such transformations would produce better outcomes for our students? What transformation would the public support? I am in favor of rethinking everything in public education, but we should be confident that we have the public's support for the solutions we produce and that the changes can produce better results for students.

One sometimes wonders whether some of the ideas put forward are mostly for the amusement of readers and other like-minded travelers. No doubt, there will be some commentators who will be disappointed that the recommendations above do not include a fundamental reimagining of public education, a bolder rethinking of the institution and what it is trying to do. The truth is that I would climb on board bolder reforms in areas where I thought they would improve things for children, but most of what I see and hear are reforms that address adult political concerns but are irrelevant to the welfare of students. Many are also big structural overhauls that say nothing about what makes schools effective or what supports good instruction. In addition, a good deal of what is proposed often has little in the way of public support or promise.

Instead of blowing up the system, as some would propose, I am suggesting a return to the fundamentals of why and how school systems can work better on behalf of their kids, actions that many urban school systems can take on their own without a broader national consensus that may never come, given our fractured politics. Keep it simple and tune out the noise. A recentering of the work of urban schools around student achievement would be revolutionary in its own way, even if the ideas behind them were anything but new.

That said, the reforms I am proffering here involve substantial upheavals in how things are currently done. Reorienting the governance work of school boards, appealing to parents, retaining high standards, sharpening the curriculum, emphasizing capacity-building efforts, expanding public-school choice, reforming collective bargaining agreements, and overhauling testing and accountability are not for the faint of heart. These and other proposals are what urban school systems that make academic progress do for their children. None of them rely on incrementalism. I hope the evidence laid out in this volume makes that clear.

As we get back to our improvement agenda, we must admit that the pandemic did real harm to the education of the nation's children. Most educators at their central offices and in classrooms did what they thought best at the time with the often-contradictory health advice they were given and the divided public they were trying to serve. I cannot fault them; no one could have done it better. They are now about the process of regaining the ground they lost. Unlike the critics of public education, I am not pessimistic about its future. In fact, I am more optimistic than ever because we know how to make things better. We have done it before and will do it—and more—again—if we have learned the right lessons and apply them faithfully. The ten to twenty years before the pandemic prove that improvement is possible and that better days lay ahead if we pay attention to what works.

I suspect that urban public education will always be in the crosshairs of our national conversations about race, choice, immigration, parent rights, and other issues. We will also be at the center of discussions about where we go as a country. We will always be a target for scrutiny and criticism. Urban public education's story, however, is that we have created the forces and expertise—with the help of others—by which we can make progress in the face of skepticism and criticism. And it is why I am more optimistic now than I have been in years. Our story is one of ongoing struggle, commitment, optimism, and perseverance to improve especially on behalf of the families and students America has often cast as outsiders or inferior.

The truth is that our urban schools are engines of upward social mobility. They are more robust and stalwart than many people think. They are a force for overcoming poverty and disadvantage. They matter to the lifeblood of our country and the health of our republic. They are a sound investment. And they contribute to the overall welfare and betterment of the nation at a time when we need every asset at our disposal to keep alive the democracy that our ancestors fought for. The nation will lose a major asset in its ability to attract talent from across the globe and advance the futures of our young people if we let these important urban public institutions falter. The enduring promise of America's Great City Schools is that we will continue to improve. We will continue to fight for both excellence and equity. We will remain the country's welcome mat. We will work to bolster the public's trust. We will continue to step in to serve the public when no one else can. And we will help the nation realize its pledge of equality and opportunity for all. Why would we not help these schools keep that promise?

Appendix

CHAPTER 2

Table A2.1 78 Members of the Council of the Great City Schools (2023–2024)

Albuquerque	Dayton	Long Beach (CA)	Portland (OR)
Anchorage	Denver	Los Angeles	Providence
Arlington (TX)	Des Moines	Memphis-Shelby County	Puerto Rico
Atlanta	Detroit	Metro-Nashville	Richmond
Aurora (CO)	District of Columbia	Miami-Dade County	Rochester (NY)
Austin	Duval County	Milwaukee	Sacramento
Baltimore City	E. Baton Rouge	Minneapolis	San Antonio
Birmingham	El Paso	New Orleans	San Diego
Boston	Fayette County (NC)	New York City	San Francisco
Bridgeport	Fort Worth	Newark	Santa Ana (CA)
Broward County	Fresno	Norfolk	Seattle
Buffalo	Guilford County (NC)	Oakland	St. Louis City
Charleston (SC)	Hawaii	Oklahoma City	St. Paul
Charlotte-Mecklenburg	Hillsborough	Omaha	Toledo
Chicago	Houston	Orange County (FL)	Tulsa

(continued)

Table A2.1 (Continued)

Albuquerque	Dayton	Long Beach (CA)	Portland (OR)
Cincinnati	Indianapolis	Palm Beach County	Washoe County (NV)
Clark County (NV)	Jackson (MS)	Philadelphia	Wichita
Cleveland	Jefferson County	Phoenix Union	Winston-Salem
Columbus (OH)	Kansas City (MO)	Pinellas County	
Dallas	Little Rock	Pittsburgh	

Rationale for Using NAEP and Critique

This volume uses the National Assessment of Educational Progress (NAEP) as the primary measure of student performance, rather than a database like the Stanford Educational Data Archive (SEDA). NAEP is based on the direct testing of students with a common assessment over a longer period. SEDA, as good as it is, is based on standardized state test scores normed on NAEP over a shorter period, making it difficult to conduct longer trend analysis like I do in this book. In some cases, moreover, SEDA is not able to maintain trend lines on some states and their respective districts because the state changes its instrument from year to year. Still, I use SEDA results in chapter 7 to determine if there has been any recovery since the pandemic because there are no NAEP data after 2022, and SEDA is an excellent database.

In addition, NAEP is widely known and accepted by academicians, the media, and practitioners as the most credible, comparable, and accessible indicator of student achievement available. Moreover, its results, like SEDA's, can be disaggregated over years at the district level by race, income, and language proficiency in ways that are of interest to readers. NAEP, moreover, is administered at the school level by federal contractors rather than local school administrators, which removes any suspicion that cheating might have occurred. And NAEP is able to retain trend lines at the national, state, and city levels. Finally, the NAEP database contains an extensive collection of background variables that other data sets do not have to the same extent.

That said, NAEP does have limitations. For instance, it does not track the achievement of individual students over time. The test is given to fourth and eighth graders every two years, so it is impossible to tell how these same students progress from year to year. Inferences of progress must be made by comparing scores of differing students in these two grades. In addition, students answer only a sample of the questions, since they take only a portion of the full assessment, meaning that part of an individual's score is dependent on the scores of like students. In addition, the public's understanding of NAEP's performance levels (e.g., Advanced, Proficient, Basic, and Below Basic) is sometimes at odds with the National Assessment Governing Board's (NAGB) use of the terms. The "Proficient" performance level, for instance, which represents solid academic performance for a given grade and competency over challenging subject matter, is often misinterpreted by the public as being on grade level. The scores that define each performance level have also been the subject of some criticism over the years, as they are established by a convening of educators and interested citizens. Still, they have been largely validated against other international measures over the years.

The national assessment has also been the subject of some criticism because it is not actually grounded in any set of standards developed nationally or by any of the states. Instead, its questions are based on a framework that is developed by a panel empowered by NAGB and open for public comment. Nonetheless, NAGB has moved the math framework closer to the standards for future testing.

How the tests are scaled in each subject and grade is sometimes critiqued as well. All scores are presented on a 0 to 500 point scale, but the full range is not used, and the scale is not directly comparable from grade to grade or subject to subject. The issue has become a point of debate when it is not always clear that we know what we need to know about students who perform below the basic level.

Finally, the national assessment has been criticized in the past for its complicated and multilayered sampling methodology. One of the critiques was over the use of large schools to draw sample students. This issue and other sampling complaints, however, have been largely resolved over the years by the National Center for Educational Statistics to ensure that students have an equal chance of being chosen for testing. Remaining challenges include the sampling of growing numbers of homeschooled children and the participation of private schools in the national assessment program.

I use the assessment in lieu of anything else because of the benefits it provides for the kinds of analysis I am doing in this book. It is a nationally, even internationally, respected assessment; it is well known and used by the practitioner community, particularly in large urban school districts; it has a lengthy trend line at all levels; and it tests students directly on a standardized framework of reading and math concepts.

Definition of Variables Used in Statistical Analysis

- **Race/ethnicity**

Student race/ethnicity information is obtained from school records and classified according to one of six categories: *White, Black, Hispanic, Asian/Pacific Islander, American Indian/Alaska Native,* or *unclassifiable*. When school-reported information was missing, student-reported data from the Student Background Questionnaire were used to establish student race/ethnicity. Using restricted NAEP data sets, we categorized as *unclassifiable* students whose race/ethnicity based on school records was *unclassifiable* or *missing* and (1) who self-reported their race/ethnicity as *multicultural* but not *Hispanic* or (2) who did not self-report race/ethnicity information.

- **Special education status**

Student has an Individualized Educational Program (IEP) for reasons other than being gifted or talented or is a student with a Section 504 Plan.

- **English language learner status**

Student is currently classified as an English language learner (ELL). (Former ELLs were not included in this category.)

- **Parental education**

Highest level of education attained by either parent: *did not complete high school, graduated high school, had some education after high school,* or *graduated college*. This variable was only available for grade 8 students.

- **Literacy materials**

The presence of reading materials in the home is associated with both socioeconomic status and student achievement. The measure reported in 2009 was based on questions in both grade 4 and grade 8 in the *Student Background Questionnaires*, which asked about the availability of computers, newspapers, magazines, and more than twenty-five books in the home. Between 2009 and 2015, the *Student Background Questionnaire* changed, and a different combination of items was used to calculate a summary score of how many materials were present. In 2011 the items included the availability of computers, magazines, and more than twenty-five books in the home (newspapers were dropped as a survey item). In 2013, 2015, 2017, and 2019, the items included the availability of computers in the home, the availability of the internet, and more than twenty-five books in the home (magazines were dropped as a survey item).[1] A summary score was created to indicate how many of these literacy materials were present in the home.[2]

- **School free or reduced-price lunch eligibility rates**

To level the influence of changing free or reduced-price lunch rates across districts, the Council research team chose to employ a school-level, rather than a student-level, school lunch indicator. Researchers did so by comparing the percentage of free or reduced-price lunch students reported in the National Center for Education Statistics Common Core of Data (CCD) files in the NAEP years prior to the Community Eligibility Program (CEP) and the NAEP reported free or reduced-price lunch percentages. When the values were within 5 percentage points of each other, researchers used the NAEP results for schools as the school-level factor. However, for large discrepancies in the data in years after CEP went into effect (values well above or well below 2012–2013 school year[3]), the CCD school lunch rate was used for the analysis.

- **Percentage of family incomes less than $15,000 per year by school zip code**

Abject poverty or concentrated poverty has been shown to impair student academic outcomes. To further control the influence of abject poverty across school districts, the research team incorporated the percentage of families making less than $15,000 per year in a school's physical zip code as a school-level poverty factor. The zip code data were taken from the US Census Bureau's American Community Survey rolling five-year average for each of the NAEP assessment years.

The following tables summarize data on each of the demographic categories.

Table A2.2 Percentages of NAEP fourth-grade sample by race/ethnicity and type of school (Large City Schools and All Other Schools), 2009 to 2022

	% Black	% Hispanic	% White
Large City Schools			
2009	29	42	21
2011	25	45	20
2013	24	44	22
2015	22	47	20
2017	22	46	20
2019	24	44	19
2022	23	45	20
All Other Schools			
2009	14	19	61
2011	14	20	59
2013	14	22	58
2015	14	22	56
2017	13	23	54
2019	13	23	53

Source: NAEP Data Explorer (NDE) based on NAEP-reported demographics for mathematics.

Table A2.3 Percentages of NAEP fourth-grade sample by FRPL-status, language-status, and IEP status and type of school (Large City Schools and All Other Schools), 2009 to 2022

	% FRPL	% ELLs	% IEPs
Large City Schools			
2009	71	20	11
2011	74	22	11
2013	73	20	12

Table A2.3 (*Continued*)

	% FRPL	% ELLs	% IEPs
2015	74	21	13
2017	70	21	13
2019	68	20	14
2022	68	23	16
All Other Schools			
2009	43	8	12
2011	48	9	12
2013	50	9	13
2015	51	10	14
2017	47	9	13
2019	47	10	14

Source: NAEP Data Explorer (NDE) based on NAEP-reported demographics for mathematics.

Table A2.4 Percentages of NAEP eighth-grade sample by race/ethnicity and type of school (Large City Schools and All Other Schools), 2009 to 2022

	% Black	% Hispanic	% White
Large City Schools			
2009	26	42	22
2011	25	44	21
2013	25	43	21
2015	25	44	21
2017	21	45	21
2019	24	45	19
2022	22	46	19
All Other Schools			
2009	14	17	63
2011	14	19	60
2013	13	20	59
2015	13	21	58
2017	12	21	58
2019	12	22	55

Source: NAEP Data Explorer (NDE) based on NAEP-reported demographics for mathematics.

Table A2.5   Percentages of NAEP eighth-grade sample by FRPL-status, language-status, and IEP status and type of school (Large City Schools and All Other Schools), 2009 to 2022

	% FRPL	% ELL	% IEP
Large City Schools			
2009	66	12	11
2011	69	11	11
2013	69	11	12
2015	71	12	13
2017	65	12	13
2019	66	13	13
2022	66	16	14
All Other Schools			
2009	39	5	10
2011	44	5	10
2013	46	4	12
2015	48	5	12
2017	42	5	12
2019	43	6	13

Source: NAEP Data Explorer (NDE) based on NAEP-reported demographics for mathematics.

Table A2.6   Percentages of NAEP eighth-grade sample whose parents had differing levels of educational attainment, 2009 to 2022

	% Did not finish high school	% Graduated high school	% Graduated college
Large City Schools			
2009	13	17	35
2011	12	17	37
2013	11	17	38
2015	12	17	38
2017	10	17	42
2019	10	16	43
2022	9	17	42
All Other Schools			
2009	7	17	47
2011	7	17	49
2013	7	16	50

Table A2.6 *(Continued)*

	% Did not finish high school	% Graduated high school	% Graduated college
2015	7	16	50
2017	6	14	57
2019	6	13	57

Source: NAEP Data Explorer (NDE) based on NAEP reported demographics for mathematics.
Note: The variable is defined as "at least one parent."

CHAPTER 3

Reports and guidance documents produced by the Council of the Great City Schools and working groups of its member districts during the COVID pandemic:

- *Addressing Unfinished Learning After COVID-19 School Closures*
- *Communications Toolkit for Reopening Schools After COVID-19*
- *Supporting English Language Learners in the COVID-19 Crisis*
- *Guidelines for Supporting Technology-Based Learning Environments*
- *Financial Issues in the Reopening of Schools During the COVID-19 Crisis*
- *Ensuring a Data-Driven Approach to Reopening Schools After COVID-19, Recommendations for Research and Assessment*
- *IDEA Best Practices During the COVID-19 Crisis*
- *Operational Issues in the Reopening of Schools During the COVID-19 Crisis—Facilities, Transportation, and Security*
- *Addressing Mental Health and Social-Emotional Wellness in the COVID-19 Crisis—A Resource Guide for School Districts*
- *Assessing Language Proficiency During Extended School Closures*
- *Council Spotlight on Identifying Signs of Suicide and Non-Suicidal Self-Injury*
- *Council Spotlight on Recognizing and Supporting Student Grief After Loss*
- *Council Spotlight on Fostering Mental Health and Wellness*
- *Council Spotlight on Water Safety in Reopened School Buildings*
- *Council Spotlight on Safeguarding the Right to Vote in the Great City Schools*
- *Increasing Ventilation and Improving Air Quality in Schools*

CHAPTER 4

The following tables present reported and reweighted TUDA math scores for fourth and eighth grades (from Enis Dogan, *Analysis of Recent NAEP TUDA Mathematics Results Based on Alignment to State Assessment Content*). Data on 2022 calculated by Dogan in subsequent analysis.

Table A4.1 Reported and reweighted TUDA means for fourth-grade mathematics by year

District	Reported scale score					Reweighted scale score				
	2013	2015	2017	2019	2022	2013	2015	2017	2019	2022
Albuquerque	234.5	230.6	229.8	229.8	223.3	233.6	231.6	231.2	231.2	223.9
Baltimore	222.9	215.0	215.3	216.5	201.0	222.7	217.0	218.3	218.5	200.5
Boston	236.9	235.5	233.3	233.8	226.8	237.4	236.6	234.5	234.8	227.6
Chicago	230.5	231.9	231.8	232.5	222.2	229.3	233.0	233.9	234.7	223.8
Clark County	NA	NA	230.2	234.5	225.3	NA	NA	231.8	236.9	226.7
DC	228.6	232.2	230.8	235.3	224.1	229.1	234.7	232.9	238.7	226.4
Fresno	219.7	217.7	221.4	224.0	NA	222.1	220.5	226.0	227.1	NA
LA	228.5	224.2	223.1	223.6	219.9	231.3	226.5	226.4	225.9	221.6
San Diego	240.9	232.8	237.4	240.2	232.0	242.8	235.2	241.0	244.2	235.4
Mean diff.						0.73	1.90	2.54	2.42	1.39

Source: Enis Dogan, *Analysis of Recent NAEP TUDA Mathematics Results Based on Alignment to State Assessment Content* (Washington, DC: National Center for Educational Statistics, 2019).

Table A4.2 Reported and reweighted TUDA means for eighth-grade mathematics by year

District	Reported scale score					Reweighted scale score				
	2013	2015	2017	2019	2022	2013	2015	2017	2019	2022
Albuquerque	273.8	270.7	269.6	266.8	260.0	274.2	271.0	270.4	267.8	261.0
Baltimore	259.8	255.2	255.5	254.1	245.3	260.0	255.2	255.9	255.0	246.2
Boston	283.1	281.1	279.7	278.8	269.9	283.4	281.9	280.6	279.7	271.3
Chicago	268.9	274.9	275.6	275.3	263.0	269.3	275.7	276.7	276.2	264.0
Clark County	NA	NA	272.2	271.6	266.8	NA	NA	273.8	273.5	268.1
DC	260.3	258.4	262.0	268.6	256.9	260.2	259.0	262.9	269.9	258.1
Fresno	259.7	256.9	254.6	253.5	NA	261.9	257.6	256.3	254.9	NA
LA	264.3	263.5	266.8	260.7	262.4	266.6	265.0	269.4	262.8	265.0
San Diego	276.9	280.4	282.8	282.6	274.4	278.7	281.9	284.2	284.7	277.3
Mean diff.	0.94						0.78	1.27	1.39	1.54

Source: Enis Dogan, *Analysis of Recent NAEP TUDA Mathematics Results Based on Alignment to State Assessment Content* (Washington, DC: National Center for Educational Statistics, 2019).

CHAPTER 5

The following tables present various bands of average income levels in the TUDA districts in 2019. Data were used in chapter 5 to explain, in part, why it takes some urban school systems longer to improve than other districts. Source: U.S. Bureau of the Census.

Table A5.1 Percentage of households by income level in TUDA districts, 2019

	% Less than $10,000	% $10,000 to $14,999	% $15,000 to $24,999	% $25,000 to $34,999	% $35,000 to $49,999	Total % of families[a] below $50,000
Cleveland Metropolitan School District	15.3	10.0	15.2	12.6	12.8	65.9
Detroit City School District	16.9	7.5	13.0	13.5	14.9	65.8
Milwaukee School District	9.6	6.3	13.6	10.5	15.9	55.9
Fresno Unified School District	10.4	6.8	11.9	13.0	13.1	55.2
Memphis-Shelby County School District	9.3	7.1	10.8	11.4	14.8	53.4
Philadelphia City School District	12.2	6.6	9.7	9.9	13.3	51.7
Baltimore City Public Schools	12.3	5.4	8.6	10.6	13.1	50.0
Guilford County Schools	7.4	4.6	9.6	9.8	14.8	46.2
Fort Worth Independent School District	8.5	4.3	8.8	11.0	13.5	46.1
Miami-Dade County School District	8.0	5.3	9.8	10.3	12.2	45.6
Houston Independent School District	8.2	4.6	10.2	9.6	12.5	45.1
Dallas Independent School District	8.6	4.0	9.0	9.0	14.4	45.0
Albuquerque Public Schools	7.9	5.0	9.3	9.5	12.6	44.3
Jefferson County School District	6.4	4.1	9.3	9.7	13.3	42.8

Table A5.1 (Continued)

	% Less than $10,000	% $10,000 to $14,999	% $15,000 to $24,999	% $25,000 to $34,999	% $35,000 to $49,999	Total % of families[a] below $50,000
Duval County School District	6.8	3.8	8.8	9.5	13.8	42.7
Chicago Public School District	8.6	5.1	9.2	9.1	10.3	42.3
Hillsborough County School District	7.0	3.4	7.9	9.3	12.9	40.5
Atlanta City School District	9.4	4.9	8.2	6.5	10.6	39.6
Clark County School District	6.6	3.8	7.7	8.3	13.2	39.6
Los Angeles Unified School District	6.4	5.0	8.3	7.9	11.0	38.6
New York City Department of Education	8.5	5.2	7.9	7.3	9.6	38.5
Charlotte-Mecklenburg Schools	4.5	3.4	6.5	8.2	12.9	35.5
Boston School District	9.8	5.3	6.7	5.7	7.5	35.0
Austin Independent School District	6.8	2.7	6.7	7.2	11.4	34.8
Denver County School District	5.5	3.6	6.6	6.9	9.8	32.4
San Diego City Unified School District	4.6	3.9	6.0	5.9	9.3	29.7
District of Columbia Public Schools	8.0	3.3	4.9	4.6	8.5	29.3

Source: U.S. Bureau of the Census.

[a] No statistical adjustments were made for family size.

Table A5.2 TUDA districts with negative district effects in four grade/subject combinations and their abject poverty levels, 2019

	District effect in grade 4 reading	District effect in grade 8 reading	District effect in grade 4 mathematics	District effect in grade 8 mathematics	Percentage of families below $15,000	Percentage of families below $50,000
Albuquerque	–1.56	–5.32	–0.81	–3.68	12.9%	44.3%
Baltimore	–7.24	–0.65	–4.84	–2.34	17.7%	50.0%
Detroit	–11.19	–3.98	–9.23	–4.68	24.4%	65.8%
Fresno	–1.39	–6.50	–3.08	–10.86	17.2%	55.2%
Los Angeles	–4.94	–3.93	–7.22	–7.39	11.4%	38.6%
Milwaukee	–10.89	–2.06	–6.97	–4.93	15.9%	55.9%
Philadelphia	–6.02	–2.99	–6.97	–4.67	18.8%	51.7%

Source: U.S. Bureau of the Census.

Table A5.3 TUDA districts with negative district effects in four grade/subject combinations and their percentage of Black students and English language learners, 2019

	District effect in grade 4 reading	District effect in grade 8 reading	District effect in grade 4 mathematics	District effect in grade 8 mathematics	Percentage of district students who were Black	Percentage of district students who were English language learners
Albuquerque	−1.56	−5.32	−0.81	−3.68	2.52%	16.98%
Baltimore	−7.24	−0.65	−4.84	−2.34	78.57%	6.81%
Detroit	−11.19	−3.98	−9.23	−4.68	82.04%	12.41%
Fresno	−1.39	−6.50	−3.08	−10.86	8.20%	18.84%
Los Angeles	−4.94	−3.93	−7.22	−7.39	8.37%	20.56%
Milwaukee	−10.89	−2.06	−6.97	−4.93	51.50%	11.95%
Philadelphia	−6.02	−2.99	−6.97	−4.67	49.24%	11.70%

Source: U.S. Bureau of the Census.

CHAPTER 7

The following graphs were prepared by Akisha Osei Sarfo and Brian Garcia, Council of the Great City Schools, using NAEP data since 2013 to compare trends in average scale scores in large city independent charters with traditional large city public schools and their charters over time.

Figure A7.1 Comparison of NAEP fourth grade reading scores of students in large city independent charters and traditional public schools and their charters (all students), 2013–2022

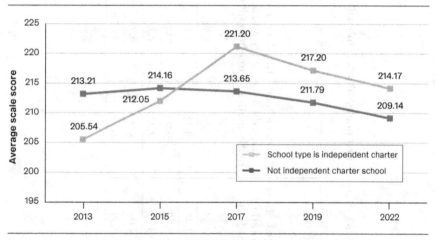

Source: Akisha Osei Sarfo and Brian Garcia, Council of the Great City Schools

Figure A7.2 Comparison of NAEP eighth grade reading scores of students in large city independent charters and traditional public schools and their charters (all students), 2013–2022

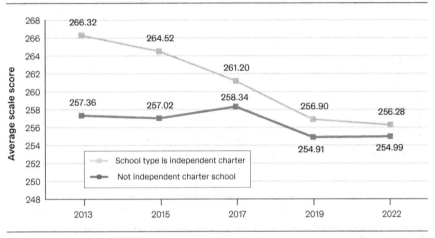

Source: Akisha Osei Sarfo and Brian Garcia, Council of the Great City Schools

Figure A7.3 Comparison of NAEP fourth grade mathematics scores of students in large city independent charters and traditional public schools and their charters (all students), 2013–2022

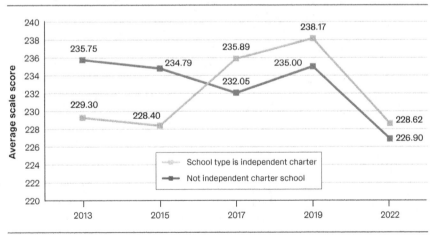

Source: Akisha Osei Sarfo and Brian Garcia, Council of the Great City Schools

Figure A7.4   Comparison of NAEP eighth grade mathematics scores of students in large city independent charters and traditional public schools and their charters (all students), 2013–2022

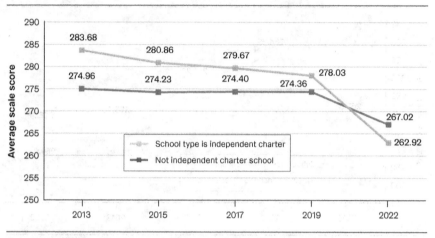

Source: Akisha Osei Sarfo and Brian Garcia, Council of the Great City Schools

Notes

Chapter 1

1. Andrew Van Dam, "The Happiest, Least Stressful Jobs on Earth," *Washington Post*, January 15, 2023.
2. Council of the Great City Schools, Enrollment Dashboard (Washington, DC: Council of the Great City Schools, 2024), www.cgcs.org/enrollmentdashboard.
3. The seventy-five city school systems that were members of the Council of the Great City Schools in 2019 were home to about 19.4 percent of the US population (63,744,443 of 328,239,523, estimated). And their public school districts enrolled about 7.5 million students, or about 15 percent of the nation's public elementary and secondary school enrollment.
4. Frederick Hess and Matthew Rice, "The Real-World Cost of Remote Learning," *National Review*, November 20, 2020, https://www.nationalreview.com/2020/11/the-real-world -cost-of-remote-learning/.
5. Jennifer Heppen, Nicholas Sorensen, Elaine Allensworth, Kirk Walters, Jordan Rickles, Suzanne Stachel Taylor, and Valerie Michelman, "The Struggle to Pass Algebra: Online vs. Face-to-Face CreditRecovery for At-Risk Urban Students," *Journal of Research on Educational Effectiveness* 10, no. 2 (2017): 272–96, https://doi.org/10.1080/19345747.2016 .1168500.
6. Michael Casserly, "Memo: Update from the Great City Schools on the Coronovirus Pandemic" (Washington, DC: Council of the Great City Schools, April 15, 2020).
7. Angelique Boutzoukas, Kanecia O. Zimmerman, Moira Inkelas, M. Alan Brookhart, Daniel K. Benjamin, Sabrina Butteris, Shawn Koval, et al. "School Masking Policies and Secondary SARS-CoV-2 Transmission," *Pediatrics* 149, no. 6 (2022), https://publications .aap.org/pediatrics/article/doi/10.1542/peds.2022-056687/185379/School-Masking -Policies-and-Secondary-SARS-CoV-2.
8. Cindy Marten's comments made at the Legislative and Policy Conference of the Council of the Great City Schools, Washington, D.C., March 20, 2022.
9. Ray Hart, Michael Casserly, Renata Uzzell, Moses Palacios, and Amanda Corcoran, *Student Testing in America's Great City Schools: An Inventory and Preliminary Analysis* (Washington, DC: Council of the Great City Schools, October 2015).

10. Center for Education Reform, "Record Education Drop is Education Malnourishment," news release, October 24, 2022, https://edreform.com/2022/10/record-education-drop-is-academic-malnourishment/.

11. Robert Pondiscio, "The Unbearable Bleakness of American Schooling" (Washington, DC: American Enterprise Institute, Ed Express, February 22, 2022).

12. Robin Lake and Paul Hill, "Can Districts Rise to the Challenge of New NAEP Results? Outlook's Not So Good," The 74, November 10, 2022, https://www.the74million.org/article/can-districts-rise-to-the-challenge-of-new-naep-results-outlooks-not-so-good/.

13. Robin Lake, "Flattening the Learning Loss Curve When School Reopens Will Take Federal Leadership, State and Local Buy-in and These Four Steps," The 74, April 30, 2020, https://www.the74million.org/article/robin-lake-flattening-the-learning-loss-curve-when-school-reopens-will-take-federal-leadership-state-and-local-buy-in-and-these-4-steps/.

14. William H. Frey, "Big Cities Saw Historic Population Losses While Suburban Growth Declined During the Pandemic," Brookings Institute, July 11, 2022, https://www.brookings.edu/articles/big-cities-saw-historic-population-losses-while-suburban-growth-declined-during-the-pandemic/.

15. Phi Delta Kappa, *PDK Poll of the Public's Attitudes toward the Public Schools*, September 2021, https://pdkpoll.org/wp-content/uploads/2021/09/Poll53_final.pdf.

16. NPR/Ipsos, "Parents Report Improvements in Their Child's Educational Attainment Compared to Last Year," April 29, 2022, https://www.ipsos.com/en-us/news-polls/NPR-Ipsos-Parent-Child-Education-04282022.

17. Erika Christakis, "Americans Have Given Up on Public Schools. That's a Mistake," *The Atlantic*, October 2017.

18. Christakis, "Americans Have Given Up."

19. Comments by David Cleary made at the Legislative and Policy Conference of the Council of the Great City Schools, Washington, DC, March 21, 2022.

20. Council of the Great City Schools, Vision Statement, Annual Report 2022–2023 (Washington, DC: Council of the Great City Schools, 2023).

21. Eric Hanushek, Guido Schwerdt, Simon Wiederhold, and Ludger Woessman, "Returns to Skills Around the World: Evidence from PIAAC," *European Economic Review* 73 (2015): 103–30.

22. Horace Mann, Twelfth Annual Report to the Secretary of the Massachusetts State Board of Education, 1848, https://genius.com/Horace-mann-twelfth-annual-report-to-the-secretary-of-the-massachusetts-state-board-of-education-1848-annotated.

Chapter 2

1. This volume uses several terms to refer to urban public schools. The term Great City Schools refers to the seventy-eight big-city school districts that currently make up the Council of the Great City Schools. To be eligible for this category, an urban public school system must be the dominant or largest school district in a city with a population of at least 250,000 people with a school district with an enrollment of 35,000 and demographic characteristics within the range of the current membership. In addition, eligibility is extended to the largest city school system in a state, regardless of the size of that district. Finally, districts may be grandfathered into membership if their enrollment falls below the formal eligibility criteria. (See the appendix for a list of the seventy-eight districts.)

The term *Large City Schools* does not refer to districts but to students enrolled in public schools in the urbanized areas of cities with populations of 250,000 or more. "Large city" is not synonymous with "inner city." Schools in participating TUDA districts are also included in the definition of Large City Schools, even though some of these districts have schools that would otherwise not be defined as Large City Schools. Large City Schools also includes both district and independent charter schools, since the two were not reported separately prior to 2013. The term TUDA refers to the Trial Urban District Assessment and included twenty-seven urban school systems in 2019: Albuquerque, Atlanta, Austin, Baltimore City, Boston, Charlotte-Mecklenburg, Chicago, Clark County (NV), Cleveland, Dallas, Denver, Detroit, the District of Columbia, Duval County (FL), Fort Worth, Fresno, Guilford County (NC), Hillsborough County (FL), Houston, Jefferson County (KY), Los Angeles, Memphis-Shelby County, Miami-Dade County, Milwaukee, New York City, Philadelphia, and San Diego. Eligibility for TUDA includes the same criteria as membership in the Great City Schools, plus the district must be large enough to support a three-subject NAEP sample. References to "big-city school districts" "urban public schools" or "public education in the nation's major cities" are meant generically. All other references are specifically footnoted.

2. This chapter and chapters 4 and 5 are based with written permission on the report by Michael Casserly, Ray Hart, Amanda Corcoran, Moses Palacios, Renata Lyons, and Eric Vignola, *Mirrors or Windows: How Well Do Large City Public Schools Overcome the Effects of Poverty and Other Barriers?* (Washington, DC: Council of the Great City Schools, 2021).

3. Results on Large City Schools are for students in public schools located in the urbanized areas of cities with populations of 250,000 or more. "Large City" is not synonymous with "inner city." Schools in participating TUDA districts are also included in the results for Large City Schools, even though some of these districts have schools that would otherwise not be defined as Large City Schools. Students in the TUDA districts represent about one-half of the students who attend Large City Schools nationally. The comparison to students in Large City Schools is made because the demographic characteristics of those students are most like the characteristics of students in urban districts.

4. NAEP results and statistically expected NAEP results for each of the TUDA districts by year are reported on pages 27, 30, 33, and 36 of the report by Casserly et al., *Mirrors or Windows*. The methodology for analyzing data is found on pages 74–80 of the same report.

5. The NCES collects parental education levels only for eighth-grade students participating in NAEP.

6. Both groups, Large City Schools and All Other Schools, included charter schools. NAEP data did not allow determination of whether a charter was independent or part of a local school system until 2013. Consequently, in this analysis, Large City Schools and All Other Schools include district-authorized charters and independent charters. When looking at individual Trial Urban District Assessment (TUDA) districts, charters were included when their district sample incorporates them, but they are excluded where charters are independent and not counted in the district's scores. More recent data that allow for separate reporting of independent charters are included in chapter 7.

7. These are the three largest racial and ethnic groups in the nation's largest urban school systems. Asian American, Pacific Islander, Native American, and Native Alaskan students make up about 10 percent of the Great City Schools enrollment.

8. Richard Florida, *The New Urban Crisis: How Our Cities Are Increasing Inequality, Deepening Segregation, and Failing the Middle Class and What We Can Do About It* (New York: Basic Books, 2017).

9. NAEP uses the ID code IEP to include students with disabilities, IEPs, or those with 504 plans.

10. There is a slight difference between "actual results" in this chapter and the results reported by the National Center for Education Statistics (NCES) because the actual results presented here omit data on any student that does not have a full complement of information on all variables examined in this analysis.

11. Data for this analysis come from the TUDA of NAEP that the Council of the Great City Schools initiated in the fall of 2000. The project was piloted in 2002 in mathematics. And in 2003, Large City Schools participated in both reading and mathematics assessments. The voluntary effort involves the oversampling of students in each participating district to obtain a district-level estimate of reading and mathematics performance in grades 4 and 8. The analysis in this chapter uses both general NAEP data as well as district-specific TUDA data.

12. Jacob Cohen, *Statistical Power Analysis for the Behavioral Sciences*, 2nd ed. (Mahway, NJ: Lawrence Erlbaum Associates, 1988); Matthew Kraft, "Interpreting Effect Sizes of Education Interventions," *Educational Researcher* 49, no. 4 (2020): 241–53, https://doi.org/10.3102/0013189X20912798. Kraft, who has applied the effect size methodology to educational settings, describes an effect size for field-based education interventions of 0.2 or above as large, between 0.2 and 0.05 as medium, and below 0.05 as small.

13. Note that changes in demographics in any individual city are reflected in the changing expected mean values. See, for example, Cleveland, District of Columbia, and Detroit.

14. Albuquerque, Dallas, and Hillsborough County began participating in TUDA in 2011, and the NCES reports trends on them for only five assessment cycles rather than six. Duval County began participating in 2015, and Milwaukee did not participate in 2015 but rejoined in 2017. Clark County, Denver, Fort Worth, Guilford County, and Shelby County began participating in 2017 and only have calculations across two testing cycles.

15. No student questionnaire data were collected on eighth graders in Denver, so it was not possible to calculate adjusted NAEP scores at this grade level in Denver.

16. We use both terms African American and Black throughout the text.

17. Chester Holland, Akisha Osei Sarfo, Brian Garcia, and Ray Hart, *Between the Lines: Large City Performance on NAEP Over the Last 20 Years (2002-2022)* (Washington, DC: Council of the Great City Schools, October 2023).

18. Jeffrey Henig, Richard C. Hula, Marion Orr, and Desiree S. Pedescleaux, *The Color of School Reform: Pace, Politics, and the Challenge of Urban Education* (Princeton, NJ: Princeton University Press, 1999).

19. Christian Barnard, "The Weighted Student Formula Yearbook, 2019" (Washington, DC: The Reason Foundation, July 2019). Weights on student enrollment in this analysis use the average weights of the districts reported by The Reason Foundation. Where districts reported a range of weights, we used the midpoint in the range for students from families with low incomes and ELLs and the low end of the range for students with disabilities. This methodology likely underestimates low-incidence, high-cost students with disabilities.

20. Eric Hanushek, Guido Schwerdt, Simon Wiederhold, and Ludger Woessman, "Returns to Skills Around the World: Evidence from PIAAC," *European Economic Review* 73 (2015): 103–30.

Chapter 3

1. Ben Willis was named by President John Kennedy to head a national commission on vocational education, which laid the groundwork for the 1963 Vocational Education Act; and Nicholas Janulis, *Chicago Schooling, Benjamin Willis, and the Fight Against Integration* (Chicago: University of Chicago, August 2022).
2. Council of the Great City Schools, *Celebrating 60 Years of Service to America's Urban Public Schools* (Washington, DC: Council of the Great City Schools, 2016).
3. United States National Commission on Excellence in Education, *A Nation at Risk: The Imperative for Education Reform* (Washington, DC: United States National Commission on Excellence in Education, 1983).
4. Peter Senge, *The Fifth Discipline: The Art and Practice of the Learning Organization* (New York: Random House Business, 2006).
5. W. Edward Deming, *Out of the Crisis* (Boston: MIT Press, 1982).
6. Kay Kendall and Glenn Bodinson, *Leading the Malcolm Baldridge Way: How World-Class Leaders Align Their Organizations to Deliver Exceptional Results* (New York: McGraw Hill, 2016).
7. Jim Collins, *Good to Great: Why Some Companies Make the Leap . . . and Others Don't* (New York: HarperCollins, 2001).
8. Tom McCarty, Lorraine Daniels, Michael Bremer, and Praveen Gupta, "Six Sigma Learning Topic: Introduction to Process Improvement Teams," *The Six Sigma Black Belt Handbook.* (New York: McGraw Hill, 2005).
9. Ronald Edmonds, "Effective Schools for the Urban Poor," *Educational Leadership* (ASCD, October 1979).
10. Anthony Bryk, Louis M. Gomez, Alicia Grunow, and Paul G. LeMahieu, *Learning to Improve: How America's Schools Can Get Better at Getting Better* (Cambridge, MA: Harvard Education Publishing, 2015).
11. Denisa R. Superville, "Urban Schools' Group Leaves Mark on K-12," *Education Week* 36, no. 1 (August 23, 2016), https://www.edweek.org/leadership/urban-schools-group-leaves-imprint-on-k-12-policy/2016/08.
12. Sam Dillon, "States Receive a Reading List: New Standards for Education," *New York Times*, June 2, 2010.
13. Council of the Great City Schools, "Urban Schools Stand Behind Common Standards," *The Urban Educator* 19, no. 5, page 1 (June/July 2010).
14. Tom Loveless, *Between the State and the Schoolhouse: Understanding the Failure of Common Core* (Cambridge, MA: Harvard Education Press, 2021).
15. Council of the Great City Schools, *National Urban Education Goals: Baseline Indicators, 1990–91* (Washington, DC: Council of the Great City Schools, 1992).
16. Council of the Great City Schools, *Beating the Odds: An Analysis of Student Performance and Achievement Gaps on State Assessments* (Washington, DC: Council of the Great City Schools, 1998 through 2008).

17. Council of the Great City Schools, *Proposal to Conduct a Trial NAEP Assessment for Large Urban School Districts to the National Assessment Governing Board (NAGB)* (Washington, DC: Council of the Great City Schools, November 17, 2000).

18. Council of the Great City Schools, *Comments on the Draft Mathematics Framework for 2025 National Assessment of Educational Progress* (Washington, DC: Council of the Great City Schools, June 7, 2019).

19. Council of the Great City Schools, *Managing for Results in America's Great City Schools: A Report of the Performance Measurement and Benchmarking Project* (Washington, DC: Council of the Great City Schools, October 2023); Council of the Great City Schools, *Academic Key Performance Indicators*, revised report (Washington, DC: Council of the Great City Schools, 2023).

20. Jason Snipes, Fred Doolittle, and Corrine Herlihy, *Foundations for Success: Case Studies of How Urban School Systems Improve Student Achievement* (New York: MDRC for the Council of the Great City Schools, 2002).

21. Amanda Horwitz, Gabriela Uro, Ricki Price-Baugh, Candace Simon, Renata Uzzell, Sharon Lewis, and Michael Casserly, *Succeeding with English Language Learners: Lessons Learned from the Great City Schools* (Washington, DC: Council of the Great City Schools, October 2009).

22. Michael Casserly, Ricki Price-Baugh, Sharon Lewis, Jessica Heppen, Steve Leinwand, Victor Bandeira de Mello, Enis Dogan, et al., *Pieces of the Puzzle: Factors in the Improvement of Urban School Districts on the National Assessment of Educational Progress* (Washington, DC: Council of the Great City Schools and the American Institutes for Research, 2011).

23. Michael Casserly, Ray Hart, Amanda Corcoran, Moses Palacios, Renata Lyons, Eric Vignola with Ricki Price-Baugh, Robin Hall, and Denise Walston, *Mirrors or Windows: How Well Do Large City Public Schools Overcome the Effects of Poverty and Other Barriers?* (Washington, DC: Council of the Great City Schools, June 2021).

24. Frederick M. Hess and Eric Osberg, eds., *Stretching the School Dollar: How Schools and Districts Can Save Money While Serving Students Best* (Cambridge, MA: Harvard Education Press, 2010).

25. Council of the Great City Schools, *Managing for Results in America's Great City Schools: A Case Study in Grants Management* (Washington, DC: Council of the Great City Schools, June 2012).

26. Council of the Great City Schools, *Managing for Results in America's Great City Schools: A Case Study in the Area of Accounts Payable* (Washington, DC: Council of the Great City Schools, March 2012).

27. Council of the Great City Schools, *Managing for Results in America's Great City Schools: A Case Study in the Area of Procurement* (Washington, DC: Council of the Great City Schools, October 2008).

28. Robert Carlson, "Managing for Results: A White Paper—What the Peer Reviews Tell Us" (white paper, Washington, DC, Council of the Great City Schools, 2023).

29. Jay Mathews, "Studies Question the Idea That Low-income Schools Are Poorly Funded," *Washington Post*, November 6, 2023.

30. Council of the Great City Schools, *Review of the Administrative Structure and Resource Allocations of the Birmingham City Schools* (Washington, DC: Council of the Great City Schools, December 2007).

31. Michael Casserly, email to the Executive Committee of the Council of the Great City Schools, February 24, 2008.

32. Bob Sims, "Mims Offers Explanation on Missing Report Pages," *Birmingham News*, March 4, 2008.

33. Marie Leech and Jeff Hansen, Birmingham Schools Hid the Bad News: Report Critical of System Altered," *Birmingham News*, February 12, 2008.

Chapter 4

1. This chapter and chapters 2 and 5 are based with written permission on the report by Michael Casserly, Ray Hart, Amanda Corcoran, Moses Palacios, Renata Lyons, and Eric Vignola, *Mirrors or Windows: How Well Do Large City Public Schools Overcome the Effects of Poverty and Other Barriers?* (Washington, DC: Council of the Great City Schools, 2021).

2. Anthony Bryk, *How a City Learned to Improve Its Schools* (Cambridge, MA: Harvard Education Press, 2023).

3. Frederick Hess, ed., *Urban School Reform: Lessons from San Diego* (Cambridge, MA: Harvard Education Press, 2005).

4. Charles Kerchner, David Menefee-Libey, Laura Mulfinger, and Stephanie Clayton, *Learning from LA: Institutional Change in American Public Education* (Cambridge, MA: Harvard Education Press, 2008).

5. Michael Pitts, *Inerasable: An Enduring Script for Quality Instruction and Quality Schools! The Real Atlanta Public Schools Story* (Alpharetta, GA: Mountain Arbor Press, 2020).

6. Mark Tucker, *Leading High-Performance School Systems: Lessons from the World's Best* (Arlington, VA: ASCD, 2019).

7. Donald McAdams and Dan Katzir, eds., *The Redesign of Urban School Systems: Case Studies in District Governance* (Cambridge, MA: Harvard Education Press, 2013).

8. Julie A. Marsh, Kerri A. Kerr, Gina S. Ikemoto, Hilary Darilek, Marika Suttorp, Ron W. Zimmer, and Healther Barney, *The Role of Districts in Fostering Instructional Improvement: Lessons from Three Urban Districts Partnered with the Institute of Learning* (Pittsburgh: Rand Corporation, 2005).

9. Karen Chenoweth, *Schools That Succeed: How Educators Marshal the Power of Systems for Improvement* (Cambridge, MA: Harvard Education Press, 2017).

10. Paul Cobb, Kara Jackson, and Erin Henrick, *Systems for Instructional Improvement: Creating Coherence from the Classroom to the District's Office* (Cambridge, MA: Harvard Education Press, 2018).

11. Stacey Childress, Richard Elmore, Allen Grossman, and Susan Moore Johnson, eds., *Managing School Districts for High Performance: Cases in Public Education Leadership* (Cambridge, MA: Harvard Education Press, 2007).

12. Heather Zavadsky, *Bringing School Reform to Scale: Five Award-Winning Urban Districts* (Cambridge, MA: Harvard Education Press, 2009).

13. Susan Moore Johnson, Geoff Marietta, Monica Higgins, Karen Mapp, and Allen Grossman, *Achieving Coherence in District Improvement: Managing the Relationship Between the Central Office and Schools* (Cambridge, MA: Harvard Education Press, 2014).

14. The Organization for Economic Cooperation and Development (OECD), *Strong Performers and Successful Reformers in Education: Lessons from PISA for the United States* (Paris: The Organization for Economic Cooperation and Development, 2020).

15. Anthony Bryk, Louis M. Gomez, Alicia Grunow, and Paul G. LeMahieu, *Learning to Improve: How America's Schools Can Get Better at Getting Better* (Cambridge, MA: Harvard Education Publishing, 2015).

16. Institute for Education Sciences, "Introduction to Improvement Science" (Institute for Education Sciences, Regional Educational Laboratory Program, REL West, December 2017).

17. Bryk, *Learning to Improve.*

18. Samuel P. Whalen, *What Is Known About the Capacity of Large Urban School Districts to Pursue Continuous Improvement Strategies? Project: Continuous Improvement of Senior Leadership Practices in a Major American Urban School District* (Chicago: University of Illinois at Chicago [UIC] Center for Urban Education Leadership, November 1, 2019); Samuel P. Whalen, *Transforming Central Office Practices for Equity, Coherence, and Continuous Improvement: Chicago Public Schools Under the Leadership of Dr. Janice K. Jackson* (Chicago: Center for Urban Education Leadership, College of Education, University of Illinois at Chicago, December 15, 2020).

19. Mona Mourshed, Chinezi Chijoke, and Michael Barber, *How the World's Most Improved School Systems Keep Getting Better* (New York: McKinsey & Company, 2010).

20. This same lesson was learned several years ago in the Charlotte-Mecklenburg public schools, which had several superintendents but who all sustained the same overall academic theories of action.

21. Michael Casserly, interview with Janice Jackson, October 31, 2017.

22. Tom Loveless, *Between the State and the Schoolhouse: Understanding the Failure of Common Core* (Cambridge, MA: Harvard Education Press, 2021).

23. Michael Cohen and Laura Slover, "Unfinished Agenda: The Future of Standards-Based School Reform" (Washington, DC: FutureEd, 2023), https://www.future-ed.org/wp-content/uploads/2022/06/STANDARDS_Movement_Essay.pdf.

24. Enis Dogan, *Analysis of Recent NAEP TUDA Mathematics Results Based on Alignment to State Assessment Content* (Washington, DC: National Center for Educational Statistics, 2019).

25. Kate Walsh, *Making a Difference: Six Places Where Teacher Evaluation Systems Are Getting Results* (Washington, DC: National Council on Teacher Quality, 2018).

26. Michael Casserly, Ricki Price-Baugh, Amanda Corcoran, Renata Uzzell, Candace Simon, Jessica Heppen, Steve Leinwand, et al., *Pieces of the Puzzle: Factors in the Improvement of Urban School Districts on the National Assessment of Educational Progress* (Washington, DC: Council of the Great City School, 2011).

27. Michael Casserly, interview with Kaya Henderson, December 18, 2023.

28. Michael Casserly, interview with Janice Jackson, December 19, 2023.

29. Bryk, *How a City Learned.*

30. Zelman v. Simmons-Harris, 536 US 639 (2002).

31. Frank G. Jackson, Cleveland's Plan for Transforming Schools: Reinventing Public Education in Our City and Serving as a Model of Innovation for the State of Ohio (Cleveland, OH: Office of the mayor of the City of Cleveland, Ohio, 2012).

32. Michael Casserly, Interview with Eric Gordon, July 5, 2022.

33. Council of the Great City Schools, *Foundations for Success in the Denver Public Schools: A Report of the Strategic Support Team of the Council of the Great City Schools* (Washington, DC: Council of the Great City Schools, 2006).

34. Michael Casserly, R. Price-Baugh, and R. Hart, memorandum to Tom Boasberg, Superintendent, Denver Public Schools, October 17, 2014.

35. We did not conduct a case study of Denver because the district had not been taking NAEP for an extended period and did not have extensive trend data using this assessment.

36. Michael Casserly, memorandum to Margie Vandeven, Commissioner, Missouri Department of Elementary and Secondary Education, December 17, 2020.

37. Michael Casserly, interview with Nikolai Vitti, April 12, 2023.

Chapter 5

1. This chapter and chapters 2 and 4 are based with written permission on the report by Michael Casserly, Ray Hart, Amanda Corcoran, Moses Palacios, Renata Lyons, and Eric Vignola, *Mirrors or Windows: How Well Do Large City Public Schools Overcome the Effects of Poverty and Other Barriers?* (Washington, DC: Council of the Great City Schools, 2021).

2. Council of the Great City Schools, *A Review of the Academic Program of the School District of Philadelphia* (Washington, DC: Council of the Great City Schools, March 26, 2020); Council of the Great City Schools, *Review of the Instructional Program of the Jackson Public Schools* (Washington, DC: Council of the Great City Schools, 2018).

3. Council of the Great City Schools, *Reforming and Improving the Detroit Public Schools: Report of the Strategic Support Teams of the Council of the Great City Schools* (Washington, DC: Council of the Great City Schools, 2008).

4. Airick Journey Crabill, *Great on Their Behalf: Why School Boards Fail, How Yours Can Become Effective*,(Austin, TX: Lioncrest Publishers, 2023).

5. Council of the Great City Schools, *Managing for Results in America's Great City Schools: Results from Fiscal Year 2020-21. A Report of the Performance Measurement and Benchmarking Project* (Washington, DC: Council of the Great City Schools, October 2022).

6. Chicago and San Diego did not report data.

7. Beth Schueler and Joshua Bleiberg, "Evaluating Education Governance: Does State Takeover of School Districts Affect Student Achievement?" *Journal of Policy Analysis and Management*, 2021.

8. Kenneth Wong and Francis Shen, "Measuring the Effectiveness of City and State Takeover as a School Reform Strategy," *Peabody Journal of Education* 78 (2003): 89–119.

9. Council of the Great City Schools, *Nashville Superintendent's Transition Team Report on Student Achievement: Summary of Findings and Recommendations* (Washington, DC: Council of the Great City Schools, 2016).

10. Council of the Great City Schools, *Next Steps in the Improvement of the Dayton Public Schools: Report of the Strategic Support Team of the Council of the Great City Schools* (Washington, DC: Council of the Great City Schools, Fall 2008).

11. Council of the Great City Schools, *Raising the Achievement of English Language Learners in the Des Moines Public Schools: A Report of the Strategic Support Team of the Council of the Great City Schools* (Washington, DC: Council of the Great City Schools, 2016).

12. Council of the Great City Schools, *Raising the Achievement of English Learners in the Providence Public Schools: Report of the Strategic Support Team of the Council of the Great City Schools* (Washington, DC: Council of the Great City Schools, 2019).

13. Council of the Great City Schools, *Raising the Achievement of English Language Learners in the Seattle Public Schools: Report of the Strategic Support Team of the Council of the Great City Schools* (Washington, DC: Council of the Great City Schools, 2008).

14. Council of the Great City Schools, *Improving Special Education Services in the Stockton Unified School District* (Washington, DC: Council of the Great City Schools, Summer, 2019).

15. Council of the Great City Schools, *Improving Special Education Services in the Buffalo Public Schools: Report of the Strategic Support Team of the Council of the Great City Schools* (Washington, DC: Council of the Great City Schools, 2014).

16. Council of the Great City Schools, *Improving Special Education Services in the Austin Independent School District: Report of the Strategic Support Team of the Council of the Great City Schools* (Washington, DC: Council of the Great City Schools, Summer 2010).

17. T. J. Sugrue, *The Origins of the Urban Crisis: Race and Inequality in Postwar Detroit* (Princeton, NJ: Princeton University Press, 2005).

18. Elizabeth Eisenhaur, "In Poor Health: Supermarket Redlining and Urban Nutrition," *GeoJournal* 53 (2001):125–33, https://doi.org/10.1023/A:105772503007.

19. Council of the Great City Schools, *A Review of the Academic Program of the School District of Philadelphia* (Washington, DC: Council of the Great City Schools, March 26, 2020); Council of the Great City Schools, *Review of the Instructional Program of the Jackson Public Schools* (Washington, DC: Council of the Great City Schools, 2018).

20. Erin Fahle, Thomas Kane, Sean Reardon, and Douglas Staiger, "The First Year of the Pandemic Recovery: A District-Level Analysis" (Center for Education Policy Research, Harvard University, and the Educational Opportunity Project, Stanford University, January 2024), ERS Report Final 1/30 2:48 (educationrecoveryscorecard.org).

Chapter 6

1. Dutch Leonard and Arnold Howitt, *Leading in Crises: Observations on the Political and Decision-Making Dimensions of Response* (Cambridge, MA: Harvard University School of Business, 2010).

2. Dutch Leonard and Robert Kaplan, *Crisis Management for Leaders* (Cambridge, MA: Seminar of the Harvard Business School, March 24, 2020), https://www.alumni.hbs.edu.

3. Emma Harville, "Twin Cities Teachers Unions Demand Schools Stay Closed This Fall," *Twin Cities Pioneer Press*, July 24, 2020.

4. Elizabeth Shockman, "Unscientific Survey Shows Most MN Families Want In-Person School, Despise Distance Learning," *MPRNews*, July 9, 2020.

5. American Federation of Teachers, "Press Release: To Ensure Students' Safety, Strikes Could be Used as a Last Resort," July 28, 2020.

6. Council of the Great City Schools, *Ensuring a Data-Driven Approach to Reopening Schools After COVID 19* (Washington, DC: Council of the Great City Schools, June 2020).

7. Council of the Great City Schools, *Legislative, Regulatory, Administrative, and Policy Recommendations for the President-elect Biden Education Transition Team* (Washington, DC: Council of the Great City Schools, 2020).

8. Catherine Gewertz, "How School Districts Can Run a COVID-19 Vaccine Clinic," *Education Week*, February 4, 2021.

9. The COVID Crisis Group, *Lessons from the COVID War: An Investigative Report* (New York: Public Affairs, 2023).

Chapter 7

1. "The Startling Evidence in Learning Loss Is In," *New York Times*, November 18, 2023.
2. Council of the Great City Schools, Enrollment Dashboard, WWW.cgcs.org/enrollment-dashboard. (The figures in this database come from the Common Core of Data, National Center for Education Statistics.)
3. PreK data include information on sixty-eight of the seventy-eight big-city school districts. The ten districts not included are the Fresno Unified School District, the Long Beach Unified School District, the Los Angeles Unified School District, the Oakland Unified School District, the Phoenix Union High School District, the Portland Public Schools, the Sacramento City Unified School district, the San Diego Unified School district, the San Francisco Unified School District, and the Santa Ana Unified School District.
4. Lauraine Langrea, "Charter School Enrollment Holds Steady After Big Early Pandemic Growth," *Education Week*, November 30, 2022.
5. Peter Jamison, Laura Meckler, Prayag Gordy, Clara Ence Morse, and Chris Alcantara, "Home-School Nation: A Remarkable Rise," *Washington Post*, November 3, 2023.
6. William Frey, *Big Cities Saw Historic Population Losses While Suburban Growth Declined During the Pandemic* (Washington, DC: The Brookings Institution, July 11, 2022).
7. Brian Garcia, Chester Holland, Akisha Osei Sarfo, and Ray Hart, *Academic Key Performance Indicators* (revised report) (Washington, DC: Council of the Great City Schools, 2023).
8. Council of the Great City Schools, *Managing for Results in America's Great City Schools: Results from Fiscal Year 2021–22* (Washington, DC: Council of the Great City Schools, October 2023).
9. Baltimore, Boston, Broward County, Columbus, East Baton Rouge, Fresno, Jefferson County, Milwaukee, Palm Beach County, and Portland.
10. The survivors at this writing included Sonja Santelisis (Baltimore City), Nikolai Vitti (Detroit), Aleesia Johnson (Indianapolis), Errick Greene (Jackson, MS), Marty Pollio (Jefferson County, KY), Keith Posley (Milwaukee, WI), Adrienne Battle (Metro-Nashville, TN), Roger Leon (Newark, NJ), Sharon Byrdsong (Norfolk, VA), Kyla Johnson-Trammell (Oakland, CA), Jason Kamras (Richmond, VA), Romulus Durant (Toledo, OH)—the dean of the urban school superintendents, and Lewis Ferebee (the District of Columbia). Two additional superintendents remain today, but they went to new districts during the pandemic. Alberto Carvahlo left the Miami-Dade County Public Schools after heading it for a dozen years and took the top post at the Los Angeles Unified School District. And Pedro Martinez left San Antonio to become CEO of the Chicago Public Schools.
11. Council of the Great City Schools, *Managing for Results in America's Great City Schools: Results from Fiscal Year 2020–21* (Washington, DC: Council of the Great City Schools, 2023).
12. Michael Casserly, Ray Hart, Amanda Corcoran, Moses Palacios, Renata Lyons, Eric Vignola with Ricki Price-Baugh, Robin Hall, and Denise Walston, *Mirrors or Windows: How Well Do Large City Public Schools Overcome the Effects of Poverty and Other Barriers?* (Washington, DC: Council of the Great City Schools, June 2021).
13. The reader should keep in mind that the national public sample used in this section includes the Large City Schools and differs from the All Other Schools variable used in chapter 2 that excluded the Large City Schools.

14. One district that had participated in 2019 did not participate in 2022: Fresno.

15. Tom Kane and Sean Reardon, "Parents Don't Understand How Far Behind Their Kids Are," *New York Times*, May 14, 2023.

16. Enis Dogan, personal emails to Michael Casserly, subject: Question, January 2, 3, and 4, 2024.

17. Brian Garcia, Chester Holland, Akisha Osei Sarfo, and Ray Hart, *Academic Key Performance Indicators* (revised report) (Washington, DC: Council of the Great City Schools, November 2023).

18. Council of the Great City Schools, *Investing American Rescue Plan Funds Strategically and Effectively: Guidance for School Districts* (Washington, DC: Council of the Great City Schools, June 2021).

19. Council of the Great City Schools, *Investing American Rescue Plan Funds Strategically and Effectively*.

20. CPS Office of Communications, "CPS Elementary Students Make Gains in Literacy and Math for 2022–23 School Year" (Chicago: Chicago Public Schools, September 19, 2023).

21. Tony B. Watlington Sr., "Promising Improvements in 2022–23 PSSA and Keystone Exam Results" (Philadelphia: School District of Philadelphia, November 10, 2023).

22. Claire Cain Miller, Sarah Mervosh, and Francesca Paris, "Students Are Making a 'Surprising' Rebound from Pandemic Closures: But Some May Never Catch Up," *New York Times*, January 31, 2024.

23. UNESCO, *COVID-19: Monitoring Impacts on Learning Outcomes* (MILO) (Paris, France: UNESCO Institute for Statistics, 2023).

24. Eric Hanushek and Ludger Woessmann, "The Economic Impacts of Learning Loss" (Paris, France: The Organization for Economic Cooperation and Development, September 2020).

25. Megan Kuhfeld, Jim Soland, Karyn Lewis, and Emily Morton, "Test Score Patterns Across Three COVID-19-Impacted School Years, working paper, 22–521 (Providence, RI: Annenberg Institute at Brown University), https://doi.org/10.26300/ga82-6v47.

26. Jens Ludwig and Jon Guryan, "Overcoming Pandemic-Induced Learning Loss" (Chicago: University of Chicago, Education Lab, 2023), https://educationlab.uchicago .edu/projects/overcoming-pandemic-induced-learning-loss.

27. "COVID-19 Learning Loss: Long-Run Macroeconomic Effects Update" (Philadelphia: University of Pennsylvania, PennWharton Budget Model, October 27, 2021).

28. Eric Hanushek and Bradley Strauss, "A Global Perspective on US Learning Losses" (Stanford, CA: Hoover Institution, Stanford University, February 2024).

29. Erin Fahle, Thomas Kane, Sean Reardon, and Douglas Staiger, "The First Year of the Pandemic Recovery: A District-Level Analysis" (Center for Education Policy Research, Harvard University, and the Educational Opportunity Project, Stanford University, January 2024), ERS Report Final 1/30 2:48 (educationrecoveryscorecard.org).

Chapter 8

1. Council of the Great City Schools, *Supporting Excellence: A Framework for Developing, Implementing, and Sustaining a High-Quality District Curriculum*, 2nd ed. (Washington, DC: Council of the Great City Schools, 2023).

2. Council of the Great City Schools, *Addressing Unfinished Learning After COVID-19 School Closures*, page 3 (Washington, DC: Council of the Great City Schools, June 2020).

3. An excellent discussion on rethinking time and technology can be found in Frederick M. Hess, *The Great School Rethink* (Cambridge, MA: Harvard Education Press, 2023). Much of this section was informed by his ideas.
4. Hess, *The Great School Rethink*.
5. Council of the Great City Schools, *A Framework for Foundational Literacy Skills Instruction of English Learners* (Washington, DC: Council of the Great City Schools, Spring 2023).

Appendix
1. The variable may not be comparable across years due to changes in the variables in the composite.
2. This summary score has been used for reporting NAEP background variables for several years and has been shown to be associated with students' achievement scores.
3. The 2012–2013 school year was the year before CEP took effect in many school districts.

Acknowledgments

No effort with as much ambition as this book entailed is accomplished alone. It is the product of lots of people who were determined to tell the story of urban public schools over the last few decades and what they did to improve America's system of public education. I am profoundly grateful to all but would like to thank several friends and colleagues in particular.

First, I thank the board of directors and the executive committee of the Council of the Great City Schools, who gave me a career that I can only describe as amazing. Few people have been so fortunate as I to work with and for individuals of such talent and dedication. Thank you.

Thank you, as well, to Ray Hart, who has most ably replaced me at the Great City Schools. He was my research director for many years and did much of the number crunching that went into the *Mirrors or Windows* report, which forms the basis for this volume. He was a great partner and friend, and we spent many long hours together working through the analysis that showed that urban schools were improving. Thank you.

I also thank Amanda Corcoran, who helped me outline this book, provided high-level editorial assistance, and talked me through the many, many choices I had as I was thinking through what to put in this book and what to leave out. If I had a muse in this work, she was it. Thank you.

Akisha Osei Sarfo deserves my special thanks. While she was handling the myriad responsibilities as the new research director of the

Council, she was endlessly patient with my requests for data and my constant questions once she supplied the data. She was the one who calculated the effect sizes in chapter 2. And she devoted countless hours working on the return-on-investment estimates in chapter 2. This was an important discussion that she deserves much credit for. I also thank her and her team for the time and care they used to check my numbers throughout the manuscript. Thank you.

I also thank Rick Hanushek for working with me and Akisha to make sure we calculated the return on investment correctly and did not go too far in our interpretations. His guidance and technical assistance were critical. Thank you, Rick.

Thank you to Brian Garcia and Chester Holland, who provided enrollment data and other information whenever I needed it. They were also most diligent in double-checking my calculations. You were more patient with me than I deserved. And thank you to Moses Palacios for analyzing data on district use of ARP funds.

I am grateful too to those who read earlier drafts of the manuscript or parts of it. They included Michael Hinojosa, Eric Gordon, Ricki Price-Baugh, Ray Hart, Gabriela Uro, A. J. Crabill, and Akisha Osei Sarfo. Their comments and critiques were invaluable in improving what was said here. Thank you. Moreover, I thank Kaya Henderson for her encouragement as I tried to tell the urban school story. Her leadership has been such an inspiration for all of us for many years.

And I would be remiss if I did not thank the talented people at the Harvard Education Press for guiding me through their very rigorous process. They improved my work immeasurably. A special thank-you to Jayne Fargnoli and Karen Adler, and Helen Wheeler at Westchester Publishing Services, for their guidance and patience, particularly when I came up short of meeting all their requirements. They are serious professionals. Thank you.

Thank you as well to Rick Hess, who introduced me to Jayne. He is not likely to agree with some things I say in these pages, but I salute his generosity and value his friendship. Thank you.

Finally, I thank my spouse, Mary Janet, who thought I had retired until I mentioned writing this book. She was most generous and supportive as I devoted day after day and too many nights to writing this work. Thank you.

Michael Casserly

About the Author

Michael Casserly has served for forty-seven years with the Council of the Great City Schools, the nation's primary coalition of large urban school districts. He spent thirty of those years as the organization's executive director, fourteen years as the group's legislative and research director, and three additional years as its strategic advisor. After being named director of the organization in 1992, Casserly remade the group's goals to focus on improving student achievement; strengthening urban school system governance, leadership, and management; and bolstering public confidence in public education in the nation's major cities.

To make progress on those goals, Casserly initiated and led hundreds of technical assistance teams to improve urban school district instruction, special and bilingual education, school board governance, organizational structure, budget and finance operations, facilities, transportation, food services, and many other district functions. Under his leadership, the organization was the first membership group in the country to support the Common Core State Standards. He initiated the Trial Urban District Assessment of NAEP in 2000 and led the development of the country's first nationwide educational performance management system with hundreds of academic and operational key performance indicators.

Casserly conducted major studies of why some urban school systems improve faster than others. He filed award-winning briefs before the US Supreme Court on cases involving desegregation and educational equity, the US Census, special education, Title I funding, and many other areas. He initiated and helped develop the Accelerating Board Capacity program at the Harvard Business School to provide professional development to the nation's urban school boards. He led the targeting of federal aid formulas in Title I, Title II, Title III, and vocational education that now result in over $1.0 billion extra each year in financial assistance to urban public schools. And he collaborated with President Obama on a pledge by the nation's largest urban school systems to improve the educational conditions for African American boys and young men.

Over the decades, Casserly worked directly with the nation's urban school leaders on many of their most difficult challenges and was viewed by many as the nation's most knowledgeable individual on urban public education. He has an annual award and scholarship named for him and is the namesake of a training institute for aspiring urban school superintendents.

Casserly has a bachelor's degree from Villanova University and a PhD from the University of Maryland. He is a US Army veteran.

Index